A Dictionary of
# Twentieth Century Quotations

Nigel Rees is a writer and broadcaster. On radio and television he has presented a large number of programmes ranging from news and current affairs to arts and entertainment. BBC Radio's *Quote . . . Unquote*, which he first devised and presented in 1976, has established him as an authority on various aspects of popular speech.

# A Dictionary of
# Twentieth Century
# Quotations

## Nigel Rees

Fontana/Collins

First published in 1987 by Fontana Paperbacks
8 Grafton Street, London W1X 3LA

Copyright © Nigel Rees Productions Ltd 1987

Set in Linotron Plantin

Made and printed in Great Britain by
William Collins Sons & Co. Ltd, Glasgow

# Preface

A dictionary of quotations can help you find the source of a saying or it can guide you towards a saying which might help you illustrate a theme.

Put another way, one approach for the dictionary compiler is to examine quotations that *actually do get quoted* and the other is for him to suggest what he thinks *ought to be quoted*.

In compiling *A Dictionary of Twentieth Century Quotations* I have, for the most part, concerned myself with the first approach – tracing the sources of well-known phrases and sayings that actually do get quoted or alluded to.

A quotation is anything written or spoken which another person chooses to repeat. I have limited my choice, however, to phrases and sayings that I have heard being quoted by someone other than myself and usually on more than one occasion.

Ten years spent devising the BBC radio programme *Quote . . . Unquote* have given me a pretty good idea of what people *do* quote and what puzzles them about modern quotations in particular. As a result of requests I have received from listeners, viewers, librarians and journalists, I have built up a store of information which I hope will lead to more accurate attribution to sources than is sometimes the case in such books.

Oddly, the more modern the quotation, the greater likelihood there seems to be of some dispute arising over its source or correct form. Classical quotations may be said to have settled in to their niches securely. In an age when there is more communication than ever before, it is paradoxically often harder to check what exactly was said last week than what was said a century ago.

I have been fortunate in having access to sound recordings of many twentieth-century speeches, film soundtracks and so on, and I hope, as a result, that I am able to give more accurate versions of some quotations than is usually the case.

On the other hand, I am aware that I may have created as many new misattributions as I have corrected old ones. I would be pleased to hear from readers who think they have superior knowledge. If previous form is anything to go by, I do not anticipate any reluctance on their part to put me right.

There are many ways in which to lay out a dictionary of quotations. I have avoided grouping the sayings into categories, as this can make it difficult to check a known quotation and is only of minor usefulness anyway. The chief aim has been to make it easy for the reader to locate the quotation he or she is interested in. By using the key-word index, this should present no problem, never mind where I have chosen to place a quotation within the book – at times somewhat arbitrarily.

On the whole, I have attributed sayings to individuals, listed in alphabetical order. But how to deal with lines from films, shows, TV programmes and advertising copy? Should I put them under the scriptwriter's name, the actor's name, or the show's name?

I have chosen to put such quotes – often the product of group creative effort – under the show's name (e.g. Bogart's sayings from *Casablanca*), though where the origination is quite clearly the responsibility of a film star or named writer, I have, in some cases, been inconsistent and put the quotation under these names.

So, the quotations are listed under author (or show) in alphabetical order or sorted into a number of specialist categories, viz.:

ANONYMOUS SAYINGS
BOOK TITLES
CATCHPHRASES
EPITAPHS
FILM TITLES
INSCRIPTIONS
PLAY TITLES
PROVERBS
SLOGANS
SONG TITLES
TELEGRAMS AND CABLES
TELEVISION PROGRAMME TITLES

I have tried to keep cross-referencing to a minimum and have chosen to mark many quotations merely 'attrib.' or 'untraced' rather than give a less than useful secondary source.

Should anyone be puzzled, both the dictionary and the index are based upon alphabetical order not of complete words but of *letter order within a sentence* (ignoring word breaks, hyphens and spaces). Within individual entries, the order of quotations is approximately chronological except where it is stated to be alphabetical.

What is to be done about common misquotations? Should they be left out? My feeling is that the usefulness of such a dictionary is increased if common misquotations are included. However, such misquotations (or frequently confused renderings) are marked by a special symbol – ## – and accompanied by a note on how the confusion has arisen.

There is a tendency in modern dictionaries of quotations, quite rightly, to include popular song lyrics. The question here is, where to stop? I have tried to limit myself to lines which have been quoted in other contexts and not simply become familiar through frequent performance.

Where possible, I have tried to give some indication of when, in this century, a line was first written or spoken. This is an almost impossible task when dealing with informally-uttered remarks. With lines from books and shows, the date is usually that of first publication or performance. In tracing quotations and allusions in the titles of books, films, and the like, I have of necessity sometimes had to go outside the century for a source. For those writers like Shaw and Kipling whose work straddled the turn of the century, I have chosen only those quotations which appear to have originated in the twentieth.

The bias of this book is towards twentieth-century quotations in the English language (British and American versions). As to why it is necessary at all, I can only admit to my own frustration (and obsessiveness) when trying to confirm a saying that has drifted into my ken and which I cannot find in a considerable library of other such dictionaries.

Another reason for the book is the splendid vagueness that people have in the use of quotations – misquoting, misattributing, mangling – nicely illustrated, I feel, by something said* by the widow of a man who had died during the D-Day 1944 landings in Normandy. Paying a

---

* Quoted in the *Observer*, 10 June 1984

visit to the battlefield forty years later, she was asked by a television interviewer why she had made the journey. She replied, 'As they said in the Bible, or in the paper, part of a foreign field is forever England.'

*As they said in the Bible, or in the paper . . .*

Ah well, that narrows it down a bit.

Should she be reading this, I think she will find the answer to her problem on page 73.

NIGEL REES
London, 1987

# A

## ACE, Goodman
US writer
(1899–   )

**1**
TV . . . is our latest medium – we call it a medium because nothing's well done.
    Letter (1954) to Groucho Marx included in *The Groucho Letters*
*See also KOVACS 263:3.*

## ACHESON, Dean
US Democratic politician
(1893–1971)

**2**
Great Britain . . . has lost an Empire and not yet found a role. The attempt to play a separate power role – that is, a role apart from Europe, a role based on a 'special relationship' with the United States, a role based on being the head of a 'Commonwealth' . . . this role is about to be played out . . . Her Majesty's Government is now attempting, wisely in my opinion, to re-enter Europe.
    Speech, Military Academy, West Point, 5 December 1962

## ACKERLEY, J.R.
British writer
(1896–1967)

**3**
I was born in 1896, and my parents were married in 1919.
    *My Father and Myself* (1968)
*Opening words.*

## ADAMS, Douglas
British writer
(1952–   )

1
Don't panic.
  Radio script, *The Hitch Hiker's Guide to the Galaxy* (1978)
*Words written on the cover of the fictional guide.*

2
I'm so depressed.
  *Ib.*

## ADAMSON, Harold
US songwriter
(1906–   )

3
Comin' in on a Wing and a Prayer.
  Title of song (1943)
*Reputedly based on words said by a pilot coming in to land with a badly damaged plane. Title of 1944 US film:* Wing and a Prayer.

## ADLER, Polly
US madam
(1900–62)

4
A House Is Not a Home.
  Title of memoirs (1954)

## AGA KHAN III
Muslim leader
(1877–1957)

5
*Defending his taste for alcohol:*
I'm so holy that when I touch wine, it turns into water.
  Attrib. by Compton Miller, *Who's Really Who* (1983)

## AGNEW, Spiro T.
US Republican politician
(1918–  )

1

I agree with you that the name of Spiro Agnew is not a household name. I certainly hope that it will become one within the next couple of months.

> Interview with Mike Wallace of ABC TV, on becoming Vice-Presidential candidate, 8/9 August 1968

2

To some extent, if you've seen one city slum you've seen them all.

> Speech, Detroit, 18 October 1968

3

*On media pundits:*

A spirit of national masochism prevails, encouraged by an effete corps of impudent snobs who characterize themselves as intellectuals.

> Speech, New Orleans, 19 October 1969

4

*On media pundits:*

In the United States today we have more than our share of the nattering nabobs of negativism. They have formed their own 4-H Club – the 'hopeless, hysterical hypochondriacs of history.'

> Speech, San Diego, 11 September 1970

*Speech written for him by William Safire.*

## AKINS, Zoë
US playwright
(1886–1958)

5

The Greeks Had a Word for It.

> Title of play (1929)

*Akins told Burton Stevenson that in dialogue cut from her play the phrase clearly referred to a type of woman. One character thinks that a 'tart' is meant, but the other corrects this and says a 'free soul' is more to the point.*

## ALBEE, Edward
US playwright
(1928–   )

**1**

I'll tell you what game we'll play. We're done with Humiliate the Host
. . . and we don't want to play Hump the Hostess . . . We'll play a
round of Get the Guests.

   *Who's Afraid of Virginia Woolf?* (1962)
*See also PLAY TITLES 342:2.*

## *ALGIERS*
*US film 1938*

**2**

\#\#   Come with me to the Casbah.
*Supposedly said by Charles Boyer to Hedy Lamarr, but not in the*
*film.*

## ALGREN, Nelson
US novelist and short story writer
(1909–81)

**3**

Never eat at a place called Mom's. Never play cards with a man called
Doc. Never go to bed with a woman whose troubles are greater than
your own.

   *A Walk on the Wild Side* (1956)

## ALI, Muhammad
(formerly Cassius Clay)
US heavyweight boxing champion
(1942–   )

**4**

I am the greatest.
   His slogan from *c.*1963

1
Float like a butterfly, sting like a bee.
  Motto
*Devised by an aide, Drew 'Bundini' Brown.*

2
*Announcing his retirement:*
I want to get out with my greatness intact.
  Quoted in the *Observer*, 4 July 1974

3
You don't want no pie in the sky when you die,
You want something here on the ground while you're still around.
  Quoted in 1978
*See also HILL 224:3.*


## ALL ABOUT EVE

*US film 1950. Script by Joseph L. Mankiewicz. With Bette Davis as Eve.*

4
*Eve:* Fasten your seatbelts. It's going to be a bumpy night.
  Soundtrack


## ALL THAT JAZZ

*US film 1979. Script by Robert Alan Arthur and Bob Fosse. With Bob Fosse as Joe Gideon.*

5
*Joe:* It's show time, folks!
  Soundtrack

## ALLEN, Fred
US comedian
(1894–1956)

**1**
Hollywood – a place where people from Iowa mistake themselves for movie stars.
Attrib.

## ALLEN, Woody
US film actor, writer and director
(1937–   )

**2**
Sex between a man and a woman can be wonderful – provided you get between the right man and the right woman.
Attrib.

**3**
Not only is there no God, but try getting a plumber on weekends.
'My Philosophy', *Getting Even* (1975)

**4**
*Woman:* You are the greatest lover I have ever known.
*Allen:* Well, I practise a lot when I'm on my own.
*Love and Death* (1975)

**5**
*On sex:*
Fun? That was the most fun I've ever had without laughing.
*Annie Hall* (1977)
*Written with Marshall Brickman. Also attrib. to Humphrey Bogart in the form 'It was the most fun I ever had without laughing.'*

**6**
Don't knock masturbation, it's sex with someone you love.
*Ib.*

1

It's not that I'm afraid to die, I just don't want to be there when it happens.

'Death (A Play)', *Without Feathers* (1978)

## ALLSOP, Kenneth
British writer and broadcaster
(1920–73)

2

In work the greatest satisfaction lies – the satisfaction of stretching yourself, using your abilities and making them expand, and knowing that you have accomplished something that could have been done only by you using your unique apparatus. This is really the centre of life, and those who never orientate themselves in this direction are missing more than they ever know.

*Letters to His Daughter* (1974)

## ALTRINCHAM, Lord
(later disclaimed peerage and known as John Grigg)
British writer
(1924–  )

3

*On Queen Elizabeth II's style of public speaking:*
Frankly a pain in the neck.

*National and English Review*, August 1958

4

The personality conveyed by the utterances which are put into her mouth is that of a priggish schoolgirl, captain of the hockey team, a prefect, and a recent candidate for confirmation. It is not thus that she will be able to come into her own as an independent and distinctive character.

*Ib.*

## AMERY, L.S.
### British Conservative MP
### (1873–1955)

1

*To the acting Opposition leader, Arthur Greenwood:*
##   Speak for England, Arthur!
   Speech, House of Commons, 2 September 1939 (interjection not
   recorded in *Hansard*)
*On the eve of war, Prime Minister Neville Chamberlain had held out
the prospect of a further Munich-type peace conference and had not
announced any ultimatum to Germany. Amery, in his account, omits
the 'Arthur'. Robert Boothby said (1964) that he (Boothby) shouted,
'You speak for Britain.'*

2

*To Neville Chamberlain:*
This is what Cromwell said to the Long Parliament when he thought it
was no longer fit to conduct the affairs of the nation: 'You have sat too
long here for any good you have been doing. Depart, I say, and let us
have done with you. In the name of God, go!'
   Speech, House of Commons, 7 May 1940
*Quoting Oliver Cromwell's words when dismissing the Rump of the
Long Parliament, 1653.*

## AMIN, Idi
### Ugandan soldier and President
### (1925–   )

3

*Public message to Lord Snowdon, on the break-up of his marriage to
Princess Margaret:*
Your experience will be a lesson to all of us men to be careful not to
marry ladies in very high positions.
   Quoted in A. Barrow, *International Gossip* (1983)

### AMIS, Kingsley
British novelist, poet and critic
(1922– )

**1**

Bowen's Beer Makes You Drunk.
   *I Like It Here* (1958)
*'Barnet Bowen' suggests this is the only type of beer slogan that will really appeal.*

**2**

*On 'the delusion that there are thousands of young people who are capable of benefiting from university training but have somehow failed to find their way there':*
I wish I could have a little tape-and-loudspeaker arrangement sewn into the binding of this magazine, to be triggered off by the light reflected from the reader's eyes on to this part of the page, and set to bawl out at several bels: MORE WILL MEAN WORSE.
   Article in *Encounter*, July 1960

### ANDREWS, Elizabeth
Royal chambermaid

**3**

*On finding intruder in Queen Elizabeth II's bedroom:*
Bloody hell, Ma'am, what's he doing here?
   Quoted in the *Daily Mail*, July 1982

### *ANIMAL CRACKERS*

*US film 1930. Script by Morrie Ryskind, from musical by himself and George S. Kaufman. With Groucho Marx.*

**4**

*Groucho:* One morning I shot an elephant in my pyjamas. How he got in my pyjamas I'll never know.
   Soundtrack

## ANKA, Paul
US singer and songwriter
(1941–  )

**1**

And now the end is near
And so I face the final curtain,
My friend, I'll say it clear,
I'll state my case of which I'm certain.
I've lived a life that's full, I've travelled each and evr'y high-way
And more, much more than this, I did it my way.

   Song, 'My Way' (1969)
*Based on a French composition, 'Comme d'habitude'.*

## *ANNA CHRISTIE*

*US film 1930. Script by Frances Marion, from the play by Eugene O'Neill. With Greta Garbo as Anna Christie.*

**2**

*Anna (to barman):* Gimme a viskey. Ginger ale on the side. And don't be stingy, baby.

   Soundtrack

**3**

Garbo Talks!

   Promotional slogan

## ANNAN REPORT ON BROADCASTING
British official inquiry

**4**

The BBC does itself untold harm by its excessive sensitivity. At the first breath of criticism the Corporation adopts a posture of a hedgehog at bay.

   Report of the Committee on the Future of Broadcasting (1977)

## ANNE, HRH the Princess
British Royal
(1950–   )


1
*To the press, a few days before her engagement to Captain Mark Phillips:*
There is no romance between us. He is here solely to exercise the horses.
   Attrib. (1973)


2
*On her first encounter with a horse:*
One was presented with a small, hairy individual and, out of general curiosity, one climbed on.
   *Princess Anne and Mark Phillips Talking Horses with Genevieve Murphy* (1976)


3
When I appear in public, people expect me to neigh, grind my teeth, paw the ground and swish my tail.
   Attrib.


4
*On pregnancy:*
It's a very boring time. I am not particularly maternal – it's an occupational hazard of being a wife.
   TV interview, quoted in the *Daily Express*, 14 April 1981


5
*To press photographers at Badminton horse trials:*
Why don't you naff off!
   Reported in the *Daily Mirror*, 17 April 1982

## ANNENBERG, Walter
US publisher and diplomat
(1908– )

**1**
*To Queen Elizabeth II, when she asked him about his accommodation as Ambassador to the Court of St James:*
We're in the Embassy residence, subject, of course, to some of the discomfiture as a result of a need for, uh, elements of refurbishment and rehabilitation.
    TV film, *Royal Family* (1969)

## ANONYMOUS SAYINGS
*(in approximate chronological order)*

**2**
It pays to advertise.
*Already current by c.1912 when Cole Porter used it as the title of an early song.*

**3**
(There were) Russians with snow on their boots.
*In September 1914, there was an unfounded rumour that a million Russian troops had landed at Aberdeen and passed through England on their way to the Western Front.*

**4**
Fifty million Frenchmen can't be wrong.
*Ironic expression which probably originated with US servicemen in France during the First World War. Used in song lyric (1927).*

**5**
My eyes are dim
I cannot see
I have not brought my specs with me.
*From trad. song, 'In the Quartermaster's Stores'.*

**1**
Never work with animals or children.
*Show business maxim.*

**2**
All of you young people [are from] a lost generation ('une generation perdue').
*French hotel owner (a Monsieur Pernollet) to an apprentice who had made a shoddy repair to Gertrude Stein's car after the First World War.*

**3**
I went to New Zealand but it was closed.
*Joke current from the 1920s.*

**4**
I know two things about the horse
And one of them is rather coarse.
*Anonymous rhyme.*

**5**
Don't tell my mother I'm in politics – she thinks I play the piano in a whorehouse.
*American saying from the Depression.*

**6**
The son-in-law also rises.
*Hollywood observation when Louis B. Mayer promoted his daughter's husband (David O. Selznick), c.1933.*

**7**
Can't act, can't sing, slightly bald. Can dance a little.
*Hollywood executive on Fred Astaire's first screen test.*

**8**
He died as he lived – at sea.
*On Ramsay Macdonald who died during a cruise (1937).*

1
Hark the herald angels sing
Mrs Simpson's pinched our king.
*Quoted by Clement Attlee in letter dated 26 December 1938.*

2
Do not fold, spindle or mutilate.
*Injunction on punched cards and computer cards, US origin, from the 1930s onwards.*

3
Overpaid, overfed, oversexed and over here.
*Second World War observation about American GIs in Europe.*

4
Go to hell, Babe Ruth – American, you die.
*Battle cry of Japanese soldiers first heard on the Pacific Islands, 1942.*

5
Hitler
Has only got one ball!
Goering
Has two, but very small!
Himmler
Has something similar,
But poor old Goebbels
Has no balls at all!
*Second World War song (to the tune of 'Colonel Bogey').*

6
You're phoney. Everything about you is phoney. Even your hair – which looks false – is real.
*American diplomat to Brendan Bracken during the Second World War.*

7
*Describing what it was like to be in a battle:*
Oh, my dear fellow, the noise . . . and the people!

*Variously attributed, but especially to a certain Captain Strahan at the Battle of Bastogne (1944).*

1

Inspiration is the act of drawing up a chair to the writing desk.
*Anonymous saying.*

2

Carnation milk is the best in the land;
Here I sit with a can in my hand –
No tits to pull, no hay to pitch,
You just punch a hole in the son of a bitch.
*Anonymous rhyme.*

3

If anything can go wrong, it will.
*'Murphy's Law' – most probably dating from the 1940s in the US. It has been suggested that Capt. E. Murphy of the California Northrop aviation firm may have formulated it.*

4

Oh no, thank you, I only smoke on special occasions.
*Labour minister when asked if he would like a cigar, while dining with King George VI.*

5

Quite so. But I have not been on a ship for fifteen years and they still call me 'Admiral'.
*Italian admiral when Eva Peron complained that she had been called a 'whore' on a visit to northern Italy.*

6

Would you buy a used car from this man?
*Joke about Richard M. Nixon, current from c.1952.*

7

The best contraceptive is a glass of cold water: not before or after, but instead.

*Delegate at International Planned Parenthood Federation Conference.*

1

Has anyone here been raped and speaks English?
*BBC television reporter to Belgian civilians waiting to escape the war in the Congo (1960).*

2

*The Times* is a tribal noticeboard.
*A candidate for the editorship of the paper's Woman's Page in the 1960s, cited 21 January 1984.*

3

Because you're in Chatham.
*Heckler's reply when Harold Wilson asked rhetorically, 'Why do I emphasize the importance of the Royal Navy?' (1964).*

4

To save the town, it became necessary to destroy it.
*American officer on the town of Ben Tre, Vietnam, during Tet offensive, 1968.*

5

Beautiful girls, walk a little slower when you walk by me.
*Graffito seen in New York City by Gordon Jenkins who included the line in his song 'This Is All I Ask' (1960s).*

6

When you've got over the disgrace of the single life, it's more airy.
*Irish woman (quoted by Joyce Grenfell in broadcasts).*

7

Anyone who isn't confused here doesn't really understand what's going on.
*Belfast citizen, 1970.*

1

Oh dear, what a pity. Nannies are so hard to come by these days.
*Aristocratic old lady, to police officer inquiring into the murder of
Lord Lucan's nanny, 1974.*

2

Ah well, they say it's not as bad as they say it is.
*Irish woman, on the situation in Ulster.*

3

We get nothing and we can't go home because you can't eat sun.
*Black Liverpudlian (on unemployment and immigration), 1976.*

4

[Alberto] Juantorena opens wide his legs and shows his class.
*British commentator at 1976 Montreal Olympics. This has been
wrongly ascribed to David Coleman; it was probably Ron Pickering.*

5

This must be the first time a rat has come to the aid of a sinking ship.
*BBC spokesman on puppet Roland Rat's success at TV-am, 1983.
See also CHURCHILL 105:7.*

6

The longest suicide note ever penned.
*Labour Shadow Cabinet member on the party manifesto, 1983.*

7

He didn't love God, he just fancied him.
*On W. H. Auden.*

8

Capitalism is the exploitation of man by man. Communism is the
complete opposite.
*Described by Laurence J. Peter as a 'Polish proverb.'*

### THE APARTMENT

*US film 1960. Script by Billy Wilder and I. A. L. Diamond. With
Shirley Maclaine as Miss Kubelik and Jack Lemmon as C. C. Baxter.*

1
*Miss Kubelik:* Why can't I ever fall in love with somebody nice like you?
*C. C. Baxter:* Yeah, well, that's the way it crumbles, cookie-wise.

## THE ARCHERS
*UK radio series (BBC) since 1951.*

2
An everyday story of country folk.
    Introductory announcement

3
Oooo arr, me ol' beauty, me ol' pal.
    Stock phrase of 'Walter Gabriel' (Chris Gittins)

## ARENDT, Hannah
German-born philosopher in the US
(1906–75)

4
The fearsome word-and-thought-defying *banality of evil.*
    *Eichmann in Jerusalem: A Report on the Banality of Evil* (1963)

## ARENS, Richard
US lawyer
(1913–69)

5
Are you now or have you ever been a member of a godless conspiracy controlled by a foreign power?
    Quoted in P. Lewis, *The Fifties*
*His version of the more usual question, 'Are you now or have you ever been a member of the Communist Party?', put to those appearing at hearings of the House of Representatives Committee on UnAmerican Activities (1947–c.1957), especially by J. Parnell Thomas.*

## *ARE YOU BEING SERVED?*

*UK TV comedy series (BBC) from 1974. Script by David Croft and Jeremy Lloyd. With John Inman as Mr Humphries.*

1
*Mr Humphries:* I'm free!
   Catchphrase

### ARMSTRONG, Neil
US astronaut
(1930–   )

2
*On lunar touch-down of space module, Apollo XI mission:*
Tranquillity Base here – the Eagle has landed.
   TV coverage, 20 July 1969

3
*On becoming the first man to step on the surface of the moon:*
That's one small step for [a] man, one giant leap for mankind.
   *Ib.*
*The 'a' was not audible, spoiling the sense. On his return from the moon, Armstrong attempted to correct the inaccuracy – with less than complete success.*

### ARNO, Peter
US cartoonist
(1904–68)

4
*Caption to* New Yorker *cartoon of designers walking away from crashed plane:*
Well, back to the old drawing board.
   Untraced
*Helped popularize, even if it did not originate, the phrase 'Back to the drawing board'.*

**1**

*Caption to cartoon of man flirting with a woman:*
Tell me about yourself – your struggles, your dreams, your telephone
number.
    Untraced

### ASKEY, Arthur
British entertainer
(1900–82)

**2**

Ay thang yew! ('I thank you!')
    Catchphrase

**3**

Big-hearted Arthur, that's me.
    Catchphrase

**4**

Doesn't it make you want to spit?
    Catchphrase

**5**

Hello, playmates!
    Catchphrase

**6**

Here and now, before your very eyes.
    Catchphrase

### ASQUITH, H.H.
(later 1st Earl of Oxford and Asquith)
British Liberal Prime Minister
(1852–1928)

**7**

*To a persistent inquirer about the Parliament Act Procedure Bill:*
You had better wait and see.
    Speech, House of Commons, 4 April 1910
*This was the fourth occasion on which he had said 'Wait and see.'*

1

*At the Westminster Abbey funeral of Bonar Law, 5 November 1923:*
It is fitting that we should have buried the Unknown Prime Minister
by the side of the Unknown Soldier.
    Attrib.


# ASQUITH, Margot
(later Countess of Oxford and Asquith)
Wife of H. H. Asquith
(1865–1945)

2

*On Lord Kitchener (1914):*
If Kitchener is not a great man, he is, at least, a great poster.
    Quoted in Sir P. Magnus, *Kitchener: Portrait of an Imperialist*

3

*On David Lloyd George:*
He can't see a belt without hitting below it.
    Quoted by Baroness Asquith in TV programme *As I Remember*,
    30 April 1967

4

*On her husband:*
His modesty amounts to deformity.
    *Ib.*

5

*On a politician:*
He always has his arm round your waist and his eye on the clock.
    *Ib.*

6

*On a US General:*
An imitation rough diamond.
    *Ib.*

1

*On Lady Desborough:*
She's as strong as an ox. She'll be turned into Bovril when she dies.
   *Ib.*

2

*On the same friend:*
She tells enough white lies to ice a wedding cake.
   *Ib.*

3

*On F. E. Smith:*
He's very clever, but sometimes his brains go to his head.
   *Ib.*

4

*On Lord Dawson of Penn:*
The King told me he would never have died if it had not been for that fool Dawson of Penn.
   Quoted in K. Rose, *George V*

5

*On Sir Stafford Cripps:*
He has a brilliant mind until he makes it up.
   Quoted in *The Wit of the Asquiths*

6

*To Jean Harlow who had asked whether the 't' was pronounced in 'Margot':*
## No. The 't' is silent – as in 'Harlow'.
*Although usually ascribed to Margot Asquith, it is more likely that the original perpetrator was Margot Grahame (1911–82), an actress who went from England to Hollywood in the 1930s and had brief success.*

## ASTOR, Nancy, Viscountess
American-born British MP
(1879–1964)

7

I married beneath me. All women do.
   Speech, Oldham, 1951

1
*On the young Shirley Williams:*
You'll never get on in politics, my dear, with *that* hair.
    Attrib.
*Confirmed by the remark's recipient (1982).*

2
*To her son, on her death bed:*
Jakie, is it my birthday or am I dying?
    Quoted in J. Grigg, *Nancy Astor: Portrait of a Pioneer*
*He replied: 'A bit of both, Mum.' Her last word was 'Waldorf' (the name of her husband).*

*See also CHURCHILL 101:1.*

## ATTLEE, Clement
British Labour Prime Minister
(1883–1967)

3
*In a letter to Harold Laski, Chairman of the Labour Party NEC, 20 August 1945:*
You have no right whatever to speak on behalf of the Government. Foreign Affairs are in the capable hands of Ernest Bevin. His task is quite sufficiently difficult without the embarrassment of irresponsible statements of the kind which you are making . . . a period of silence on your part would be welcome.
    Quoted in *British Political Facts 1900–75*

4
*On himself:*
Few thought he was even a starter
There were many who thought themselves smarter
But he ended PM, CH and OM
An Earl and a Knight of the Garter.
    Lines written on 8 April 1956
    Quoted in K. Harris, *Attlee*

## AUDEN, W.H.
British-born poet
(1907–73)

**1**
Private faces in public places
Are wiser and nicer
Than public faces in private places.
   Marginalia (1932)

**2**
August for the people and their favourite islands.
   'Birthday Poem' (1935)

**3**
This is the Night Mail crossing the Border
Bringing the cheque and the postal order.
   'Night Mail' (1935)
*Commentary for Post Office documentary film.*

**4**
Look, stranger, at this island now.
   'Look, Stranger' (1936)
*Another version is ' . . . on this island'.*

**5**
We must love one another or die.
   'September 1, 1939'
*Auden tried to suppress this line. A 1955 anthology has: 'We must love one another and die.'*

**6**
Lay your sleeping head, my love,
Human on my faithless arm.
   'Lullaby' (1940)

**1**
To the man-in-the-street, who, I'm sorry to say
Is a keen observer of life,
The word Intellectual suggests straight away
A man who's untrue to his wife.
    'Note on Intellectuals' (1947)

**2**
Most people enjoy the sight of their own handwriting as they enjoy the smell of their own farts.
    'Writing', *The Dyer's Hand* (1962)
*See also PROVERBS 351:3.*

**3**
*To reporter:*
Your cameraman might enjoy himself, because my face looks like a wedding cake left out in the rain.
    Quoted in H. Carpenter, *W. H. Auden*

**4**
A professor is one who talks in someone else's sleep.
    Quoted in *The Treasury of Humorous Quotations*

**AUSTIN, Warren R.**
US diplomat
(1877–1962)

**5**
*In a debate on the Middle East:*
[Jews and Arabs should settle their differences] like good Christians.
    Attrib.

# AXELROD, George
US screenwriter
(1922–   )

1
The Seven Year Itch.
   Title of play (filmed 1955)
*Axelrod commented (1979): 'There was a phrase which referred to a somewhat unpleasant disease [but] nobody had used it in a sexual context before. I do believe that I invented it in that sense.'*

# B

## BADEN-POWELL, Robert
(later Lord Baden-Powell)
British soldier and founder of the Boy Scouts
(1857–1941)

**1**
Be Prepared . . . the meaning of the motto is that a scout must prepare himself by previous thinking out and practising how to act on any accident or emergency so that he is never taken by surprise; he knows exactly what to do when anything unexpected happens.
   *Scouting for Boys* (1908)
*Motto of the Scout movement.*

**2**
On my honour I promise that I will do my best . . . to do my duty to God and the King . . . to help other people at all times . . . to obey the Scout Law.
   'Scout's oath' in *ib.*

**3**
A Scout smiles and whistles under all circumstances.
   Part of 'The Scout Law' in *ib.*

**4**
*On masturbation:*
It is called in our schools 'beastliness', and this is about the best name for it . . . should it become a habit it quickly destroys both health and spirits; he becomes feeble in body and mind, and often ends in a lunatic asylum.
   *Ib.*

**5**
Dyb-dyb-dyb.
   Shout used by Wolf Cubs
*Meaning 'Do your best'.*

## BAGNOLD, Enid
British playwright
(1889–1981)

**1**

The great and terrible step was taken. What else could you expect from a girl so expectant? 'Sex,' said Frank Harris, 'is the gateway to life.' So I went through the gateway in an upper room in the Cafe Royal.

*Enid Bagnold's Autobiography* (1969)

## BAIRNSFATHER, Bruce
British cartoonist
(1888–1959)

**2**

Well, if you knows of a better 'ole, go to it.

Caption to cartoon in *Fragments from France* (1915)
*Said by 'Ol' Bill', up to his waist in mud on the Somme. A film (US 1926), based on the character, was called* The Better 'Ole.

## BAKER, Hylda
British entertainer
(1908–86)

**3**

*Of her silent foil, 'Cynthia':*
She knows, you know!

Catchphrase, from 1950s onwards

## BALDWIN, James
US novelist
(1924–   )

**1**

If we do not now dare everything, the fulfillment of that prophecy, re-created from the Bible in song by a slave, is upon us: *God gave Noah the rainbow sign, No more water, the fire next time!*
*The Fire Next Time* (1963)

## BALDWIN, Stanley
(later 1st Earl Baldwin of Bewdley)
British Conservative Prime Minister
(1867–1947)

**2**

*Of the House of Commons in 1918:*
They are a lot of hard-faced men . . . who look as if they had done well out of the war.
  Quoted in J. M. Keynes, *Economic Consequences of Peace*
*Baldwin is assumed to have been the 'Conservative politician' Keynes quoted.*

**3**

*Attacking the press lords during a by-election campaign:*
The papers conducted by Lord Rothermere and Lord Beaverbrook are not newspapers in the ordinary acceptance of the term. They are engines of propaganda, for the constantly changing policies, desires, personal wishes, personal likes and dislikes of two men . . . What the proprietorship of these papers is aiming at is power, and power without responsibility – the prerogative of the harlot throughout the ages.
  Speech, London, 18 March 1931
*His cousin, Rudyard Kipling, was the originator of this remark. Harold Macmillan recalled that his father-in-law, the Duke of Devonshire, exclaimed at this point, 'Good God, that's done it, he's lost us the tarts' vote.'*

**1**

The bomber will always get through.

Speech, House of Commons, 10 November 1932

**2**

*On becoming Prime Minister in 1933:*
I met Curzon in Downing Street, from whom I got the sort of greeting a corpse would give to an undertaker.

Attrib.

**3**

There is a wind of nationalism and freedom blowing round the world, and blowing as strongly in Asia as elsewhere.

Speech, London, 4 December 1934

**4**

*On the Abyssinia crisis:*
## I shall be but a short time tonight. I have seldom spoken with greater regret, for my lips are sealed.

Speech, House of Commons, 10 December 1935
*Actually, he said, 'my lips are not yet unsealed.'*

**5**

I put before the whole House my own view with appalling frankness . . . supposing I had gone to the country and said . . . that we must rearm, does anybody think that this pacific democracy would have rallied to that cry at that moment? I cannot think of anything that would have made the loss of the election from my point of view more certain.

Speech, House of Commons, 12 November 1936

**6**

*On his resignation:*
Once I leave, I leave. I am not going to speak to the man on the bridge, and I am not going to spit on the deck.

Statement to the Cabinet, 28 May 1937, later released to the press

**7**

You will find in politics that you are much exposed to the attribution of false motives. Never complain and never explain.

To Harold Nicolson, 21 July 1943, quoting Disraeli

## BALFOUR, Arthur
(later 1st Earl of Balfour)
British Conservative Prime Minister
(1848–1930)

1

*To Frank Harris who had claimed that Christianity and journalism
were the two main curses of civilization:*
Christianity, yes, but why journalism?
Quoted in M. Asquith, *Autobiography*

2

*As Foreign Secretary, to Lord Rothschild:*
His Majesty's Government looks with favour upon the establishment
in Palestine of a national home for the Jewish people.
Letter, 2 November 1917
*The 'Balfour Declaration'.*

3

History does not repeat itself. Historians repeat each other.
Attrib.
*Compare GUEDALLA 203:3.*

4

Nothing matters very much and very few things matter at all.
Attrib.

## BALL, Bobby
British comedian
(1944–    )

5

*To partner, Tommy Cannon:*
Rock on, Tommy!
Catchphrase, from 1970s onwards

## BANKHEAD, Tallulah
US actress
(1903–68)

**1**

I tell you cocaine isn't habit-forming and I know because I've been taking it for years.
   Quoted in L. Hellman, *Pentimento*

**2**

*On the play* Aglavaine and Selysette *by Maurice Maeterlinck:*
There's less in this than meets the eye.
   Remark, 3 January 1922

**3**

*On being greeted by a former admirer after many years:*
I thought I told you to wait in the car.
   Attrib.

**4**

*To admirer:*
I'll come and make love to you at five o'clock. If I'm late start without me.
   Quoted in E. Morgan, *Somerset Maugham*

**5**

*On herself:*
I'm as pure as driven slush.
   Quoted in the *Observer*, 24 February 1957


## BARNES, Clive
British-born theatre and ballet critic
(1927–   )

**6**

*On* Oh, Calcutta! *(1969):*
This is the kind of show that gives pornography a bad name.
   Attrib.

## BARNES, Peter
British playwright
(1931–   )

1

I know I am God because when I pray to him I find I'm talking to myself.
   *The Ruling Class* (1968)


## BARRIE, J.M.
(later Sir James)
British playwright
(1860–1937)

2

Every time a child says 'I don't believe in fairies', there's a little fairy somewhere that falls down dead.
   *Peter Pan* (1904)

3

To die will be an awfully big adventure.
   *Ib.*

4

Do you believe in fairies? Say quick that you believe. If you believe, clap your hands!
   *Ib.*

5

Second to the right, and straight on till morning.
   *Ib.*

6

*Last words of 'Captain Hook':*
Floreat Etona!
   *Ib.*

*Motto of Eton College. In* Peter Pan and Wendy, *the novel (1911), he merely says, 'Bad form!'*

**1**

There are few more impressive sights in the world than a Scotsman on the make.

What Every Woman Knows (1908)

**2**

I know I'm not clever but I'm always right.

*Ib.*

**3**

Every man who is high up likes to feel that he has done it himself; and the wife smiles, and let's it go at that. It's our only joke. Every woman knows that.

*Ib.*

**4**

Never ascribe to an opponent motives meaner than your own.

Rectorial Address, St Andrews, 3 May 1922

**5**

*To H. G. Wells:*

It is all very well to be able to write books, but can you waggle your ears?

Quoted in J. A. Hamerton, *Barrie: The Story of a Genius*

## BARRYMORE, John
US actor
(1882–1942)

**6**

*Throwing a sea-bass to a noisily coughing audience:*

Busy yourselves with *this*, you damned walruses, while the rest of us proceed with the libretto.

Quoted in B. Cerf, *Try and Stop Me*

## BARTON, Bruce
US advertising executive and Republican politician
(1886–1967)

1

[Jesus] picked up twelve men from the bottom ranks of business and forged them into an organization that conquered the world.
  *The Man Nobody Knows: A discovery of the real Jesus* (1924)

## BARUCH, Bernard
US financier and Presidential adviser
(1870–1965)

2

Let us not be deceived – we are today in the midst of a cold war.
  Speech, South Carolina, 16 April 1947
*The phrase was suggested to him by his speechwriter Herbert Bayard Swope who had been using it privately since 1940.*

## BATCHELOR, Horace
British businessman
(1898–1977)

3

*For details of Infra-Draw method of winning football pools:*
Send now to Horace Batchelor, Dept 1, Keynsham – spelt K-E-Y-N-S-H-A-M, Keynsham, Bristol.
  Radio advertisements, from 1950s onwards
*Usually spoken by another voice.*

## BATEMAN, H.M.
British cartoonist
(1887–1970)

4

The Man Who . . . [committed some solecism or other]
  Caption of cartoons in the 1920s/30s

*e.g.: 'The Man Who Missed the Ball on the First Tee at St Andrews',
'The Man Who Lit His Cigar Before the Royal Toast', 'The Girl Who
Ordered a Glass of Milk at the Café Royal', and, 'The Man Who
Asked for "A Double Scotch" in the Grand Pump Room at Bath'.*

## BAX, Sir Arnold
British composer
(1883–1953)

1

*Quoting an anonymous Scotsman:*
One should try everything once, except incest and folk-dancing.
  *Farewell to My Youth* (1943)

## BAYLIS, Lilian
British theatre owner and producer
(1874–1937)

2

O God, send me some good actors – cheap.
  Quoted in the *Guardian*, 1 March 1976

3

*On a less than adequate performance in* King Lear:
Quite a sweet little Goneril, don't you think?
  *Ib.*

## 'BEACHCOMBER'
(J. B. Morton)
British humorist
(1893–1979)

1

Hush, hush
Nobody cares!
Christopher Robin
Has
  Fallen
    Down-
      Stairs.
  'Now We Are Sick', *By the Way* (1931)

2

Erratum. In my article on the Price of Milk, 'Horses' should have read 'Cows' throughout.
  *The Best of Beachcomber* (1963)

3

Gone to that country from whose Bourne no Hollingsworth returns.
  Attrib.

4

Justice must not only be seen to be done but has to be seen to be believed.
  Attrib.

5

Wagner is the Puccini of music.
  Attrib.

## BEATTY, Sir David
(later 1st Earl Beatty)
British admiral
(1871–1936)

6

*To his Flag Captain, Ernle Chatfield, at the Battle of Jutland, 31 May 1916:*
There seems to be something wrong with our bloody ships today.

*Quoted in* The Oxford Dictionary of Quotations (1953)
*Chatfield discounted any other wording.*


## BEAVERBROOK, Lord
(Maxwell Aitken)
Canadian-born politician and newspaper proprietor
(1879–1964)

**1**
I am the cat that walks alone.
   Saying, quoted in A. J. P. Taylor, *Beaverbrook*
*See KIPLING 260:4.*


**2**
*To Winston Churchill of Edward VIII during the Abdication crisis:*
Our cock won't fight.
   Quoted in F. Donaldson, *Edward VIII*


**3**
*As Minister of Aircraft Production:*
Let me say that the credit belongs to the boys in the back rooms. It
isn't the man who sits in the limelight like me who should have the
praise. It is not the men who sit in prominent places. It is the men in
the back rooms.
   Radio broadcast, 19 March 1941
*His inspiration for this phrase was Marlene Dietrich singing 'The
Boys in the Back Room' in the film* Destry Rides Again *(1939).*
*See LOESSER 279:3.*


**4**
*Frequent inquiry at his newspaper office:*
Who's in charge of the clattering train?
*Quoting a nineteenth-century poem.*


**5**
*To Godfrey Winn:*
Go out and speak for the inarticulate and the submerged.
   Quoted in E. Morgan, *Somerset Maugham*

**1**

*When asked why Winn was paid more than the rest of the staff:*
Because he shakes hands with people's hearts.
  *Ib.*

**2**

*On Earl Haig:*
With the publication of his Private Papers in 1952, he committed suicide twenty-five years after his death.
  *Men and Power* (1956)

**3**

*On David Lloyd George:*
He did not care which direction the car was travelling, so long as he was in the driver's seat.
  *The Decline and Fall of Lloyd George* (1963)

## BECKETT, Samuel
### Irish playwright
### (1906–  )

**4**

Nothing happens, nobody comes, nobody goes, it's awful!
  *Waiting for Godot* (1954)

**5**

*Vladimir:* That passed the time.
*Estragon:* It would have passed in any case.
*Vladimir:* Yes, but not so rapidly.
  *Ib.*

## BEECHAM, Sir Thomas
### British orchestral conductor
### (1879–1961)

**6**

*To Utica Welles:*
I don't like your Christian name. I'd like to change it.

Attrib. remark
*She replied, 'You can't, but you can change my surname.' And so they were married (1903).*

1
*To a man called 'Ball':*
Ball . . . how very singular.
    Quoted in N. Cardus, *Sir Thomas Beecham*

2
*On Elgar's A Flat Symphony:*
The musical equivalent of the towers of St Pancras station – neo-Gothic, you know.
    *Ib.*

3
There are two golden rules for an orchestra: start together and finish together. The public doesn't give a damn what goes on in between.
    Quoted in H. Atkins and A. Newman, *Beecham Stories*

4
*On Beethoven's 7th Symphony:*
What can you do with it? – it's like a lot of yaks jumping about.
    *Ib.*

5
*On Herbert von Karajan:*
[He's a kind] of musical Malcolm Sargent.
    *Ib.*


**BEERBOHM, Sir Max**
British writer
(1872–1956)

6
'I don't,' she added, 'know anything about music, really. But I know what I like.'
    *Zuleika Dobson* (1911)

1
*On Pinero's eyebrows:*
[Like] the skins of some small mammal just not large enough to be
used as mats.
   Quoted in C. Hassall, *Edward Marsh*


**BELL, Daniel**
US sociologist
(1919–    )

2
The Coming of Post-Industrial Society.
   Title of book (1973)


**BELLOC, Hilaire**
British writer
(1870–1953)

3
The chief defect of Henry King
Was chewing little bits of string.
   'Henry King', *Cautionary Tales* (1907)

4
They answered, as they took their fees,
'There is no cure for this disease.'
   *Ib.*

5
And always keep a hold of Nurse
For fear of finding something worse.
   'Jim' in *ib.*

**1**
My language fails
Go out and govern new South Wales.
    'Lord Lundy' in *ib*.

**2**
When I am dead, I hope it may be said:
'His sins were scarlet, but his books were read.'
    'On His Books', *Epigrams*

## BENCHLEY, Robert
US humorist
(1889–1945)

**3**
I must get out of these wet clothes and into a dry martini.
    Line delivered in film *The Major and the Minor* (1942)
*Sometimes attributed to Alexander Woollcott, this line may actually
have originated with Benchley's press agent or with his friend Charles
Butterworth.*

**4**
*Capsule criticism of long-running play:*
See Hebrews 13:8.
    Attrib.
*The text reads: 'Jesus Christ the same yesterday, and today, and for
ever.'*

**5**
*Suggested epitaph for actress:*
She sleeps alone at last.
    Attrib.

**6**
*Telegram to the* New Yorker *on arriving in Venice:*
STREETS FULL OF WATER. PLEASE ADVISE.
    Attrib.

### BENDA, Julien
French writer and philosopher
(1868–1956)

1

La trahison des clercs ('The intellectuals' betrayal').
    Title of book (1927)
*The phrases denotes a compromise of intellectual integrity by writers, artists and thinkers.*

### BENN, Tony
(formerly Viscount Stansgate)
British Labour politician
(1925–   )

2

I am on the right wing of the middle of the road and with a strong radical bias.
    Remark, from the 1950s

3

*When Minister of Technology:*
Broadcasting is really too important to be left to the broadcasters and somehow we must find some new way of using radio and television to allow us to talk to each other.
    Speech, *c.*1970
*Compare CLEMENCEAU 111:3 and DE GAULLE 134:3.*

### BENNETT, Alan
British playwright
(1934–   )

4

Life, you know, is rather like opening a tin of sardines. We're all of us looking for the key.
    'Take a pew', *Beyond the Fringe* (1961)

1

*On Sidney and Beatrice Webb:*
Two of the nicest people if ever there was one.
   *Forty Years On* (1969)
*Not in the published script.*

2

Sapper, Buchan, Dornford Yates, practitioners in that school of Snobbery with Violence that runs like a thread of good-class tweed through twentieth-century literature.
   *Ib.*
*An obituary in* The Times *for Colin Watson (21 January 1983) credited him with the origination of the phrase 'snobbery with violence'. His book of that title did not appear, however, until 1971.*

3

*In Bulldog Drummond parody:*
A divorced woman on the throne of the House of Windsor would be a pretty big feather in the cap of that bunch of rootless intellectuals, alien Jews and international pederasts who call themselves the Labour Party.
   *Ib.*

4

Why is it always the intelligent people who are socialists?
   *Ib.*

5

*Of Arianna Stassinopoulos, Greek-born writer:*
So boring you fall asleep halfway through her name.
   Quoted in the *Observer*, 18 September 1983

## BENNETT, Arnold
British writer
(1867–1931)

6

'What great cause is he identified with?' 'He's identified . . . with the great cause of cheering us all up.'
   *The Card* (1911)

**1**

Journalists say a thing that they know isn't true, in the hope that if they keep on saying it long enough it *will* be true.

    *The Title* (1918)

**2**

Mr Lloyd George spoke for a hundred and seventeen minutes, in which period he was detected only once in the use of an argument.

    'After the March Offensive', *Things That Have Interested Me* (1921–5)

### BENNY, Jack
US comedian
(1894–1974)

**3**

*In reply to robber demanding 'You're money or your life!':*
I'm thinking it over.
*His basic joke, from the 1930s onwards.*

### BENSON, A.C.
British writer
(1862–1925)

**4**

Land of Hope and Glory, Mother of the Free,
How shall we extol thee, who are born of thee?
Wider still and wider shall thy bounds be set;
God who made thee mighty, make thee mightier yet.

    Song (1902)
*Sung to music by Sir Edward Elgar.*

### BENSON, E.F.
British novelist
(1867–1940)

**5**

Au reservoir!
    *Passim* in his 'Lucia' novels of the 1930s
*A reasonably common catchphrase of the period.*

## BENTLEY, E.C.
British writer
(1875–1956)

1

Sir Christopher Wren
Said, 'I am going to dine with some men.
If anybody calls
Say I am designing St Paul's.'
  *Biography for Beginners* (1905)

## BENTLEY, Nicolas
British cartoonist and writer
(1907–78)

2

*Of Henry Campbell-Bannerman:*
He is remembered chiefly as the man about whom all is forgotten.
  *An Edwardian Album* (1974)

3

His was the sort of career that made the Recording Angel think seriously about taking up shorthand.
  Attrib.

4

No news is good news; no journalists is even better.
  Attrib.

5

One should not exaggerate the importance of trifles. Life, for instance, is much too short to be taken seriously.
  Attrib.

## BERLIN, Irving
US composer and lyricist
(1888–   )

1
The song is ended
But the melody lingers on.
   'The Song Is Ended', *Ziegfeld Follies* (1919)

2
We joined the Navy to see the world,
And what did we see? We saw the sea.
   'We Saw the Sea', *Follow the Fleet* (1936)

3
I'm dreaming of a white Christmas.
   'White Christmas', *Holiday Inn* (1942)

4
Got no cheque books, got no banks.
Still I'd like to express my thanks –
I got the sun in the mornin' and the moon at night.
   'I Got the Sun in the Mornin'', *Annie Get Your Gun* (1946)

5
There's No Business Like Show Business.
   Title of song in *ib.*

6
Doin' What Comes Natur'lly.
   Title of song in *ib.*

7
Anything You Can Do, I Can Do Better.
   Title of song in *ib.*

8
The Hostess with Mostes' on the Ball.
   Title of song, *Call Me Madam* (1950)

## BERNERS, Lord
### British writer and composer
### (1853–1950)

**1**
*On T. E. Lawrence:*
He's always backing into the limelight.
  Attrib.

## BERRA, Yogi
### US baseball player
### (1925–  )

**2**
The game isn't over till it's over.
  Attrib.

## BERRY, Chuck
### US singer/songwriter
### (1931–  )

**3**
Roll Over Beethoven.
  Title of song (1956)

## BETJEMAN, Sir John
### British Poet Laureate
### (1906–84)

**4**
Broad of Church and broad of mind,
Broad before and broad behind,
A keen ecclesiologist,
A rather dirty Wykehamist.
  'The Wykehamist' (1932)

1

Spirits of well-shot woodcock, partridge, snipe
Flutter and bear him up the Norfolk sky.
'Death of King George V' (1937)

2

Come, friendly bombs, and fall on Slough
It isn't fit for humans now.
'Slough' (1937)

3

Miss J. Hunter Dunn, Miss J. Hunter Dunn
Furnish'd and burnish'd by Aldershot sun.
'A Subaltern's Love-song' (1945)

4

Phone for the fish knives, Norman,
As Cook is a little unnerved.
'How to Get on in Society' (1954)

5

*When asked if he had any regrets:*
Yes, I haven't had enough sex.
*Time With Betjeman*, BBC TV, February 1983


**BEVAN, Aneurin**
Welsh Labour politician
(1897–1960)

6

Listening to a speech by Chamberlain is like paying a visit to
Woolworths; everything in its place and nothing over sixpence.
In *Tribune* (1937)

7

*Recalling the inter-war Depression:*
That is why no amount of cajolery, and no attempts at ethical or social

seduction, can eradicate from my heart a deep and burning hatred for
the Tory Party that inflicted those experiences on me. So far as I am
concerned they are lower than vermin.
   Speech, Manchester, 4 July 1948

1

In Place of Fear.
   Title of book about disarmament (1952)

2

We know what happens to people who stay in the middle of the road.
They get run over.
   Quoted in the *Observer*, 9 December 1953

3

I know that the right kind of political leader for the Labour Party is a
desiccated calculating machine.
   Speech at meeting during Labour Party Conference, 29 September
   1954
*Taken as referring to Hugh Gaitskell though Bevan denied this.*

4

*Wishing to address the Prime Minister (Harold Macmillan) rather
than the Foreign Secretary (Selwyn Lloyd) in a post-Suez debate:*
I am not going to spend any time whatsoever in attacking the Foreign
Secretary. Quite honestly I am beginning to feel extremely sorry for
him. If we complain about the tune, there is no reason to attack the
monkey when the organ grinder is present.
   Speech, House of Commons, 16 May 1957
*Also attrib. to Churchill during the Second World War – replying to a
query from the British Ambassador as to whether he should raise a
question with Mussolini or Count Ciano, his Foreign Minister.*

5

*Speaking against a motion proposing unilateral disarmament:*
If you carry this resolution . . . you will send a Foreign Secretary –
whoever he may be – naked into the conference chamber.
   Speech, Labour Party Conference, 3 October 1957

**1**
And you call that statesmanship. I call it an emotional spasm.
   *Ib.*

**2**
Socialism in the context of modern society (means) the conquest of the commanding heights of the economy.
   Speech, two-day Labour Conference, November 1959
   *Quoting an earlier use by him of the phrase.*

**3**
I read the newspaper avidly. It is my one form of continuous fiction.
   Quoted in the *Observer*, 3 April 1960

**BEVIN, Ernest**
British Labour politician
(1881–1951)

**4**
*On being told that another Labourite was 'his own worst enemy':*
Not while I'm alive, he ain't.
   Quoted in M. Foot, *Aneurin Bevan 1945–60*
   *Reputedly levelled at Aneurin Bevan, Herbert Morrison, Emanuel Shinwell and others.*

**5**
*On the cliché-ridden content of a speech by another politician (possibly Anthony Eden):*
It was clitch after clitch after clitch.
   Attrib.

**BEYOND OUR KEN**

*UK radio comedy series (BBC), from 1954. Script by Eric Merriman. With Kenneth Horne and Kenneth Williams.*

**1**
*'Arthur Fallowfield' (Williams):*
I think the answer lies in the soil.
   Catchphrase

**2**
*'Fallowfield':*
I'm looking for someone to love.
   Catchphrase

**3**
*Old man (Williams), when asked how long he had been doing anything:*
Thirty-five years!
   Catchphrase

**BINYON, Laurence**
British poet
(1869–1943)

**4**
They shall grow not old, as we that are left grow old:
Age shall not weary them, nor the years condemn.
At the going down of the sun and in the morning
We will remember them.
   'For the Fallen', printed in *The Times*, 21 September 1914
   *Frequently misquoted as 'They shall not grow old . . . '*

**BIRCH, Nigel**
(later Lord Rhyl)
British Conservative MP
(1906–81)

**5**
For the second time the Prime Minister has got rid of a Chancellor of the Exchequer who tried to get expenditure under control. Once is more than enough.
   Letter, *The Times*, 14 July 1962

1

*On Harold Macmillan during the Profumo scandal:*
I myself feel that the time will come very soon when my right hon.
friend ought to make way for a much younger colleague . . . I
certainly will not quote at him the savage words of Cromwell, but
perhaps some of the words of Browning might be appropriate in his
poem on 'The Lost Leader', in which he wrote:

> 'Let him never come back to us!
> There would be doubt, hesitation and pain.
> Forced praise on our part – the glimmer of twilight,
> Never glad confident morning again!'

Speech, House of Commons, 17 June 1963

## BIRT, John
British TV executive
(1944–    )

2

There is a bias in television journalism. It is not against any particular
party or point of view – it is a bias against *understanding*.
    Article in *The Times*, 28 February 1975
*This launched a series of articles written jointly with Peter Jay.*

## BLAKE, Eubie
US jazz musician
(1883–1983)

3

If I'd known I was gonna live this long, I'd have taken better care of
myself.
    Quoted in the *Observer*, 13 February 1983
*Five days after marking his centennial, he died.*

## BLANCH, Lesley
British novelist
(1907–   )

**1**
The Wilder Shores of Love.
Title of novel (1954)

## BLEASDALE, Alan
British playwright
(1946–   )

**2**
*Stock phrase of unemployed character, 'Yosser Hughes':*
Gi' us a job, I could do that.
TV play, *The Boys from the Blackstuff* (1982)

## BLUNT, Alfred
British bishop
(1879–1957)

**3**
*On King Edward VIII:*
The benefit of the King's Coronation depends under God upon . . .
the faith, prayer and self-dedication of the King himself . . . We hope
that he is aware of this need. Some of us wish that he gave more
positive signs of such awareness.
   Address to diocesan conference, 1 December 1936
*With these words the Bishop unwittingly triggered off press comment
on the Abdication crisis.*

### BLYTHE, Ronald
British writer
(1922–   )

1

As for the British churchman, he goes to church as he goes to the bathroom, with the minimum of fuss and no explanation if he can help it.
   *The Age of Illusion* (1963)

### BOGART, Humphrey
US film actor
(1899–1957)

2

##   Tennis, anyone?
*Wrongly said to have been the sole line he spoke in his first play. An ABC TV programme, broadcast 9 May 1974, using old film, contained a denial by Bogart.*

*See also* CASABLANCA *pp. 86–7.*

### BOLITHO, William
British writer
(1890–1930)

3

The shortest way out of Manchester is notoriously a bottle of Gordon's gin.
   Quoted in *The Treasury of Humorous Quotations*

## BOOK TITLES
*(and where they come from)*

4

All the President's Men (Bob Woodward and Carl Bernstein)

*Alluding to the line 'All the king's horses/And all the king's men,/Couldn't put Humpty together again' from the nursery rhyme 'Humpty Dumpty' but also perhaps to the book and film about Huey Long,* All the King's Men, *and to a saying of Henry Kissinger's at the time of the 1970 Cambodia invasion: 'We are [all] the President's men and we must behave accordingly.'*

1

Boldness Be My Friend (Richard Pape)
*From Shakespeare,* Cymbeline.

2

Breakfast of Champions (Kurt Vonnegut)
*From the slogan for Wheaties, the US breakfast cereal.*

3

A Bridge Too Far (Cornelius Ryan)
*From a remark made by Lieut. General Sir Frederick Browning to Field Marshal Montgomery about the airborne landings in the Netherlands (1944) to capture eleven bridges needed for the invasion of Germany: 'But, sir, we may be going a bridge too far.'*

4

Bury My Heart at Wounded Knee (Dee Brown)
*From Stephen Vincent Benét, 'American Names' (1927).*

5

A Confederacy of Dunces (John Kennedy Toole)
*From Jonathan Swift's* Thoughts on Various Subjects *(1706): 'Many a true genius appears in the world – you may know him by this sign, that the dunces are all in confederacy against him.'*

6

A Dance to the Music of Time (Anthony Powell)
*From the title given to a painting by Nicolas Poussin in the Wallace Collection, London.*

**1**

Diamonds Are Forever (Ian Fleming)
*Alluding to the slogan 'A Diamond is Forever' for De Beers
Consolidated Mines (since 1939).*

**2**

Do You Sincerely Want To Be Rich? (Charles Raw, *et al*)
*Question posed to his salesmen, during training, by Bernie Cornfeld
(1928–   ) who made his name and fortune selling investment plans.*

**3**

Eating People Is Wrong (Malcolm Bradbury)
*From the song 'The Reluctant Cannibal' by Michael Flanders and
Donald Swann.*

**4**

Fun in a Chinese Laundry (Josef Von Sternberg)
*From the title of an early Edison film.*

**5**

God Protect Me From My Friends (Gavin Maxwell)
*'I can look after my enemies, but God protect me from my friends' is a
proverb common to many languages.*

**6**

Gone With the Wind (Margaret Mitchell)
*From Ernest Dowson's poem* Non Sum Qualis Eram *(1896): 'I have
forgot much, Cynara! Gone with the wind . . . '*

**7**

The Heart Is a Lonely Hunter (Carson McCullers)
*From William Sharp's 'The Lonely Hunter' – 'My heart is a lonely
hunter that hunts on a lonely hill.'*

**8**

I Never Promised You a Rose Garden ('Hannah Green'/Joanne
Greenberg)
*The phrase appears to be original to this book (1964). A song 'Rose*

Garden' by Joe South incorporated it in 1968 and a film with this title followed in 1977.


1

Look Homeward, Angel! (Thomas Wolfe)
*From 'Lycidas' by John Milton.*


2

Love Is a Many-Splendoured Thing (Han Suyin)
*Alluding to Francis Thompson, 'The Kingdom of God': ''Tis ye, 'tis your estranged faces,/That miss the many-splendoured thing.'*


3

The Moon's a Balloon (David Niven)
*From E. E. Cummings, '& N &': 'Who knows if the moon's a balloon, coming out of a keen city in the sky – filled with pretty people?'*


4

The Moon and Sixpence (Somerset Maugham)
*From a review in the* Times Literary Supplement *of Of Human Bondage which said the main character, 'Like so many young men, was so busy yearning for the moon that he never saw the sixpence at his feet.'*


5

The Night Has a Thousand Eyes (Cornell Woolrich)
*From the title of a poetic work by Francis Bourdillon (1878). Also used as a song title.*


6

None But the Lonely Heart (Richard Llewellyn)
*Adapted from the English title of Tchaikowsky's song 'None But the Weary Heart' (original words by Goethe).*


7

Nostalgia Isn't What It Used To Be (Simone Signoret)
*From a graffito.*

**1**

Of Human Bondage (Somerset Maugham)
*From the title of one of the books in Spinoza's* Ethics *(1677).*

**2**

A Postillion Struck by Lightning (Dirk Bogarde)
*This is said to be a line from a nineteenth-century phrase book, but is possibly apocryphal.*

**3**

Random Harvest (James Hilton)
*From an error in a German official report which claimed that a town called 'Random' had been attacked, following a British official report that 'Bombs fell at Random'.*

**4**

The Singer Not the Song (Audrey Erskine Lindop)
*From a West Indian calypso.*

**5**

Tender Is the Night (F. Scott Fitzgerald)
*From the 'Ode to a Nightingale' by John Keats – 'Already with thee! tender is the night.'*

**6**

To Serve Them All My Days (R. F. Delderfield)
*Not a quotation, although it contains echoes of 'And to serve him truly all the days of my life' from the Catechism in the* Book of Common Prayer *and 'Serve him all my days' from the Sunday school hymn 'I Must Like a Christian . . . '*

**7**

Tread Softly for You Tread on My Jokes (Malcolm Muggeridge)
*Alluding to 'Tread softly because you tread on my dreams' from 'He Wishes for the Cloths of Heaven' (1899) by W. B. Yeats.*

**8**

When the Kissing Had to Stop (Constantine FitzGibbon)

*From Robert Browning, 'A Toccata at Galuppi's': 'What of soul was left, I wonder, when the kissing had to stop.'*

**1**
Whistle Down the Wind (Mary Hayley Bell)
*Not intended as a quotation, but echoing Shakespeare,* Othello: *'I'd whistle her off and let her down the wind' (a hawking metaphor). Also a nautical expression.*

## BORGES, Jorge Luis
### Argentinian novelist
### (1899–1986)

**2**
*On the war with Britain over the Falklands, 1982:*
The Falklands thing was a fight between two bald men over a comb.
  Quoted in *Time*, 14 February 1983

## BOSSIDY, John Collins
### US oculist
### (1860–1928)

**3**
And this is good old Boston,
The home of the bean and the cod,
Where the Lowells talk only to Cabots,
And the Cabots talk only to God.
  Toast at Harvard dinner (1910)

## BOTHAM, Ian
### British cricketer
### (1955–   )

**4**
*On Pakistan:*
The sort of place everyone should send his mother-in-law for a month, all expenses paid.
  BBC Radio 2 interview, March 1984

## BOTTOMLEY, Horatio
British journalist
(1860–1933)

1

*When sewing mail-bags in prison and greeted by a visitor with the words, 'Ah, Bottomley, sewing':*
No, reaping.
  Attrib.

2

If it's in *John Bull*, it is so.
  Attrib.

## BOWRA, Sir Maurice
British academic
(1898–1971)

3

I am a man more dined against than dining.
  Attrib. in J. Betjeman, *Summoned by Bells*

4

*On the wedding of a well-known literary couple in 1956:*
Splendid couple – slept with both of them.
  Attrib.

## BRADBURY, Malcolm
British novelist
(1932–   )

5

The History Man.
  Title of novel (1975)

## BRADLEY, Omar
US General
(1893–1981)

1

*On Gen. MacArthur's proposal to carry the Korean war into China:*
The wrong war, at the wrong place, at the wrong time, and with the wrong enemy.
Senate inquiry, May 1951

## BRAINE, John
British novelist
(1922–86)

2

Room at the Top.
Title of novel (1957)
*Braine re-popularized this phrase. In reply to advice not to become a lawyer because it was an overcrowded profession, Daniel Webster (1782–1852) replied, 'There is always room at the top.'*

## BRANDO, Marlon
US film actor
(1924–   )

3

An actor's a guy who, if you ain't talking about him, ain't listening.
Quoted in the *Observer*, January 1956

## BRECHT, Bertholt
German playwright
(1898–1956)

4

Mack the Knife (transl. of 'Mackie Messer').
*The Threepenny Opera* (1928)

## BRESSLAW, Bernard
British actor
(1933–    )

1
Hello, it's me, Twinkletoes.
    Catchphrase from radio series, *Educating Archie*, in the 1950s

2
I only arsked!
    Catchphrase from TV series, *The Army Game* (1957–62)

## THE BRIDGES AT TOKO-RI
*US film 1954. Based on the novel by James Michener. With William Holden.*

3
*Holden, as admiral, seeing men off on a mission from which they will not return, in the Korean war:*
Where did we get such men?
    Soundtrack
*Adapted by Ronald Reagan in 1984 as 'Where do we find such men?'*

## BRIDSON, D.G.
British radio producer
(19??–80)

4
*On disc jockeys:*
The wriggling ponces of the spoken word.
    Attrib.

## BRIEN, Alan
British journalist
(1925–    )

5
Violence is the repartee of the illiterate.
    Article in *Punch*, 7 February 1973

## BRITTAIN, Ronald
British Regimental Sergeant-Major
(1899?–1981)

1

*Although he denied ever saying it, he was associated with:*
You 'orrible little man!
    Attrib. in his obituary, *The Times*, 12 January 1981

2

Wake up there!
    *Ib.*

## 'BRITTON, Colonel'
(Douglas Ritchie)
British propagandist
(1905–67)

3

*In broadcast to resistance workers in occupied Europe:*
You wear no uniforms and your weapons differ from ours – but they
are not less deadly. The fact that you wear no uniforms is your
strength. The Nazi official and the German soldier don't know you.
But they fear you . . . The night is your friend. The 'V' is your sign.
    Radio broadcast, summer of 1941

## BROOKE, Rupert
British poet
(1887–1915)

4

Unkempt about those hedges blows
An unofficial English rose.
    'The Old Vicarage, Grantchester' (1912)

5

For Cambridge people rarely smile,
Being urban, squat, and packed with guile.
    *Ib.*

1
Stands the Church clock at ten to three?
And is there honey still for tea?
   *Ib.*


2
Now, God be thanked who has matched us with His hour,
And caught our youth, and wakened us from sleeping.
   'Peace' (1914)


3
If I should die, think only this of me:
That there's some corner of a foreign field
That is for ever England.
   'The Soldier' (1914)


4
A pulse in the eternal mind, no less
Gives somewhere back the thoughts by England given.
Her sights and sounds; dreams happy as her day;
And laughter, learnt of friends; and gentleness,
In hearts at peace, under an English heaven.
   *Ib.*


5
The cool kindliness of sheets, that soon
Smooth away trouble; and the rough male kiss of blankets.
   'The Great Lover' (1914)


6
*On Cathleen Nesbitt, the actress:*
Incredibly, inordinately, devastatingly, immortally, calamitously,
hearteningly, adorably beautiful.
   Quoted in C. Hassall, *Rupert Brooke*
*In a letter to her, responding to criticism that he was 'in love with
words'.*

## BROOKNER, Anita
British novelist
(1928–   )

**1**

*On the tortoise and hare myth:*
In real life, of course, it is the hare who wins. Every time. Look around you. And in any case it is my contention that Aesop was writing for the tortoise market . . . Hares have no time to read. They are too busy winning the game.
   *Hotel du Lac* (1984)

## BROWN, George
(later Lord George-Brown)
British Labour politician
(1914–85)

**2**

Most British statesmen have either drunk too much or womanized too much. I never fell into the second category.
   Quoted in the *Observer*, 11 November 1974

## BROWN, Helen Gurley
US journalist
(1922–   )

**3**

Sex and the Single Girl.
   Title of book (1962)

**4**

Good girls go to heaven, bad girls go everywhere.
   Promotional line for *Cosmopolitan* magazine
*She relaunched the magazine in 1965.*

## BROWN, James
US singer/songwriter
(1934–   )

1

Say It Loud, 'I'm Black and I'm Proud.'
  Title of song (1968)

## BROWN, John Mason
US critic
(1900–69)

2

*On Tallulah Bankhead as Shakespeare's Cleopatra (in 1937):*
Tallulah Bankhead barged down the Nile last night and sank. As the
Serpent of the Nile she proves to be no more dangerous than a garter
snake.
  Quoted in *Current Biography* (1941)

3

Some television programmes are so much chewing gum for the eyes.
  Interview, 28 July 1955

## BROWN, Coral
Australian-born actress
(1913–   )

4

*To companion when an enormous phallus was revealed as the
centrepiece of the National Theatre production of* Oedipus *(1968):*
Nobody we know, dear.

5

*To Hollywood writer who had criticized the work of Alan Bennett:*
Listen, dear, you couldn't write fuck on a dusty venetian blind.
  Attrib. in the *Sunday Times Magazine*, 18 November 1984

## BRUCE, Lenny
US satirist
(1923–66)

1

*Leaping out of a second floor window:*
I'm Super-jew!
   Quoted in the *Observer*, 21 August 1966
*He only sustained a broken leg.*


## BUCHAN, John
(later Lord Tweedsmuir)
British politician and writer
(1875–1940)

2

An atheist is a man who has no invisible means of support.
   Attrib.


## BUCKLE, Richard
British ballet critic
(1916–   )

3

*On the Beatles:*
The greatest composers since Beethoven.
   Review in the *Sunday Times*, 29 December 1963


## BULMER-THOMAS, Ivor
British Labour, then Conservative, MP
(1905–   )

4

*On Harold Wilson:*
If ever he went to school without any boots it was because he was too
big for them.
   Remark, Conservative Party Conference, 1949
*See WILSON 456:1.*

## BUNUEL, Luis
Spanish film director
(1900–83)

1

I am still an atheist, thank God.
  Attrib.

## BURNS, George
US comedian
(1896–   )

2

*Exchange with wife (Gracie Allen):*
*Burns:* Say goodnight, Gracie.
*Allen:* Goodnight, Gracie.
  Customary ending of TV series, *The Burns and Allen Show*, 1950s

## BURNS, John
British Labour politician
(1858–1943)

3

I have seen the Mississippi. That is muddy water. I have seen the St
Lawrence. That is crystal water. But the Thames is liquid history.
  Attrib.

## BUTLER, R.A.
(later Lord Butler)
British Conservative politician
(1902–82)

4

*On Sir Anthony Eden, who had been described as the offspring of a*
*mad baronet and a beautiful woman:*
That's Anthony for you – half mad baronet, half beautiful woman.
  Attrib.

**1**
*On Sir Anthony Eden:*
## The best Prime Minister we have.
Press Association report, December 1955
*At the time of attacks on Eden's performance as Prime Minister, Butler was boarding an aircraft when a reporter asked him, 'Mr Butler, would you say that this is the best Prime Minister we have?' Butler's 'hurried assent' was converted into the above statement. In due course, Butler himself became known as 'the best Prime Minister we never had'.*

**2**
I think the Prime Minister has to be a butcher, and know the joints. That is perhaps where I have not been quite competent enough in knowing the ways that you cut up a carcass.
Interviewed on BBC television, June 1966
*cf. Gladstone: 'The first essential for a Prime Minister is to be a good butcher.'*

**3**
## Politics is the art of the possible.
*Butler's memoirs* The Art of the Possible *(1971) caused him to be credited with the origination of this phrase. However, in the preface to the paperback edition he pointed out that it had previously been attributed to Bismarck, Cavour, Pindar and Camus, among others.*


**BUTLER, Samuel**
British writer
(1835–1904)

**4**
*Last words:*
Have you brought the cheque book, Alfred?
Quoted in P. Henderson, *Samuel Butler: The Incarnate Bachelor*
*To Alfred Cathie, his servant and friend.*

## BUTZ, Earl
US politician
(1909–    )

1

*On the Pope's attitude to birth control:*
He no play-a da game. He no make-a da rules!
    Remark, 1974
*Repeating this joke of the time led to his losing his job.*

## BYGRAVES, Max
British entertainer
(1922–    )

2

Big 'ead.
    Catchphrase from BBC radio series, *Educating Archie*, 1950s

3

A good idea, son!
    Catchphrase in *ib.*

4

I've arrived and, to prove it, I'm here.
    Catchphrase in *ib.*

5

\## I wanna tell you a story.
*Catchphrase supplied by Mike Yarwood in impressions of Bygraves and taken up by Bygraves.*

## *BY ROCKET TO THE MOON*
*German film 1928. Directed by Fritz Lang (1890–1976).*

1
Five – four – three – two – one.
   Attrib.
*Believed to be the origin of the reverse countdown for rocket launchings.*

# C

## CAGNEY, James
### US actor
### (1899–1986)

1
## You dirty rat!
*The nearest he came to uttering this phrase was in the film* Blonde
Crazy *(1931) when he says, 'You dirty, double-crossing rat.'*

2
Don't get me mad, see!
   Characteristic expression in gangster role

*See also* WHITE HEAT *p. 451.*

## CAHN, Sammy
### US lyricist
### (1913–   )

3
Love and marriage, love and marriage,
Go together like a horse and carriage.
   Song 'Love and Marriage', *Our Town* (1955)

## CAINE, Michael
### British actor
### (1933–   )

4
Not many people know that.
   Characteristic expression, from 1970s onwards

## CALLAGHAN, James
British Labour Prime Minister
(1912–    )

1

## A lie can be halfway round the world before the truth has got its boots on.
Speech, House of Commons, 1 November 1976
*In fact he was misquoting the 19th century Baptist preacher, the Rev. C. H. Spurgeon, who said: 'A lie travels round the world while truth is putting on her boots.' 'A lie can travel halfway round the world while truth is putting on its shoes' has also been attributed to Mark Twain.*

2

*On return from Guadaloupe summit to face widespread strikes:*
## Crisis? What crisis?
Press conference, London airport, 10 January 1979
*In answer to a reporter's question, 'What . . . of the mounting chaos in the country at the moment?' Callaghan replied: 'I don't think that other people in the world would share the view that there is mounting chaos.' The Sun (11 January) encapsulated the remark in the above form and used it as a headline.*

## CAMPBELL, Mrs Patrick
British actress
(1865–1940)

3

*On a homosexual affair between two actors (1901):*
I don't care what people do, as long as they don't do it in the street and frighten the horses.
Quoted in M. Peters, *The Life of Mrs Pat*

4

*To a man:*
Do you know why God withheld the sense of humour from women?
That we may love you instead of laughing at you.
Quoted in *ib.*

1

*On marriage:*

The deep, deep peace of the double-bed after the hurly-burly of the chaise longue.

Quoted in *ib.*

2

When you were quite a little boy somebody ought to have said 'hush' just once.

Letter to Bernard Shaw, 1 November 1912

### CAPONE, Al
US gangster
(1899–1947)

3

I don't even know what street Canada is on.

Attrib.

### CAPOTE, Truman
US writer
(1924–84)

4

Venice is like eating an entire box of chocolate liqueurs at one go.

Quoted in the *Observer*, 26 November 1961

5

*On Jack Kerouac:*

That's not writing, that's typing.

Attrib.

### CARNEY, Don
US broadcaster
(1897–1954)

6

*Thinking he was off the air after a children's radio show:*

I guess that'll hold the little bastards.

Attrib.

## CARNEGIE, Dale
US writer
(1888–1955)

1

How to Win Friends and Influence People.
Title of book (1938)

## CARSON, Frank
Ulster comedian
(1926–   )

2

It's the way I tell 'em.
Catchphrase, from 1970s onwards

## CARTER, Howard
British archaeologist
(1873–1939)

3

*On opening the tomb of Tutankhamun, 1912:*
As my eyes grew accustomed to the light, details of the room within
emerged slowly from the mist, strange animals, statues and gold –
everywhere the glint of gold . . . Lord Carnavon, unable to stand the
suspense any longer, inquired anxiously, 'Can you see anything?' It
was all I could do to get out the words, 'Yes, wonderful things.'
*The Tomb of Tut-ankh-Amen* (1933)

## CARTER, Jimmy
US Democratic President
(1924–   )

4

Why not the best?

Campaign slogan, 1976
*From a question posed to Carter by Admiral Hyman Rickover in 1948*
*as to why Carter had not done his best at Naval Academy.*

1

My name is Jimmy Carter and I'm running for President.
   Stock phrase during campaign, 1976

2

I've looked on a lot of women with lust. I've committed adultery in my
heart many times. God recognizes I will do this and forgives me.
   Interview with *Playboy*, November 1976

3

*Of Bert Lance, government official:*
He is competent, honest, trustworthy, a man of integrity. Bert, I'm
proud of you.
   Remark, 1977

4

*On a visit to north-east of England, using trad. Georgie greeting:*
Hawae the lads!
   Speech, 1977

5

*On a visit to Poland:*
## I desire the Poles carnally.
   Quoted in the *Daily Mail*, 29 December 1978
*This was the inadequate translation into Polish by an American*
*interpreter of Carter's 'I have come to learn your opinions and*
*understand your desires for the future.'*

6

*Seeking to evoke the name of Hubert Horatio Humphrey:*
[The] great president who might have been – Hubert Horatio
Hornblower.
   Speech accepting renomination, Democratic Convention, New
   York, 15 August 1980

## CARTER, Mrs Lillian
US mother of President Carter
(1898–1983)

1
Sometimes when I look at my children I say to myself, 'Lillian, you should have stayed a virgin.'
 Remark, 1980

## *CASABLANCA*

*US film 1942. Script by Julius J. Epstein, Philip G. Epstein, Howard Koch, from an unproduced play* Everybody Comes To Rick's *by Murray Burnett and Joan Alison. With Humphrey Bogart as Rick, Ingrid Bergman as Ilsa, Dooley Wilson as Sam and Claude Rains as Capt. Louis Renaud.*

2
## *Rick/Ilsa:* Play it again, Sam.
*Not said as such in the film. See following entries.*

3
*Ilsa:* Play it once, Sam, for old time's sake.
*Sam:* I don't know what you mean, Miss Ilsa.
*Ilsa:* Play it, Sam. Play, 'As Time Goes By'.
 Soundtrack

4
*Rick:* Of all the gin joints in all the towns in all the world, she walks into mine!
 Soundtrack

5
*Rick:* You played it for her, and you can play it for me.
*Sam:* Well, I don't think I can remember it.
*Rick:* If she can stand it, I can. Play it.
 Soundtrack

1
*Rick (to Ilsa):* Here's looking at you, kid.
  Soundtrack

2
*Rick:* We'll always have Paris.
  Soundtrack

3
## *Rick:* Drop the gun, Louis.
*Not spoken in the film but often used by Bogart impersonators. What he says is, 'Not so fast, Louis.'*

4
*Rick:* Louis, I think this is the beginning of a beautiful friendship.
  Soundtrack
*Last words of film.*


### 'CASSANDRA'
(William Connor)
British journalist
(1909–67)

5
*On resuming his column after the Second World War:*
As I was saying when I was interrupted, it is a powerful hard thing to please all the people all the time.
  *Daily Mirror*, September 1946

*See also* DAILY MIRROR *129:3.*


### CASTLE, Ted
(later Lord Castle)
British journalist
(1907–79)

6
In Place of Strife.

Title of White Paper on industrial relations legislation (1969)
*He suggested the title of this ill-fated proposal, put forward by his wife, Barbara. Compare BEVAN 58:1.*

## CASTLING, Harry
British songwriter

**1**
Let's all go down the Strand – have a banana.
    Song, 'Let's All Go Down the Strand', (1904)
*The words 'Have a banana' were interpolated by audiences. Although not part of the original lyrics, the words were included in later versions.*

## CATCHPHRASES
*(in alphabetical order)*

**2**
Any gum, chum?
*Child's cry to American GIs in the Second World War.*

**3**
Anyone for tennis?
*Other forms: 'Who's for tennis?', 'Tennis, anyone?'*
*There is no single source for this popular phrase, often used to denote the light dramas of the 1920s and 30s. An early example of the form can be found in Shaw's* Misalliance *(1910).*
*See also BOGART 63:2.*

**4**
Are we downhearted? – No!
*Popular at the start of the First World War, but current before. Also incorporated in a song.*

**5**
'Arf a mo, Kaiser!

*Originally a caption on a First World War recruiting poster which showed a British 'Tommy' lighting his pipe prior to going into action.*

1
Back to square one.
*Meaning to go right back to the beginning – possibly derived from BBC radio football commentators of the 1930s who would describe the game in relation to a numbered plan of the pitch. Equally, it could come from a board game like Snakes and Ladders.*

2
Boom, boom!
*Way of underlining the punchline of a joke, used by Billy Bennett, Morecambe and Wise, Basil Brush and others.*

3
The butler did it!
*i.e. as the solution to a 'whodunit'. There is no obvious source for this expression, though it was in use by 1916.*

4
Goody, goody, gumdrops.
*Phrase used by Humphrey Lestocq as host of children's TV series, Whirligig, 1950s.*

5
Heeeeere's Johnny!
*Introduction to Johnny Carson on NBC-TV's Tonight show in the US, from 1961. Spoken by the announcer Ed McMahon.*

6
Hi-yo, Silver!
*Call to horse, by the Lone Ranger on US radio from 1933 and subsequently in films and TV series.*

7
Hoots mon, there's a moose loose aboot this hoose./
It's a braw bricht moonlicht nicht.

*Cod Scotticisms used on the 1958 British hit 'Hoots Mon' (comp.
Robertson), performed by Lord Rockingham's XI.
See also LAUDER 268:4.*


1
I'm sorry I'll read that again.
*Customary BBC radio newsreader's apology for making an error. Also
used as the title of a radio comedy series, from 1964.*


2
Is everybody happy?
*Customary inquiry addressed to holiday camp visitors. Also used by
Ted Lewis, the 'Top Hatted Tragedian of Jazz' in music-hall.*


3
It's a bird! It's a plane! It's Superman!
*Part of introduction to US radio version of the Superman comic strips
(from 1940 onwards).*


4
[Superman], disguised as Clark Kent, mild-mannered reporter for a
great metropolitan newspaper, fights a never-ending battle for truth,
justice, and the American way.
   *Ib.*


5
I was only obeying orders.
*Often used as a defence by those charged with war crimes after the
Second World War, this phrase became much parodied in skits
thereafter. The defence of 'superior orders' was specifically ruled out
by military tribunals, as at Nuremberg 1945–6.*


6
Kookie, Kookie, lend me your comb.
*From the TV series 77 Sunset Strip (late 1950s/early 60s), in which
'Kookie' (Edd Byrnes) was always combing his hair. Also featured in a
song (1960).*

1
Let's get on with it!
*Used in the variety act of Nat Mills (1900– ) and Bobbie, from the early years of the Second World War onwards.*

2
Nice legs, shame about the face.
*The title of a pop song performed by The Monks in 1979 gave rise to the format, 'Nice —, shame about the —.'*

3
No comment.
*Response to journalistic questioning, probably of American mid-century origin. Churchill appeared only to become aware of it in 1946.*

4
[That's the] sixty-four dollar question!
*Meaning the question that would solve the problem if only we could answer it. Derived from CBS radio quiz Take It or Leave It (1941–8). Later, allowing for inflation, it became the title of TV quizzes, The $64,000 Question, The $64,000 Challenge, etc.*

5
Some of my best friends are Jews/Jewish.
*Possibly originated in untraced cartoon caption in the New Yorker, 1930s.*

6
Take me to your leader.
*Customary line spoken by Martian invaders, possibly originating in strip cartoons of the 1950s.*

7
There's gold in them thar hills.
*Possibly this phrase was established (from US gold-mining) by the end of the nineteenth century. It seems to have had a resurgence in the 1930s/40s, possibly through Western films. A Laurel and Hardy short called Them Thar Hills appeared in 1934. The melodrama Gold in the*

Hills *by J. Frank Davis has been performed every season since 1936 by the Vicksburg Theatre Guild in Mississippi.*

1

This week's deliberate mistake.
*A genuine error was covered up by saying this on the BBC radio show Monday Night at Seven (c.1938) and the phrase stuck.*

2

Up there, Cazaly!
*Crowd encouragement to Australian Rules footballer Roy Cazaly (1893–1963).*

3

What's up, Doc?
*From 'Bugs Bunny' cinema cartoons (1937–63).*

4

Who shot J.R.?
*Question posed by last episode of TV soap opera Dallas, in 1979–80 season, referring to character, J. R. Ewing.*

**CAVELL, Edith**
British nurse
(1865–1915)

5

*'Message to the world', given to Revd Stirling Gahan the day before Cavell was executed by the Germans for 'conducting soldiers to the enemy':*
This I would say, standing as I do in view of God and Eternity: I realize that patriotism is not enough; I must have no hatred and bitterness towards anyone.
    11 October 1915

## CHAMBERLAIN, Joseph
British Liberal, then Conservative, politician
(1836–1914)

1

We are not downhearted. The only trouble is, we cannot understand what is happening to our neighbours.
  Speech, 1906

## CHAMBERLAIN, Neville
British Conservative Prime Minister
(1869–1940)

2

*On Czechoslovakia:*
How terrible, fantastic, incredible it is that we should be digging trenches and trying on gas-masks here because of a quarrel in a faraway country between people of whom we know nothing.
  Radio broadcast, 27 September 1938

3

*On returning from signing the Munich agreement:*
This morning I had another talk with the German Chancellor, Herr Hitler, and here is the paper which bears his name upon it as well as mine . . . 'We regard the agreement signed last night – and the Anglo-German Naval Agreement – as symbolic of the desire of our two peoples never to go to war with one another again.'
  Speech, Heston airport, 30 September 1938

4

My good friends, this is the second time in our history that there has come back from Germany to Downing Street peace with honour. I believe it is peace for our time. Go home and get a nice quiet sleep.
  Remarks to crowd, Downing Street, London, 30 September 1938
  *He was alluding to Disraeli's 'Peace with honour'. Note, he did not say 'peace in our time'.*

**1**

This morning the British Ambassador in Berlin handed the German Government a final note stating that, unless we heard from them by eleven o'clock that they were prepared at once to withdraw their troops from Poland, a state of war would exist between us. I have to tell you that no such undertaking has been received, and that consequently this country is at war with Germany.

Radio broadcast from Downing Street, London, 3 September 1939

**2**

Whatever may be the reason, whether it was that Hitler thought he might get away with what he had got without fighting for it, or whether it was that, after all, the preparations are not sufficiently complete, one thing is certain – he missed the bus.

Speech to Conservative Central Council, 5 April 1940

## CHAMBERLAIN, Office of the Lord
British theatre censor until 1968

**3**

*Alterations ordered to script of* The Bed-Sitting Room *(by John Antrobus and Spike Milligan) (1963):*
Omit 'You get all the dirt off the tail of your shirt.' Substitute 'You get all the dirt off the front of your shirt . . . ' Omit the song 'Plastic Mac Man' and substitute 'Oh you dirty young devil, how dare you presume to wet the bed when the po's in the room. I'll wallop your bum with a dirty great broom when I get up in the morning.'

Quoted in K. Tynan, *Tynan Right and Left*

## CHANDLER, Raymond
US novelist
(1888–1959)

**4**

Down these mean streets a man must go who is not himself mean.

'The Simple Art of Murder', *Pearls Are a Nuisance* (1950)

**1**
It was a blonde. A blonde to make a bishop kick a hole in a stained-glass window.
*Farewell, My Lovely* (1940)

**2**
Hollywood is a world with all the personality of a paper cup.
Atrrib.

### CHAPLIN, Charles
(later Sir Charles)
British-born film comedian
(1889–1977)

**3**
All I need to make a comedy is a park, a policeman and a pretty girl.
*My Autobiography* (1964)

### CHARLES, HRH the Prince
Heir to the British throne
(1948–  )

**4**
The one advantage about marrying a princess – or someone from a royal family – is that they do know what happens.
Attrib.

**5**
I have fallen in love with all sorts of girls and I fully intend to go on doing so.
Quoted in the *Observer*, 21 December 1975

**6**
*When asked if he was 'in love' upon getting engaged:*
Yes . . . whatever that may mean.
TV news interview, February 1981

1

*On a proposed extension to the National Gallery:*
A kind of vast municipal fire station . . . like a monstrous carbuncle on the face of a much-loved and elegant friend.
  Quoted in the *Observer*, 3 June 1984

## CHARLIE BUBBLES

*UK film 1968. Script by Shelagh Delaney. With Albert Finney as Charlie and Joe Gladwin as the waiter.*

2

*Waiter:* Do you just do your writing now – or are you still working?
*Charlie:* No . . . I just do the writing.
  Soundtrack

## CHASEN, Dave
### US restaurateur

3

Bogart's a helluva nice guy till 11.30 p.m. After that he thinks he's Bogart.
  Quoted in L. Halliwell, *The Filmgoer's Book of Quotes*

## CHESTERTON, G.K.
### British writer
### (1874–1936)

4

'My country, right or wrong' is a thing no patriot would ever think of saying except in a desperate case. It is like saying, 'My mother, drunk or sober'.
  *The Defendant* (1901)

1
*Telegram to wife:*
Am in Market Harborough. Where ought I to be?
  Quoted in M. Ward, *Return to Chesterton*
*Other venues have been suggested, but this was the original.*

2
Thieves respect property; they merely wish the property to become
their property that they may more perfectly respect it.
  Attrib.

3
Before the Roman came to Rye or out to Severn strode,
The rolling English drunkard made the rolling English road.
  'The Rolling English Road'

4
For there is good news yet to hear and fine things to be seen,
Before we go to Paradise by way of Kensal Green.
  *Ib.*

5
The only way of catching a train I ever discovered is to miss the train
before.
  Attrib.

6
The human race, to which so many of my readers belong, has been
playing at children's games from the beginning, and will probably do
it till the end, which is a nuisance for the few people who grow up.
  *The Napoleon of Notting Hill* (1904)
*Opening words.*

7
Individually, men may present a more or less rational appearance,
eating, sleeping and scheming. But humanity as a whole is changeful,
mystical, fickle and delightful. Men are men, but Man is a woman.
  *Ib.*

**1**

Mr [Bernard] Shaw is (I suspect) the only man on earth who has never written any poetry.
  *Orthodoxy* (1908)

**2**

If a thing is worth doing it is worth doing badly.
  'Folly and Female Education', *What's Wrong with the World* (1910)

**3**

Are they clinging to their crosses,
            F. E. Smith?
  *Antichrist, or the Reunion of Christendom*

**4**

Talk about the pews and steeples
  And the cash that goes therewith!
But the souls of Christian peoples . . .
  Chuck it, Smith!
  *Ib.*

**5**

Journalism largely consists in saying 'Lord Jones Dead' to people who never knew Lord Jones was alive.
  'The Purple Wig', *The Wisdom of Father Brown* (1914)

## CHEVALIER, Maurice
French entertainer
(1888–1972)

**6**

I prefer old age to the alternative.
  Remark, 1962

## CHILDERS, Erskine
British-born author and Irish patriot
(1870–1922)

1
*Last words before being executed by firing squad, 24 November 1922:*
Take a step forward, lads. It will be easier that way.
Quoted in A. Boyle, *The Riddle of Erskine Childers*

## CHRISTIE, Agatha
(later Dame Agatha)
British detective novelist
(1891–1976)

2
[Hercule Poirot] tapped his forehead. 'These little gray cells, It is "up to them" – as you say over here.'
*The Mysterious Affair at Styles* (1920)

3
I believe that a well-known anecdote exists to the effect that a young writer, determined to make the commencement of his story forcible and original enough to catch the attention of the most blasé of editors, penned the first sentence:
' "Hell!" said the Duchess.'
*The Murder on the Links* (1923)

4
## An archaeologist is the best husband any woman can have; the older she gets, the more interested he is in her.
News report, 8 March 1954, also quoted in the *Observer* 2 January 1955
*She denied having said it.*

## CHURCHILL, Randolph
British politician and journalist
(1911–68)

**1**
*While reading the Bible from cover to cover in response to a bet:*
Isn't God a shit.
    Quoted in E. Waugh, *Diaries* (entry for 11 November 1944)

**2**
*During papal audience:*
I expect you know my friend, Evelyn Waugh who, like you, your holiness, is a Roman Catholic.
    Attrib.

**3**
*In a letter to a hostess whose dinner party he had ruined with one of his displays of drunken rudeness:*
I should never be allowed out in private.
    Quoted in B. Roberts, *Randolph*

## CHURCHILL, Winston
(later Sir Winston)
British Conservative Prime Minister
(1874–1965)

**4**
*In response to the charge that the Government had brought the reputation of the country into contempt by describing the employment of Chinese indentured labour in South Africa as 'slavery':*
It cannot in the opinion of His Majesty's Government be classified as slavery in the extreme acceptance of the word without some risk of terminological inexactitude.
    Speech, House of Commons, 22 February 1906
*The phrase 'terminological inexactitude' is sometimes wrongly quoted as a long-winded way of saying 'lie'.*

1

*To Lady Astor who had said, 'If you were my husband, I'd poison your coffee', c.1912:*
If you were my wife, I'd drink it.
   Quoted in E. Langhorne, *Nancy Astor and Her Friends*

2

*In response to Bernard Shaw's offer of tickets for the first night of* St Joan *'for yourself and a friend, if you have one', Churchill expressed regret at being unable to attend and asked for tickets on the second night:*
If there is one.
   Attrib.

3

*On Ramsay MacDonald:*
[At Barnum's Circus] the exhibit on the programme I most desired to see was the one described as the Boneless Wonder. My parents judged that the spectacle would be too revolting and demoralizing for my youthful eyes, and I have waited fifty years to see the boneless wonder sitting on the Treasury bench.
   Speech, House of Commons, 28 January 1931

4

*When Gandhi was released from gaol to take part in a Round Table conference:*
[It is] alarming and also nauseating to see Mr Gandhi, a seditious Middle Temple lawyer, now posing as a fakir of a type well-known in the East, striding half-naked up the steps of the vice-regal palace.
   Speech, Epping, 23 February 1931

5

*To A. P. Herbert, 1935:*
Call that a maiden speech? I call it a brazen hussy of a speech.
   Quoted in L. Frewin, *Immortal Jester*

6

*On being asked by Somerset Maugham if he had ever had homosexual affairs:*

*Churchill:* I once went to bed with a man to see what it was like.
*Maugham:* Who was it?
*Churchill:* Ivor Novello.
*Maugham:* And what was it like?
*Churchill:* Musical . . .
    Quoted in E. Morgan, *Somerset Maugham*

1

I cannot forecast to you the action of Russia. It is a riddle wrapped in a mystery inside an enigma.
    Broadcast, 1 October 1939

2

*On becoming Prime Minister:*
I would say to the House, as I said to those who have joined this Government: I have nothing to offer but blood, toil, tears and sweat.
    Speech, House of Commons, 13 May 1940

3

You ask, what is our aim? I can answer in one word: victory, victory at all costs, victory in spite of all terror, victory, however long and hard the road may be.
    *Ib.*
*Compare CLEMENCEAU 111:4.*

4

Come then, let us go forward together, with our united strength.
    *Ib.*

5

*After the evacuation of Allied troops from Dunkirk:*
We shall fight on the beaches, we shall fight on the landing grounds, we shall fight in the fields and in the streets, we shall fight in the hills; we shall never surrender.
    Speech, House of Commons, 4 June 1940

6

If we can stand up to [Hitler], all Europe may be free and the life of the world may move forward into broad, sunlit uplands.

Speech, House of Commons, 18 June 1940
*'Broad, sunlit uplands' was an image often invoked by Churchill.*


1

Let us therefore brace ourselves to our duties, and so bear ourselves that, if the British Empire and its Commonwealth last for a thousand years, men will say, This was their finest hour.
*Ib.*


2

*Instruction on the establishment of the Special Operations Executive to co-ordinate acts of subversion against enemies overseas:*
Set Europe ablaze.
Attrib. remark, July 1940


3

*On RAF pilots in the Battle of Britain:*
Never in the field of human conflict was so much owed by so many to so few.
Speech, House of Commons, 20 August 1940


4

*On co-operation with the US:*
Like the Mississippi, it just keeps rolling along. Let it roll. Let it roll on full flood, inexorable, irresistible, benignant, to broader lands and better days.
*Ib.*
*Alluding to HAMMERSTEIN 208:2.*


5

Français, c'est moi – Churchill – qui vous parle.
Broadcast, London, 21 October 1940


6

Here is the answer which I will give to President Roosevelt . . . Give us the tools, and we will finish the job.
Broadcast, 9 February 1941

1

We must just KBO ('Keep Buggering On').
   Remark, December 1941, quoted in M. Gilbert, *Finest Hour*

2

What kind of people do they [the Japanese] think we are?
   Speech to US Congress, 26 December 1941

3

When I warned [the French] that Britain would fight on alone . . .
their General [Weygand] told their Prime Minister . . . in three weeks
England will have her neck wrung like a chicken – some chicken,
some neck.
   Speech, Canadian Parliament, 30 December 1941

4

*On Charles de Gaulle:*
[He is] like a female llama surprised in her bath.
   Attrib.

5

*On Charles de Gaulle:*
##    The Cross of Lorraine is the heaviest cross I have had to bear.
   Attrib.
*Churchill told Alexander Korda in 1948 that he had never said it.*

6

I have not become the King's First Minister in order to preside over
the liquidation of the British Empire.
   Speech, Mansion House, London, 10 November 1942

7

Now this is not the end. It is not even the beginning of the end. But it
is, perhaps, the end of the beginning.
   *Ib.*

8

This is *your* victory.
   Speech, London, 8 May 1945

1

*On his defeat in the 1945 General Election:*
If this is a blessing, it is certainly *very* well disguised.
    Quoted in R. Nixon, *Memoirs of Richard Nixon*

2

*On Soviet influence in post-war Europe:*
From Stettin in the Baltic to Trieste in the Adriatic, an iron curtain
has descended across the Continent.
    Speech, Fulton, Miss., 5 March 1946
*The phrase 'iron curtain' in this context dates back to the 1920s and
Churchill had already used it in telegrams to President Truman and in
the House of Commons.*

3

Would a special relationship between the United States and the
British Commonwealth be inconsistent with our over-riding loyalty to
the World Organization?
    *Ib.*

4

It is all right to rat, but you can't re-rat.
    Attrib.

5

*When a proud mother said her baby looked like him:*
Madam, all babies look like me.
    Attrib.

6

*To Bessie Braddock MP who told him he was drunk:*
And you, madam, are ugly. But I shall be sober in the morning.
    Attrib.

7

*On Air Vice Marshal Bennett who had joined the Liberals:*
It [is] the first time that [I have] heard of a rat actually swimming out
to join a sinking ship.

Quoted in M. Muggeridge, *Like It Was* (diary entry for 14 February 1948)

**1**

*When someone said that Stanley Baldwin 'might as well be dead':*
Not dead . . . but the candle in that great turnip has gone out.
   Quoted in H. Nicolson, *Diaries* (17 August 1950)

**2**

*On Clement Attlee:*
## A sheep in sheep's clothing.
   Attrib.
*Churchill told Sir Denis Brogan that he had said it not about Attlee but about Ramsay MacDonald (perhaps echoing a 'Beachcomber' remark).*

**3**

*On Clement Attlee:*
## An empty taxi arrived at 10 Downing Street, and when the door was opened Attlee got out.
   Attrib.
*Churchill told John Colville he would never make such a remark about Attlee.*

**4**

*On Sir Stafford Cripps:*
There, but for the grace of God, goes God.
   Attrib.

**5**

*On Sir Alfred Bossom MP:*
Bossom? What an extraordinary name. Neither one thing nor the other!
   Quoted in L. Frewin, *Immortal Jester*

**6**

Do not criticize your government when out of the country. Never cease to do so when at home.
   Attrib.

1
*On Ian Mikardo MP:*
He's not as nice as he looks.
   Attrib.

2
*On a long-winded memorandum by Sir Anthony Eden:*
## As far as I can see, you have used every cliché except 'God is love' and 'Please adjust your dress before leaving'.
   Quoted in M. Edelman, *The Mirror: A Political History*
*Churchill said: 'This offensive story is wholly devoid of foundation.'*

3
*Marginal comment on a document:*
This is the sort of English up with which I will not put.
   Quoted in Sir E. Gowers, *Plain Words*

4
In war, resolution; in defeat, defiance; in victory, magnanimity; in peace, goodwill.
   'Moral of the Work', *The Second World War*, Vol. 1 (1948)

5
*On becoming Prime Minister in 1939:*
I felt as if I were walking with destiny, and that all my past life had been but a preparation for this hour and this trial.
   *Ib.*

6
Quand je regarde mon derrière, je vois qu'il est divisé en deux partie.
   Attrib.
*What Churchill meant by 'mon derrière' was not his backside but his past.*

7
*On being asked what he would do if he saw Picasso walking ahead of him down Piccadilly:*
I would kick him up the arse, Alfred.

Quoted by Sir Alfred Munnings in speech at Royal Academy dinner, 1949

*Munnings actually used the euphemism 'kick him up the something-something'.*

**1**

*On his 75th birthday:*
I am ready to meet my Maker. Whether my Maker is ready for the ordeal of meeting me is another matter.

Speech, 30 November 1949

**2**

*On plans for commercial television in Britain:*
Why do we need this peep-show?

Attrib. remark, *c*.1951

*Alternatively, 'tuppenny Punch and Judy show'.*

**3**

Here at the summit of our worldwide community is a lady whom we respect because she is our Queen, and whom we love because she is herself.

Broadcast, 2 June 1953

**4**

*On Field Marshal Montgomery:*
In defeat unbeatable; in victory unbearable.

Quoted in E. Marsh, *Ambrosia and Small Beer*

**5**

Talking jaw to jaw is better than going to war.

At White House lunch, 26 June 1954

**6**

*When, as an old man, a colleague told him his fly-buttons were undone:*
Dead birds don't fall out of nests.

Attrib.

*Also alluded to in* The Lyttelton Hart-Davis Letters, Vol. 2 (for 1957).

1

*On his 80th birthday:*
I have never accepted what many people have kindly said, namely that
I inspired the nation. It was the nation and the race dwelling all round
the globe that had the lion heart. I had the luck to be called upon to
give the roar.
Speech, Westminster Hall, 30 November 1954

2

*On being presented with his portrait painted by Graham Sutherland:*
The portrait is a remarkable example of modern art. It certainly
combines force and candour. These are qualities which no active
member of either house can do without or should fear to meet.
*Ib.*

3

*On the same portrait:*
I look as if I was having a difficult stool.
Remark, quoted in E. Morgan, *Somerset Maugham*

4

*Last words:*
I'm so bored with it all.
Quoted in M. Soames, *Clementine*

## CIANO, Count Galeazzo
Italian Foreign Minister
(1903–44)

5

As always, victory finds a hundred fathers, but defeat is an orphan.
Diary entry for 9 September 1942 (pub. 1946)

## *CITIZEN KANE*

*US film 1941. Script by Herman J. Mankiewicz and Orson Welles.
With Orson Welles as Kane, Dorothy Comingore as Susan and
George Couloris as Thatcher.*

**1**
*Kane:* Rosebud!
*His last word, the first word in the film, referred to passim.*

**2**
*Thatcher (quoting Kane):* I think it would be fun to run a newspaper.

**3**
*Kane:* I've talked to the responsible leaders of the Great Powers –
England, France, Germany, and Italy. They're too intelligent to
embark on a project which would mean the end of civilization as we
now know it. You can take my word for it: there'll be no war!
*A good example of the Hollywood cliché, 'The end of civilization etc'
in use.*

**4**
*Kane, replying to a war correspondent's message, 'Could send you
prose poems about scenery but . . . there is no war in Cuba':*
Dear Wheeler, you provide the prose poems. I'll provide the war.
*This is based on an 1898 exchange between the newspaper artist
Frederic Remington and his proprietor, William Randolph Hearst.
Remington asked to be allowed home from Cuba because there was no
war for him to cover. Hearst cabled: 'Please remain. You furnish the
pictures and I will furnish the war.'*

**5**
*Susan:* I'm the one who has to do the singing. I'm the one who gets the
raspberries.

### CLARK, Brian
British playwright
(1932–   )

**6**
Don't half-quote me to reinforce your own prejudices.
  *Kipling* (1984)

## CLARK, Kenneth
(later Lord Clark)
British art critic
(1903–83)

**1**

What could be more agreeable?

Remark attrib. by *Private Eye* following TV series, *Civilization* (1969)

**2**

One may be optimistic, but one can't exactly be joyful at the prospect before us.

The end of *Civilization*

## CLEMENCEAU, Georges
French politician
(1841–1929)

**3**

War is too serious a business to be left to the generals.

Attrib.

*One of his most famous observations (probably dating from the last century). Others have said similar things. See BENN 51:3 and DE GAULLE 134:3.*

**4**

My home policy? I wage war. My foreign policy? I wage war. Always, everywhere, I wage war.

Speech to the Chamber of Deputies, 8 March 1918

**5**

*To General Mordacq, 11 November 1918:*
We have won the war: now we have to win the peace, and it may be more difficult.

Quoted in D. R. Watson, *Clemenceau*

1

*On President Wilson's Fourteen Points (1918):*
The good Lord has only ten.
   Attrib.

2

*On David Lloyd George:*
Ah, si je pouvais pisser comme il parle! ('If I could piss the way he speaks!')
   Attrib.

3

*On the US:*
The only country in history which miraculously has gone directly from barbarism to degeneration without the usual interval of civilization.
   Attrib.


## THE COCOANUTS

*US film 1929. Written by George S. Kaufman and Morrie Ryskind. With the Marx Brothers.*

4

*Groucho:* Believe me, you have to get up early if you want to get out of bed.
   Soundtrack


### COGGAN, Rt. Rev. Donald
(later Lord Coggan)
British Archbishop of Canterbury
(1909–   )

5

We listened to these words of Jesus [St Matthew 7:24] a few moments ago. How right he was!
   Sermon, St Paul's Cathedral, London, 7 June 1977
*At Queen Elizabeth II's Silver Jubilee.*

### COHAN, George M.
US entertainer
(1878–1942)

1
I don't care what you say about me, as long as you say *something* about me, and as long as you spell my name right.
Quoted in J. McCabe, *George M. Cohan*

### COHEN, Sir Jack
British supermarket trader
(1898–1979)

2
Pile it high, sell it cheap.
Business motto

### COHN, Irving and SILVER, Frank

3
Yes, we have no bananas,
We have no bananas today.
Song 'Yes, We Have No Bananas' (1923)
*The line came from a cartoon strip by Tad Dorgan and not, as the composers claimed, from a Greek fruit-store owner.*

### COLLINS, Norman
British broadcasting executive and novelist
(1907–82)

4
Steam radio.
Attrib. in A. Briggs, *History of Broadcasting in the United Kingdom*, Vol. III

## COLSON, Charles
US Watergate conspirator
(1931– )

1

*To campaign staff, 1972:*
I would walk over my grandmother if necessary to get Nixon re-elected!
  Recounted in *Born Again* (1976)


## COMPTON-BURNETT, Ivy
British novelist
(1884–1969)

2

*On a certain woman's age:*
Pushing forty? She's clinging on to it for dear life.
  Attrib.


## CONNOLLY, Cyril
British writer
(1903–74)

3

*On Sir Alec Douglas-Home at Eton:*
In the eighteenth century he would have become Prime Minister before he was thirty; as it was he appeared honourably ineligible for the struggle of life.
  *Enemies of Promise* (1938)

4

Imprisoned in every fat man a thin one is wildly signalling to be let out.
  *The Unquiet Grave* (1944)
*See also ORWELL 328:1.*

**1**
Whom the gods wish to destroy they first call promising.
*Ib.*

**2**
It is closing time in the gardens of the West and from now on an artist will be judged only by the resonance of his solitude or the quality of his despair.
In the final issue of *Horizon* magazine (1949)

**3**
*On V. Sackville-West:*
She looked like Lady Chatterley above the waist and the gamekeeper below.
Attrib.

**4**
*On George Orwell:*
He would not blow his nose without moralizing on conditions in the handkerchief industry.
*The Evening Colonnade* (1973)

### CONRAD, Joseph
Polish-born novelist
(1857–1924)

**5**
The Heart of Darkness.
Title of novel (1902)

**6**
The horror! The horror!
*Ib.*

**7**
Mistah Kurtz – he dead.
*Ib.*

## COOK, A.J.
British miners' leader
(1885–1931)

1

Not a penny off the pay, not a minute on the day.
Slogan prior to General Strike, 1926

## COOK, Peter
British humorist
(1937–   )

2

*Impersonating Harold Macmillan:*
We exchanged many frank words in our respective languages.
'T.V.P.M.', *Beyond the Fringe* (1961)

3

You know, I go to the theatre to be entertained . . . I don't want to see
plays about rape, sodomy and drug addiction . . . I can get all that at
home.
Cartoon caption in the *Observer*, 8 July 1962

4

*On the British satire boom of the early 1960s:*
[Britain must be] about to sink sniggering beneath the watery main.
Attrib. 1962/3

5

Spotty Muldoon, Spotty Muldoon
He's got spots all over his face.
Spotty Muldoon, Spotty Muldoon,
He's got spots all over the place.
Song, 'The Ballad of Spotty Muldoon' (1965)

1
*On being told that the person sitting next to him at a dinner party was
'writing a book':*
Neither am I.
   Attrib. 1984


## *COOL HAND LUKE*

*US film 1967. Script by Donn Pearce and Frank Pierson. With
Strother Martin as Captain and Paul Newman as Luke.*

2
*Captain to Luke:*
What we've got here is failure to communicate. Some men you just
can't reach.
   Soundtrack


## COOLIDGE, Calvin
US Republican President
(1872–1933)

3
*On being asked to elaborate on a clergyman's sermon about sin:*
##   He was against it.
   Attrib.
*A popular story from the 1920s – Coolidge denied it.*

4
*To the President of the American Federation of Labour:*
There is no right to strike against the public safety by anybody,
anywhere, at any time.
   Telegram, 14 September 1919
*Coolidge was Governor of Massachusetts during the Boston police
strike.*

1

*On the Allies' war debt, 1925:*
They hired the money, didn't they?
   Attrib.

2

The chief business of the American people is business.
   Speech to newspaper editors, 17 January 1925

3

I do not choose to run for President in 1928.
   Remark to newsmen, 2 August 1927

4

*When a girl told him her father had bet her she could not get more
than two words out of Coolidge:*
Poppa wins.
   Attrib.

5

*When a woman said 'I could give you tit for tat any time':*
Tat!
   Attrib.

### CORNFORD, Frances
British poet
(1886–1960)

6

Magnificently unprepared
For the long littleness of life.
   'Rupert Brooke' (1915)

7

O why do you walk through the fields in gloves,
Missing so much and so much?
O fat white woman whom nobody loves.
   'To a Fat Lady Seen from a Train' (1915)

## COSTELLO, Lou
US comedian
(1906–59)

1
I'm a ba-a-a-a-d boy.
   Catchphrase in films with Bud Abbott, from 1930s onwards

## COTTON, Billy
British band leader
(1900–69)

2
Wakey-wakey!
   Catchphrase in broadcasts, from 1949 onwards

## COUE, Emile
French psychologist
(1857–1926)

3
Every day and in every way I am getting better and better ('Tous les jours, à tous les points de vue, je vais de mieux en mieux').
   Catchphrase, from the 1920s
*Derived from his system of 'Self-Mastery Through Conscious Auto-Suggestion' or 'Couéism'.*

## COWARD, Noel
(later Sir Noel)
British entertainer and writer
(1899–1973)

4
*To Lady Diana Cooper who told him she had not laughed once at his comedy* The Young Idea:

How strange, when I saw you acting in *The Glorious Adventure* [a film about the Great Fire of London], I laughed all the time!
  Quoted in *The Noel Coward Diaries* (note to 13 March 1946)
*This is the original form of a much-told put down.*

1
*Requirements for acting:*
Just know your lines and don't bump into the furniture.
  Attrib.
*Also attributed to Spencer Tracy.*

2
I was photographed and interviewed and photographed again. In the street. In the park. In my dressing-room. At my piano. With my dear old mother. Without my dear old mother and on one occasion sitting up in an over-elaborate bed looking like a heavily-doped Chinese illusionist.
  Quoted in D. Richards, *The Wit of Noel Coward*

3
Poor Little Rich Girl.
  Title of song, *Charlot's Revue* (1926)
*The phrase had been used for a Mary Pickford film in 1917, re-made in 1936.*

4
A room with a view – and you
  And no one to worry us
No one to hurry us.
  Song, *This Year of Grace* (1928)

5
I'll see you again,
Whenever spring breaks through again.
  Song, *Bittersweet* (1929)

6
*In response to telegram from Gertrude Lawrence saying 'Nothing*

wrong that can't be fixed', concerning her part in Private Lives:
Nothing to be fixed except your performance.
    Quoted in *Noel Coward and his Friends*

1
Very flat, Norfolk.
    *Private Lives* (1930)

2
Certain women should be struck regularly like gongs.
    *Ib.*

3
Moonlight can be cruelly deceptive.
    *Ib.*

4
You are looking very lovely in this damned moonlight, Amanda.
    *Ib.*

5
Strange how potent cheap music is.
    *Ib.*
*Some texts of the play employ 'extraordinary' instead of 'strange' but
the above is what Gertrude Lawrence says in the record she made with
Coward in 1930.*

6
That one day this country of ours, which we love so much, will find
dignity and greatness and peace again.
    The toast from *Cavalcade* (1931)
*See also THATCHER 422:5.*

7
In spite of the troublous times we are living in, it is still pretty exciting
to be English.
    His curtain speech at the first night of *Cavalcade*, Drury Lane
Theatre, London, 1931

1

*Writing to T. E. Lawrence in the RAF:*
Dear 338171 (May I call you 338?)
   Included in *Letters to T. E. Lawrence*


2

Mad dogs and Englishmen go out in the midday sun.
   Song, 'Mad Dogs and Englishmen', *Words and Music* (1932)


3

The Party's Over Now.
   Title of song in *ib.*


4

I believe that since my life began
The most I've had is just
A talent to amuse.
   Song, 'If Love Were All', *Bitter Sweet* (1932)


5

Don't put your daughter on the stage, Mrs Worthington.
   Song, 'Mrs Worthington' (1935)


6

*On Randolph Churchill:*
Dear Randolph, utterly unspoiled by failure.
   Attrib.


7

The Stately Homes of England
How beautiful they stand,
To prove the upper classes
Have still the upper hand.
   Song, 'The Stately Homes of England', *Operette*, (1938)
*Based on a song by Felicia Dorothea Hemans (d. 1835).*

1

*Telegram to Gertrude Lawrence on her marriage to Richard S. Aldrich:*
Dear Mrs A., hooray hooray,
At last you are deflowered
On this as every other day
I love you. Noel Coward.

2

Don't Let's Be Beastly to the Germans.
   Title of song (1943)

3

Chase me, Charlie.
   Title of song, *Ace of Clubs* (1950)

4

*On an American production of* The Cherry Orchard *set in the Deep South:*
A Month in the Wrong Country.
   *Diaries* (entry for 4 September 1950)

5

*Watching the 1953 Coronation on TV, Coward was asked who the man was riding in a carriage with the portly Queen of Tonga:*
Her lunch.
   Attrib.

6

*On the musical* Camelot:
It's like *Parsifal* without the jokes.
   Attrib.

7

*On being told that a certain person had just blown his brains out:*
He must have been an incredibly good shot.
   Quoted in D. Richards, *The Wit of Noel Coward*

1

Television is for appearing on, not looking at.
   Attrib.


2

The only way to enjoy life is to work. Work is much more fun than
fun.
   Quoted in the *Observer*, 21 June 1963


3

She could eat an apple through a tennis racquet.
   *Come Into the Garden, Maud* (1966)


4

*On a child star, in a long-winded play:*
Two things should be cut: the second act and the child's throat.
   Quoted in D. Richards, *The Wit of Noel Coward*


5

*On an inadequate portrayal of Queen Victoria:*
It made me feel that Albert had married beneath his station.
   *Ib.*


6

*To William Fairchild who wrote the dialogue for the part of Coward in
the film* Star:
Too many Dear Boys, dear boy.
   Quoted in C. Lesley, *The Life of Noel Coward*


7

*On child star Bonnie Langford in a musical of* Gone with the Wind
*(1972), when a real horse messed up the stage:*
If they'd stuffed the child's head up the horse's arse, they would have
solved two problems at once.
   Quoted in N. Sherrin, *Cutting Edge*

1

*To Rex Harrison:*
If you weren't the best light comedian in the country, all you'd be fit for would be the selling of cars in Great Portland Street.
   Attrib.

2

*To Laurence Olivier's five-year-old daughter, Tamsin, when she asked what two dogs were doing together:*
The doggie in front has suddenly gone blind, and the other one has very kindly offered to push him all the way to St Dunstan's.
   Quoted in K. Tynan, *Two Hands Clapping*

3

*Last words:*
Goodnight, my darlings. I'll see you tomorrow.
   Quoted in C. Lesley, *The Life of Noel Coward*

## CRICK, Francis
### British scientist
### (1916–   )

4

*On discovering the structure of DNA, 1953:*
We have discovered the secret of life!
   Recounted in J. D. Watson, *The Double Helix*

## CRISP, Quentin
### British celebrity
### (1908–   )

5

There was no need to do any housework at all. After the first four years the dirt doesn't get any worse.
   *The Naked Civil Servant* (1968)

**1**
I became one of the stately homos of England.
  *Ib.*

## CRITCHLEY, Julian
British Conservative politician and writer
(1930–   )

**2**
I was told when a young man . . . that the two occupational hazards of
the Palace of Varieties [Westminster] were alcohol and adultery. 'The
Lords,' he said severely, 'has the cup for adultery' . . . The hurroosh
that follows the intermittent revelation of the sexual goings-on of an
unlucky MP has convinced me that the only safe pleasure for a
parliamentarian is a bag of boiled sweets.
  Article in the *Listener*, 10 June 1982

## CRONKITE, Walter
US broadcaster
(1916–   )

**3**
And that's the way it is.
  Stock phrase
*Concluding CBS TV news broadcasts, 1962–81.*

## CROSSMAN, Richard
British Labour politician
(1907–74)

**4**
*Describing his first day in office as a Cabinet Minister, October 1964:*
Already I realize the tremendous effort it requires not to be taken over
by the Civil Service. My Minister's room is like a padded cell, and in
certain ways I am like a person who is suddenly certified a lunatic and

put safely into this great vast room, cut off from real life . . . Of course, they don't behave *quite* like nurses because the Civil Service is profoundly deferential – 'Yes, Minister! No, Minister! If you wish it, Minister!'

*The Diaries of a Cabinet Minister 1964–70* Vol. 1 (1975)
*Hence the title of the TV series,* Yes, Minister.


## CUMMINGS, E.E.
US poet
(1894–1962)

**1**
a politician is an arse upon
which everyone has sat except a man.
  'a politician'


## CUNARD, Lady (Maud) 'Emerald'
American-born society figure in Britain
(1872–1948)

**2**
*To Somerset Maugham, who had said he was leaving early 'to keep his youth':*
Then why didn't you bring him with you? I should be delighted to meet him.
  Quoted in D. Fielding, *Emerald and Nancy*


## CURZON, George Nathaniel
(later Marquis Curzon)
British Conservative politician
(1859–1925)

**3**
*On seeing soldiers bathing:*
I never knew the lower classes had such white skins.
  Attrib.

# D

## DAD'S ARMY

*UK TV comedy series (BBC), from 1968. Script by David Croft and Jimmy Perry. With Arthur Lowe as Captain Mainwaring, John Le Mesurier as Sergeant Wilson and Clive Dunn as Lance-Corporal Jones.*

1

*Wilson:* Excuse me, sir, do you think that's wise?
   Catchphrase

2

*Jones:* Permission to speak, sir?
   Catchphrase

3

*Mainwaring:* Stupid boy!
   Catchphrase

## DAILY EXPRESS
### London newspaper

4

Britain will not be involved in a European war this year, or next year either.
   Headline, 30 September 1938
   *Inspired by Lord Beaverbrook.*

5

MARTIN BORMANN ALIVE
   Headline, 25 November 1972

1
CHARLES TO MARRY ASTRID – Official.
   Headline, 17 June 1977

## DAILY MIRROR
### London newspaper

2
Forward with the people.
   Slogan, from c. 1935–59.
   *Later, 'Forward with Britain'.*

3
'The price of petrol has been increased by one penny' – Official.
   Caption to cartoon by Philip Zec, 6 March 1942
   *The cartoon showed a torpedoed sailor adrift on a raft. The caption was suggested by 'Cassandra' (William Connor). Together they led to the paper almost being suppressed by the government.*

4
'Here you are – don't lose it again.'
   Caption to cartoon by Philip Zec, 8 May 1945
   *The cartoon showed a wounded soldier proferring 'Victory and peace in Europe'.*

5
WHOSE FINGER?
   Front page headline, 25 October 1951
   *This, being General Election day, saw the culmination of a campaign. Earlier, the paper had asked, 'Whose finger do you want on the trigger when the world situation is so delicate?' The choice was between Churchill and Attlee.*

6
Enough is enough.
   Front page headline, 10 May 1968

*Headline on article by Cecil H. King, Chairman of the International Publishing Corporation, referring to the Government of Harold Wilson.*

1

*On Michael Foot, then Labour party leader:*
A good man fallen among politicians.
   Editorial, 28 February 1983

## DAILY TELEGRAPH
### London newspaper

2

*On the premiership of Sir Anthony Eden:*
Most Conservatives, and almost certainly some of the wiser Trade Union leaders, are waiting to feel the smack of firm government.
   Editorial comment, 3 January 1956
*Written by Donald McLachlan.*

3

*Reviewing Alan Sillitoe's novel* Saturday Night and Sunday Morning:
A novel of today with a freshness and raw fury that makes 'Room at the Top' look like a vicarage tea-party.
   Book review, 1958

## DALEY, Richard J.
### US Democratic politician and Mayor of Chicago
### (1902–76)

4

*To the press, concerning riots during Democratic Convention, 1968:*
Gentlemen, get the thing straight once and for all. The policeman isn't there to *create* disorder, the policeman is there to *preserve* disorder.
   Audio source

## DANIELS, Paul
British entertainer
(1938– )

1
You'll like this. Not a lot, but you'll like it.
Catchphrase

## *DARLING*

*UK film 1965. Script by Frederic Raphael. With Dirk Bogarde as Robert Gold and Julie Christie as Diana Scott.*

2
*Robert (to Diana):* Your idea of fidelity is not having more than one man in the bed at the same time . . . You're a whore, baby, that's all, just a whore, and I don't take whores in taxis.
Soundtrack

## DARROW, Clarence
US lawyer
(1857–1938)

3
I have never killed a man, but I have read many obituaries with a lot of pleasure.
*Medley*

4
When I was a boy I was told that anybody could become President; I'm beginning to believe it.
Attrib.

## DAUGHERTY, Harry
US Republican supporter
(1860–1941)

**1**

*On choosing the party's Presidential candidate, Chicago, June 1920,*
*when the convention failed to make up its mind:*
[A group of senators] bleary eyed for lack of sleep [will have to] sit
down about two o'clock in the morning around a table in a
smoke-filled room in some hotel and decide the nomination.

Quoted in W. Safire, *Political Dictionary*
*Daugherty, however, denied he used the phrase 'smoke-filled'.*

## DAVIES, W.H.
British poet
1871–1940

**2**

What is this life, if full of care,
We have no time to stand and stare?
'Leisure' (1911)

## DAVIS, Bette
US film actress
(1908– )

**3**

*On a starlet:*
I see – she's the original good time that was had by all.
Attrib.

## DAVIS, Sammy, Jnr
US entertainer
(1925– )

**4**

I'm a coloured, one-eyed Jew – do I need anything else?
*Yes I Can* (1966)

## DAWSON OF PENN, Viscount
British doctor
(1864–1945)

**1**

*On his dying patient, George V:*
The King's life is moving peacefully towards its close.
   Medical bulletin, 20 January 1936
*Taken up and broadcast by the BBC.*

## A DAY AT THE RACES

*US film 1937. Script by Robert Pirosh, George Seaton and George Oppenheimer. With the Marx Brothers.*

**2**

*Groucho:* Have the florist send some roses to Mrs Upjohn and write 'Emily I love you' on the back of the bill.
   Soundtrack

**3**

*Groucho (taking pulse):* Either this man is dead or my watch has stopped.
   Soundtrack

## DE COUBERTIN, Baron Pierre
French founder of modern Olympics
(1863–1937)

**4**

The most important thing in the Olympic Games is not winning but taking part, just as the most important thing in life is not the triumph but the struggle. The essential thing in life is not conquering but fighting well.
   Translation of speech, London, 24 July 1908

## DEAN, John
US Presidential counsel
(1938–  )

**1**

*At White House meeting with President Nixon, 21 March 1973, on the Watergate scandal:*
We have a cancer within, close to the Presidency, that is growing. It is growing daily.

Revealed in *The White House Transcripts* (1974)

## DEDERICH, Charles
US founder of anti-heroin centres

**2**

Today is the first day of the rest of your life.
Attrib. slogan *c.* 1969
*Also known in the form 'Tomorrow is . . .' as a wall slogan, graffito, etc.*

## DE GAULLE, Charles
French general and President
(1890–1970)

**3**

Politics is too important to be left to the politicians.
Attrib.
*See also BENN 51:3 and CLEMENCEAU 111:3.*

**4**

*Broadcast appeal from London to Frenchmen betrayed by Pétain's armistice with the Germans:*
I, General de Gaulle, now in London, call on all French officers and men who are at present on British soil, or may be in the future, with or without arms . . . to get in touch with me.

Translation of script broadcast 18 June 1940 (no recording exists)

1

La France a perdu une bataille! Mais la France n'a pas perdu la
guerre! ('France has lost a battle, but France has not lost the war!')
   Proclamation dated 18 June 1940, circulated later in the month
*The phrase was not used in the broadcast, only in the proclamation.*

2

*To his wife, at the burial of their mentally retarded daughter, Anne:*
Come. Now she is like the others.
   Quoted in B. Crozier, *De Gaulle The Statesman*

3

Toute ma vie je me suis fait une certaine idée de la France. ('All my
life I have had a certain view of France.')
   *Les Mémoires de Guerre* (1954)

4

How can you govern a country which produces 246 different kinds of
cheese?
   Quoted in E. Mignon, *Les Mots du Général* (1962)
*Another source dates this as 1951 and has 265 as the number.*

5

*On being compared with Robespierre:*
I always thought I was Jeanne d'Arc and Buonaparte – how little one
knows oneself.
   Quoted in *Figaro Littéraire* (1958)

6

Je vous ai compris . . . Vive l'Algérie française! ('I have understood
you . . . Long live French Algeria!')
   Speech to rally in Algiers, 4 June 1958
*Here de Gaulle spoke with forked tongue – as he later led France out
of its colonial link with Algeria.*

1
## Non!
   Press conference, Paris, 14 January 1963
*His rejection of British attempts to join the European Common Market was not rendered so briefly, though this was the popular (British) way of characterizing his attitude.*

2
*On Jackie Kennedy:*
I can see her in about ten years from now on the yacht of a Greek petrol millionaire.
   Attrib. after her husband's assassination

3
Vive le Québec libre! ('Long live free Quebec!')
   Speech, Montreal, 25 July 1967
*The Federal Canadian government found these words offensive and de Gaulle had to cut short his visit.*

4
La réforme, oui; la chienlit, non. ('Reform, yes; bed-shitting, no.')
   Remark at Cabinet meeting, 19 May 1968, etc.
*Reported to the press by his Prime Minister, Georges Pompidou.*

5
Old age is a shipwreck.
   Quoted in H. Brogan, *The Life of Arthur Ransome*

### DELLA FEMINA, Jerry
US advertising executive
(1936–   )

6
*Suggested slogan for Japanese product:*
From those wonderful folks who gave you Pearl Harbor.
   Recounted in book with that title (1970)

7
Advertising is the most fun you can have with your clothes on.
   *Ib.*

### DEMPSEY, Jack
US heavyweight boxer
(1895–1983)

1

*To wife, on losing his World Heavyweight title to Gene Tunney, 23 September 1926:*
Honey, I just forgot to duck.
   Recounted in his *Autobiography* (1977)

2

Kill the other guy before he kills you.
   Motto, quoted in *The Times*, 2 June 1983

3

Keep punching.
   *Ib.*

### DENNING, Lord
British lawyer
(1899–   )

4

To every subject of this land, however powerful, I would use Thomas Fuller's words over three hundred years ago, 'Be ye never so high, the law is above you.'
   In a High Court ruling against the Attorney-General, January 1977

5

*On the difference between a diplomat and a lady:*
When a diplomat says yes, he means perhaps. When he says perhaps he means no. When he says no, he is not a diplomat. When a lady says no, she means perhaps. When she says perhaps, she means yes. But when she says yes, she is no lady.
   Speech at meeting of Magistrates Association, 14 October 1982
   *Based on a possibly apocryphal saying of Bismarck's.*

### DENT, Alan
British critic
(1905–78)

**1**

This is the tragedy of a man who could not make up his mind.
Introduction to film *Hamlet* (1948)

### DIAGHILEV, Serge
Russian ballet impresario
(1872–1929)

**2**

*To Jean Cocteau, 1912:*
Etonne-moi! ('Astonish me!')
Quoted in J. Cocteau, *Journals*

### DIANA, HRH the Princess
British Royal
(1961–   )

**3**

*When asked what her impression of Prince Charles was on first meeting her future husband in 1977:*
Pretty amazing.
Remark, 1981

### DIETZ, Howard
US writer and film executive
(1896-1983)

**4**

*Motto of Metro-Goldwyn-Mayer, devised c. 1916:*
Ars Gratia Artis ('Art for Art's sake').
Recalled in *Dancing in the Dark* (1974)

**1**
A day away from Tallulah [Bankhead] is like a month in the country.
  *Ib.*

**2**
*Slogan for MGM:*
More Stars Than There Are In Heaven.
  Attrib.

**3**
That's Entertainment.
  Title of song, *The Band Wagon* (1953)

**4**
The world is a stage
The stage is a world of entertainment.
  *Ib.*


## DINNER AT EIGHT

*US film 1933. Script by Frances Marion and Herman J. Mankiewicz.*
*With Jean Harlow as Kitty and Marie Dressler as Carlotta Vance.*

**5**
*Kitty:* The guy said that machinery is going to take the place of every profession?
*Carlotta:* That's something you need never worry about.
  Soundtrack


### DISNEY, Walt
US film-maker
(1901–66)

**6**
All the world owes me a living.
  *The Grasshopper and the Ant*

*So credited by Graham Greene in* England Made Me (1935). *In 1944 there was a UK film with the title* The World Owes Me a Living.

**1**
Girls bored me – they still do. I love Mickey Mouse more than any woman I've ever known.
    Quoted in W. Wagner, *You Must Remember This*

**DODD, Ken**
British comedian
(1927–   )

**2**
Freud never played the second house at Glasgow Empire on a Friday night.
    Quoted in the *Observer Magazine*, 16 December 1984
*His remark has appeared in several versions over the years.*

**3**
By Jove, I needed that!
    Catchphrase

**4**
Hello, Mrs!
    Catchphrase

**5**
How tickled I am!
    Catchphrase

**6**
Nikky, nokky, noo!
    Catchphrase

**7**
Where's me shairt?
    Catchphrase

## DOUGLAS-HOME, Sir Alec
(Later Lord Home)
British Conservative Prime Minister
(1903–  )

1

When I have to read economic documents I have to have a box of matches and start moving them into position to illustrate and simplify the points to myself.

Interview in the *Observer*, 1962, quoted in A. Howard and R. West, *The Making of the Prime Minister 1964*

2

As far as [being] the 14th Earl is concerned, I suppose Mr Wilson, when you come to think of it, is the 14th Mr Wilson.

TV interview, 21 October 1963

3

There are two problems in my life. The political ones are insoluble and the economic ones are incomprehensible.

Speech, January 1964

4

*On Stanley Baldwin:*
A large pipe and thick country tweeds gave the image of a yeoman squire living close to the soil. It was very clever, because in fact he was at his happiest in a room, preferably facing north, with the windows shut, reading Mary Webb.

*The Way the Wind Blows* (1976)

## DOYLE, Sir Arthur Conan
British writer
(1859–1930)

5

Come, Watson, come! The game is afoot.

'The Adventure of the Abbey Grange', *The Return of Sherlock Holmes* (1904)

*See also* THE RETURN OF SHERLOCK HOLMES *p. 361.*

## DRAGNET

*US radio series from 1949, TV series 1951–8, 1967–9. Starring, produced and directed by Jack Webb as Police Sergeant Joe Friday.*

1
*Friday:* Ladies and gentlemen, the story you are about to hear/see is true. Only the names have been changed to protect the innocent . . . I'm a cop . . . My name's Friday.
    Soundtrack.
*Standard preamble.*

2
*Friday:* All we want is the facts, ma'am.
    Stock phrase

### DRAKE, Charlie
British comedian
(1925–    )

3
Hello, my darlings.
    Catchphrase, from 1950s onwards

### DRAPER, Ruth
US entertainer
(1884–1956)

4
Wonderful, I imagine that we're going to find that this is *full* of quotations.
    Sketch, 'The Italian Lesson'

## DR WHO

*UK TV science fiction series (BBC), from 1963. Script (originally) by Terry Nation.*

1
Exterminate, exterminate!
  *Passim*, cry of Daleks

## DUBCEK, Alexander
Czechoslovakian politician
(1921–   )

2
Socialism [or Communism] with a human face.
  Translation of a report in *Rudé právo*, 14 March 1968

## DUCK SOUP
*US film 1933. Script by various. With the Marx Brothers.*

3
*Groucho:* I could dance with you till the cows come home. On second thoughts I'd rather dance with the cows till you came home.
  Soundtrack

4
*Groucho:* Go, and never darken my towels again!
  Soundtrack

## DULLES, John Foster
US politician
(1888–1959)

5
The ability to get to the verge without getting into the war is the necessary art. If you cannot master it, you inevitably get into war. If

you try to run away from it, if you are scared to go to the brink, you are lost.

Quoted in *Life*, 16 January 1956
*This was the origin of the term 'brinkmanship' popularized by Adlai Stevenson during the 1956 US Presidential campaign.*

## DU MAURIER, Daphne
British novelist
(1907–   )

1
Last night I dreamt I went to Manderley again.
*Rebecca* (1938)

## DUNCAN, Isadora
US dancer and choreographer
(1878–1927)

2
*Last words:*
Adieu, mes amis, je vais à la gloire ('Goodbye, my friends, I go on to glory').
Attrib.
*She was about to test-drive a Bugatti and was strangled when the scarf she was wearing caught in the spokes of a wheel.*

## DURANT, Will
US teacher, philosopher and historian
(1885–1982)

3
There is nothing in Socialism that a little age or a little money will not cure.
Attrib.

## DURANTE, Jimmy
US entertainer
(1893–1980)

1
Dese [or 'dems'] are de conditions dat prevail.
   Catchphrase

2
Everybody wants to get into da act.
   Catchphrase

3
Goodnight, Mrs Calabash – wherever you are.
   Catchphrase
*Referring to his late wife.*

4
Stoppa da music!
   Catchphrase


## DUROCHER, Leo
US baseball manager
(1906–   )

5
Nice guys finish last.
   Attrib.
*Or 'Nice guys don't finish first.'*


## DURRELL, Lawrence
British writer
(1912–   )

6
*Of the Mona Lisa:*
She has the smile of a woman who has just dined off her husband.
   Attrib.

# DYLAN, Bob
## US singer/songwriter
## (1941–   )

1

The answer, my friend, is blowin' in the wind.
   Song 'Blowin' in the Wind' (1962)

2

The Times They Are A-Changin'.
   Title of song (1963)

3

How does it feel
To be without a home
Like a complete unknown
Like a rolling stone.
   Song, 'Like a Rolling Stone' (1965)

4

Keep a clean nose
Watch the plain clothes
You don't need a weather man
To know which way the wind blows.
   Song, 'Subterranean Homesick Blues' (1965)

5

I ain't gonna work on Maggie's farm no more.
   Song, 'Maggie's Farm' (1965)

6

*When asked for 'a good quote' by a French journalist on a cold night:*
If I had a good quote, I'd be wearing it.
   Quoted in *The Times*, July 1981

## DYSON, Will
British cartoonist

1

*Clemenceau noticing a child bewailing the breakdown of the peace efforts at the Versailles conference:*
Curious! I seem to hear a child weeping!
    Caption to cartoon in *Daily Herald* 1919
*The child is prophetically labelled '1940 Class'.*

# E

## E.T.

*US film 1982. Script by Melissa Mathison. With Henry Thomas as Elliott.*

1
*Elliott:* How do you explain school to a higher intelligence?
   Soundtrack

2
*The extra-terrestrial:* E.T., phone home!
   Soundtrack

## EDEN, Sir Anthony
### (later 1st Earl of Avon)
### British Conservative Prime Minister
### (1897–1977)

3
We are not at war with Egypt. We are in armed conflict.
   Quoted in the *Observer*, 4 November 1956

## EDEN, Clarissa, Lady
### British wife of Sir Anthony Eden
### (1920– )

4
During the past few weeks I have felt sometimes that the Suez Canal was flowing through my drawing-room.
   Speech, Gateshead, 20 November 1956

## EDGAR, Marriott
British writer
(1880–1951)

1

A grand little lad was young Albert,
  All dressed in his best; quite a swell
With a stick with an 'orse's 'ead 'andle,
  The finest that Woolworth's could sell.
  'The Lion and Albert' (1932)
*Written with Wolseley Charles.*

## EDISON, Thomas Alva
US inventor
(1847–1931)

2

Genius is one per cent inspiration and ninety-nine per cent perspiration.
  Quoted in *Life* (1932)

## EDWARD VIII
(later Duke of Windsor)
British sovereign
(1894–1972)

3

The young business and professional men of this country must get together round the table, adopt methods that have proved sound in the past, adapt them to the changing needs of the times and, whenever possible, improve them.
  Speech, British Industries Fair, Birmingham, 1927
*Adopted as the motto of the Round Table movement in the form 'Adopt, adapt, improve'.*

1

Perhaps one of the only positive pieces of advice that I was ever given was that supplied by an old courtier who observed: 'Only two rules really count. Never miss an opportunity to relieve yourself; never miss a chance to sit down and rest your feet.'

A King's Story (1951)

*The 'old courtier' may have been his father, George V, to whom this advice has also been attributed.*

2

*To official at Bessemer steel works, South Wales, where 9,000 men had been made unemployed:*

These works brought all these people here. Something must be done to find them work.

News reports, November 1936

3

I have found it impossible to carry the heavy burden of responsibility and to discharge my duties as King as I would wish to do without the help and support of the woman I love.

Radio broadcast after abdication, 11 December 1936

4

The thing that impresses me most about America is the way parents obey their children.

Attrib.

## EHRLICHMAN, John D.
US Presidential aide
(1925–   )

5

*Yardstick for judging whether policies would appeal to 'Middle America', 1968:*

It'll play in Peoria.

Quoted in W. Safire, *Political Dictionary*

1

*Of Patrick Gray, Acting Director of the CBI, who did not know his commission had been withdrawn:*
Let him twist slowly, slowly in the wind.
　Telephone remark to John Dean, 7/8 March 1973

## EHRMANN, Max
US writer
(d. 1945)

2

Go placidly amid the noise and haste, and remember what peace there may be in silence. As far as possible without surrender be on good terms with all persons. Speak your truth quietly and clearly; and listen to others, even the dull and ignorant; they too have their story. Avoid loud and aggressive persons, they are vexations to the spirit.
　*Desiderata* (1927)
*In the 1960s and 70s, these words were marketed anonymously as having come from Old St Paul's Church, Baltimore, and dating from 1692.*

## EINSTEIN, Albert
German-born US scientist
(1879–1955)

3

$E=mc^2$ (Energy = mass × the speed of light squared.)
　Statement (1905)

4

When a man sits with a pretty girl for an hour, it seems like a minute. But let him sit on a hot stove for a minute – and it's longer than any hour. That's relativity.
　Attrib.

## EISENHOWER, Dwight D.
US general and Republican President
(1890–1969)

1

I shall go to Korea and try to end the war.
    Campaign promise, in speech, 24 October 1952

2

You have a row of dominoes set up. You knock over the first one and what will happen to the last one is that it will go over very quickly.
    Remark at press conference, April 1954
*The 'domino theory' had, however, first been applied to South-East Asia by the columnist Joseph Alsop.*

3

In the councils of government, we must guard against the acquisition of unwarranted influence, whether sought or unsought, by the military-industrial complex. The potential for the disastrous rise of misplaced power exists and will persist.
    Farewell address, 17 January 1961

## EKLAND, Britt
Swedish actress
(1942–   )

4

I say I don't sleep with married men, but what I mean is that I don't sleep with happily married men.
    Attrib. in January 1980

## ELIOT, T.S.
American-born poet
(1888–1965)

5

Let us go then, you and I
When the evening is spread out against the sky
Like a patient etherised upon a table.
    'The Love Song of J. Alfred Prufrock' (1917)

1

In the room the women come and go
Talking of Michelangelo.
   *Ib.*

2

The yellow fog that rubs its back upon the window panes.
   *Ib.*

3

I have measured out my life with coffee spoons.
   *Ib.*

4

Here I am, an old man in a dry month,
Being read to by a boy, waiting for rain.
   'Gerontion' (1920)

5

The hippopotamus's day
Is passed in sleep; at night he hunts;
God works in a mysterious way –
The Church can feed and sleep at once.
   'The Hippopotamus' (1920)

6

Webster was much possessed by death
And saw the skull beneath the skin.
   'Whispers of Immortality' (1920)

7

April is the cruellest month, breeding
Lilacs out of the dead land.
   *The Waste Land* (1922)

8

O O O O that Shakespeherian Rag
It's so elegant
So intelligent.
   *Ib.*

*Based on 'That Shakespearian Rag' by Buck, Ruby and Stamber, published in the US, 1912.*

1
These fragments have I shored against my ruins.
  *Ib.*

2
We are the hollow men
We are the stuffed men
Leaning together.
  *The Hollow Men* (1925)

3
This is the way the world ends
Not with a bang but a whimper.
  *Ib.*

4
Between the idea
And the reality
Between the motion
And the act
Falls the shadow.
  *Ib.*

5
Pray for us now and at the hour of our birth.
  'Animula' (1929)

6
Time present and time past
Are both perhaps present in time future,
And time future contained in time past.
  'Burnt Norton', *Four Quartets* (1935)

7
At the still point of the turning world. Neither flesh nor fleshless;

Neither from nor towards; at the still point, there the dance is,
But neither arrest nor movement.
>     *Ib.*

1
Go go go said the bird.
>     *Ib.*

2
In my beginning is my end.
>     'East Coker' in *ib*. (1940)

3
In my end is my beginning.
>     *Ib.*

4
He always has an alibi, and one or two to spare:
At whatever time the deed took place – Macavity wasn't there.
>     'Macavity: The Mystery Cat', *Old Possum's Book of Practical Cats*
>     (1939)


## ELIZABETH THE QUEEN MOTHER, HM Queen
### British Royal
### (1900–   )

5
*After the bombing of Buckingham Palace, September 1940:*
I'm glad we've been bombed. It makes me feel I can look the East End
in the face.
>     Attrib.

6
*On whether her children would leave England after the bombing of*
*Buckingham Palace:*
The children will not leave unless I do. I shall not leave unless their

father does, and the King will not leave the country in any circumstances whatever.

Attrib.

1

My favourite programme is 'Mrs Dale's Diary'. I try never to miss it because it is the only way of knowing what goes on in a middle-class family.

Untraced report from the London *Evening News*

2

*When a fishbone lodged in her throat:*
The salmon are striking back.

Attrib. November 1982

3

*On President Carter:*
He is the only man since my dear husband died, to have the effrontery to kiss me on the lips.

Attrib. February 1983

4

*To her daughter, when the Queen accepted a second glass of wine at lunch:*
Do you think it's wise, darling? You know you've got to rule this afternoon.

Attrib. 1984

## ELIZABETH II, HM Queen
### British sovereign
(1926–    )

5

*When a girl:*
I should like to be a horse.

Attrib.

1

*To her sister, at end of radio talk to children evacuated to North America:*
Come on, Margaret!
   Broadcast, 13 October 1940

2

*On her 21st birthday:*
I declare before you all that my whole life, whether it be long or short, shall be devoted to your service, and the service of our great imperial family to which we all belong.
   Broadcast from South Africa, 21 April 1947

3

My husband and I left London a month ago . . .
   Christmas broadcast from New Zealand, 25 December 1953
*The phrase 'My husband and I' was used for many years.*

4

*At Silver Wedding banquet:*
I think everybody really will concede that on this, of all days, I should begin my speech with the words, 'My husband and I'.
   Speech, Guildhall, London, 20 November 1972

5

I have to be seen to be believed.
   Attrib.

6

*On Princess Michael of Kent:*
She's more royal than we are.
   Attrib. in *Sunday* magazine, 14 April 1985
*Compare the saying from the time of Louis XVI: 'Il ne faut pas être plus royaliste que le roi' ('You mustn't be more royalist than the king').*

**ELLINGTON, Duke**
US musician and composer
(1899–1974)

7

Love you madly.
   Stock phrase

## EMERY, Dick
British comedian
(1917–83)

**1**

Oooh, you are awful . . . but I like you!
  Catchphrase
*As character 'Mandy'.*

## ENGLISH, Arthur
British comedian
(1919–   )

**2**

Mum, mum, they are laughing at me.
  Catchphrase, from 1940s

**3**

Play the music and open the cage.
  Catchphrase, from 1940s

## EPITAPHS

**4**

*On Captain 'Titus' Oates, in the Antarctic, 1912:*
Hereabouts died a very gallant gentleman.
*Composed by E.L. Atkinson and Apsley Cherry-Garrard.*

**5**

Their Name Liveth for Evermore.
*Standard epitaph over lists of war dead, written after the First World
War by Rudyard Kipling and based on Ecclesiasticus 44:14.*

**6**

A Soldier of the Great War Known unto God.
*Standard epitaph over graves of the unknown dead from the First
World War.*

1

They buried him among the Kings because he had done good toward
God and toward his house.
*On the tomb of the Unknown Soldier in Westminster Abbey, buried*
*1920 – echoing 2 Chronicles 24:16.*

**ERWIN, Dudley**
Australian politician
(1917–   )

2

*When asked the reason for his dismissal as Air Minister, 1969:*
It is shapely, it wiggles, and it's name is Ainslie Gotto.
   Quoted in *Dictionary of Australian Quotations*
*Ms Gotto was the secretary of Prime Minister John Gorton, and said*
*to exert undue influence.*

**EVANS, Dame Edith**
British actress
(1888–1976)

3

*On being told that Nancy Mitford had been lent a villa so that she*
*could finish a book:*
Oh really. What exactly is she reading?
   Attrib.

4

*To a salesgirl at Fortnum and Mason who insisted on giving her*
*threepence change:*
Keep the change, my dear. I trod on a grape as I came in.
   Quoted in B. Forbes, *Ned's Girl*

## EVERETT, Kenny
British entertainer
(1944–  )

1
It's all done in the best *possible* taste!
  Catchphrase, *Kenny Everett Television Show* (from 1981 onwards)
*As American film star 'Cupid Stunt'.*

## EWER, W.N.
British journalist
(1885–1976)

2
How odd
Of God
To choose
The Jews.
  Quoted in the *Week-end Book* (1924)
*In conversation at the Savage Club, London.*

# F

## THE FACE OF FU MANCHU

*UK film 1965. Script by Peter Welbeck. With Christopher Lee as Fu Manchu.*

1
*Fu Manchu:* The world shall hear from me again!
*Last words of film, Fu Manchu having been blown up. The character had been created in a 1911 novel by Sax Rohmer.*

## FAIRLIE, Henry
British journalist
(1924–  )

2
I have several times suggested that what I call the 'Establishment' in this country is today more powerful than ever before. By the 'Establishment' I do not mean only the centres of official power – though they are certainly part of it – but rather the whole matrix of official and social relations within which power is exercised . . . the 'Establishment' can be seen at work in the activities of, not only the Prime Minister, the Archbishop of Canterbury and the Earl Marshal, but of such lesser mortals as the Chairman of the Arts Council, the Director-General of the BBC, and even the editor of the *Times Literary Supplement*, not to mention dignitaries like Lady Violet Bonham-Carter.
    Article in *Spectator*, 23 September 1955
*A.J.P. Taylor had also used the phrase 'Establishment' in its modern sense in a review for the* New Statesman *in 1953.*

## FAROUK, King
Egyptian Royal
(1920–65)

1

There will soon be only five kings left – the Kings of England, Diamonds, Hearts, Spades and Clubs.
  Remark to Lord Boyd-Orr, 1951

### *THE FATAL GLASS OF BEER*

*US film 1933. Script by W.C. Fields. With W.C. Fields.*

2

*Fields:* 'Tain't a fit night out for man or beast.
  Soundtrack

## FAULKNER, William
US novelist
(1897–1962)

3

The Long Hot Summer.
  Title of a film based on his short stories (1958) and of a TV series (1965–6)
*He had originated the phrase in 1928.*

4

*On Henry James:*
The nicest old lady I ever met.
  Quoted in E. Stone, *The Battle and the Books*

### *FAWLTY TOWERS*

*UK TV comedy series (BBC), from 1975–9. Script by John Cleese and Connie Booth. With John Cleese as Basil Fawlty and Andrew Sachs as Manuel, the Spanish waiter.*

**1**
*On the shortcomings of Manuel:*
*Basil:* I'm sorry. He's from Barcelona.
   Stock phrase (variable)

**2**
*Manuel:* ¿Que?
   Stock phrase

## FERBER, Edna
US writer
(1887–1968)

**3**
Being an old maid is like death by drowning, a really delightful
sensation after you cease to struggle.
   Quoted in R.E. Drennan, *Wit's End*

## FERLINGHETTI, Laurence
US poet
(1919– )

**4**
The world is a beautiful place
   to be born into
if you don't mind some people dying
   all the time
or maybe only starving
   some of the time
which isn't half so bad
   if it isn't you.
   *Pictures of the Gone World* (1955)

1
Yes
    but then right in the middle of it
comes the smiling
    mortician.
    *Ib.*


# FIELDS, Dorothy
US lyricist
(1904–74)

2
I Can't Give You Anything But Love.
    Title of song, *Delmar's Revels* (1927)·


# FIELDS, W.C.
US comedian
(1880–1946)

3
Never give a sucker an even break.
    Quoted in *The Concise Oxford Dictionary of Proverbs* (1982)
*Popularized by Fields, though attributed to various people. It was
already associated with him by 1925 and may have been used in the
musical comedy* Poppy *(1923). Used as the title of one of his films,
1941.*

4
##   On the whole I'd rather be in Philadelphia.
*What the comedian actually submitted as a suggested epitaph to*
Vanity Fair *magazine in 1925 was: 'Here lies W.C. Fields. I would
rather be living in Philadelphia.' It does not appear on his actual
gravestone. The saying evolved from the older expression 'Sooner
dead than in Philadelphia.'*

1

I went to Philadelphia and found that it was closed.
    Attrib.
*See also ANONYMOUS 21:3.*

2

## Any man who hates dogs and babies can't be all bad.
*In fact, this was said by Leo Rosten (1908–  ) about Fields at a Masquer's Club dinner, 16 February 1939. Often 'children' is substituted for 'babies'.*

3

*When asked why he did not drink water:*
Fish fuck in it.
    Attrib.

4

*When asked whether he liked children:*
Boiled or fried?
    Attrib.

5

*When a gambler asks, 'Is this a game of chance'?:*
*'Cuthbert J. Twillie':* Not the way I play it.
    Film, *My Little Chickadee* (1939)

6

I was in love with a beautiful blonde once – she drove me to drink – 'tis the one thing I'm indebted to her for.
    Attrib.

7

Horse sense is a good judgement which keeps horses from betting on people.
    Attrib.

8

*During his last illness:*

I have spent a lot of time searching through the Bible for loopholes.
   Attrib.

*See also* THE FATAL GLASS OF BEER *162:2*


# FILM TITLES

1
Blonde Bombshell (US 1933)
*Title of a Jean Harlow vehicle (1933), known simply as* Bombshell *in the UK.*


2
The Days of Wine and Roses (US 1962)
*From Ernest Dowson (d. 1900),* Vitae Summa Brevis.


3
Do Not Fold Spindle or Mutilate (US 1971)
*From the instruction on punched cards, from 1930s.*


4
Heaven's Gate (US 1980)
*Alluding to the song 'Hark, hark, the lark' from Shakespeare's* Cymbeline *or his Sonnet XXIX.*


5
La Grande Illusion (France 1937)
*From the revised title of Norman Angell's book* The Great Illusion *(1910).*


6
A Fool There Was (US 1914)
*From Rudyard Kipling's poem 'The Vampire' (1897). It was through this film that Theda Bara popularized the notion of the female 'vamp'.*


7
If It's Tuesday, This Must be Belgium (US 1969)
*Title of film about US tourists rushing around Europe.*

**1**
In Which We Serve (UK 1942)
*From* The Book of Common Prayer, *'Forms of Prayer to Be Used at Sea'.*

**2**
Now Voyager (US 1942)
*(And the original Olive Higgins Prouty novel), from Walt Whitman's line: 'Now voyager, sail thou forth to seek and find.'*

**3**
An Officer and a Gentleman (US 1982)
*See PLAY TITLES 341:3.*

**4**
One Flew Over the Cuckoo's Nest (US 1975)
*(And the original Ken Kesey novel), from the US nursery rhyme 'One flew east, one flew west/One flew over the cuckoo's nest.'*

**5**
Les Quatre Cents Coups (The Four Hundred Blows) (France 1958)
*From a French slang expression – 'faire les quatre cents coups' – meaning either 'to paint the town red' or 'to be up to all sorts of tricks'.*

**6**
Situation Hopeless But Not Serious (US 1965)
*Probably derived from: 'The situation in Germany is serious but not hopeless; the situation in Austria is hopeless but not serious.' This is described as 'an Austrian proverb collected by Franklin Pierce Adams' in A. Andrews,* Quotations for Speakers and Writers.

**7**
Somebody Up There Likes Me (US 1956)
*Title of film based on life of boxer, Rocky Graziano (b. 1922)*

**8**
Straw Dogs (UK 1971)
*'Heaven and Earth are not humane. They regard all things as straw dogs' (used in sacrifices) – Lao-tzu (c. 604 – c. 531 BC).*

1

Tirez Sur Le Pianiste (France 1960)
*Translated as 'Shoot the Pianist/Piano-Player' – echoing the notice once reported by Oscar Wilde from a bar in the US Rocky Mountains – 'Please do not shoot the pianist. He is doing his best.' (In 1972, Elton John had a record album entitled, 'Don't Shoot Me, I'm Only the Piano-Player'.)*

2

A View to a Kill (UK 1985)
*The title of Ian Fleming's original short story was 'From a View to a Kill', alluding more directly to the line 'From a view to a death' in the hunting song, 'D'ye Ken John Peel' (1832).*

3

What's New Pussycat? (US/France 1965)
*From a phrase said to have been coined by Warren Beatty for whom the film was originally written.*

4

Where Were You When the Lights Went Out? (US 1968)
*Alluding perhaps to the old (US?) rhyme 'Where was Moses when the lights went out?/Down in the cellar eating sauerkraut.'*

**FISHER, Lord**
British admiral
(1841–1920)

5

The British navy always travels first class.
    Quoted in W. Churchill, *The Second World War*, Vol.1

6

Fear God and Dread Nought.
    His motto when elevated to the peerage

**1**

[Some day the Empire will go down because it is] Buggins's turn.

Letter (8 January 1917), printed in his *Memories* (1919)

*He also used the expression in a letter in 1901, though he may not have originated it.*

**2**

*On the ruinous cost of the Fleet and those responsible:*

You must be ruthless, relentless, and remorseless! Sack the lot!

Letter, *The Times*, 2 September 1919

**3**

*Signing off correspondence:*

Yours till charcoal sprouts.

Quoted in C. Hassall, *Edward Marsh*

*His other salutations included, 'Yours till hell freezes over' and 'Yours to a cinder'.*

**4**

Never complain and never apologise.

Attrib.

*Compare Benjamin Disraeli: 'Never complain and never explain.'*


**FITZGERALD, F. Scott**
US novelist
(1896–1940)

**5**

Tales of the Jazz Age.

Title of book (1922)

**6**

So we beat on, boats against the current, borne back ceaselessly into the past.

*The Great Gatsby* (1925)

*Last line.*

**1**

In a real dark night of the soul it is always three o'clock in the morning.

*The Crack-Up* (1936)

*The phrase 'Noche oscura' – meaning a period of spiritual aridity suffered by a mystic – had been used as the title of a Spanish work by St John of the Cross in the sixteenth century.*

## FITZPATRICK, James A.
US travel film-maker
(1902–  )

**2**

And so we say farewell.

Customary signing-off line in *Fitzpatrick Traveltalks*, from 1920s onwards

## FITZSIMMONS, Bob
British boxer
(1862–1917)

**3**

*Referring to an opponent of larger build (James L. Jeffries):*
## The bigger they come, the harder they fall.

Attrib.

*Also attributed to John L. Sullivan. Probably of earlier proverbial origin in any case.*

## FLANDERS, Michael
British entertainer
(1922–75)

**4**

Mud, mud, glorious mud,
Nothing quite like it for cooling the blood.

'The Hippopotamus Song' (1953)

**1**

Eating people is wrong.
  Song, 'The Reluctant Cannibal', *At the Drop of a Hat* (1957)

**2**

Have Some Madeira, M'Dear
  Song, 'Madeira, M'Dear' in *ib.*

**3**

Gnot a gnother gnu?
  Song, 'The Gnu' in *ib.*

**4**

If God had intended us to fly, he'd never have given us the railways.
  'By Air', *At the Drop of Another Hat* (1963)

**5**

It all makes work for the working man to do.
  'The Gas-Man Cometh' in *ib.*

**6**

The purpose of satire it has been rightly said is to strip off the veneer of
comforting illusion and cosy half-truth and our job, as I see it, is to put
it back again.
  *Ib.*

**7**

Pee po belly bum drawers.
  Title of (a very rude) song (pub. 1977)
*Supposedly based on a traditional child's remark.*


**FLETCHER, Cyril**
British entertainer
(1913–   )

**8**

I'm dreaming, oh my darling love, of thee.
  Catchphrase, following broadcast in 1938
*From poem 'Dreaming of Thee' by Edgar Wallace.*

1

Pin back your lugholes.
  Catchphrase
*Preparing to recite one of his 'Odd Odes'.*


# FOCH, Ferdinand
French soldier
(1851–1929)

2

*To General Joffre, during the second battle of the Marne (July/August 1918):*
Mon centre cède, ma droite recule, situation excellente. J'attaque! ('My centre gives way, my right retreats; situation excellent. I shall attack!')
  Attrib.


# FOOT, Paul
British journalist
(1937–   )

3

If you don't know what's going on in Portugal, you must have been reading the papers.
  Attrib. 1975.


# FORD, Gerald R.
US Republican President
(1913–   )

4

*On becoming Vice-President:*
I am a Ford, not a Lincoln. My addresses will never be as eloquent as Mr Lincoln's. But I will do my very best to equal his brevity and his plain speaking.
  Speech, Washington, 6 December 1973

1

*On becoming President:*
I believe that truth is the glue that holds government together, not only our government but civilization itself . . . Our long national nightmare is over. Our Constitution works. Our great Republic is a government of laws and not of men. Here, the people rule.

    Speech, Washington, 9 August 1974

2

*Proposing a toast to Anwar Sadat:*
[To] the great people and the government of Israel . . . Egypt, excuse me . . .

    Speech, Washington, December 1975

3

There is no Soviet domination of Eastern Europe and there never will be under a Ford administration.

    TV debate with Jimmy Carter, 1976

## FORD, Henry
US industrialist
(1863–1947)

4

We're going to try to get the boys out of the trenches before Christmas. I've chartered a ship, and some of us are going to Europe.

    Statement, 1915

*The* New York Tribune *put it this way: 'GREAT WAR ENDS CHRISTMAS DAY. FORD TO STOP IT.'*

5

History is more or less bunk. It's tradition.

    Interview with the *Chicago Tribune*, 25 May 1916

*Popularly remembered as 'History is bunk.'*

**1**

*On the Model T Ford motor car:*
People can have it any colour – so long as it's black.
 Quoted in Hill and Nevins, *Ford: Expansion and Challenge*

### FORMBY, George (Jnr)
British entertainer
(1904–61)

**2**

[It's] turned out nice again.
 Catchphrase, from 1930s onwards.
*He starred in a film (UK 1941) with the title* Turned Out Nice Again.

### FORMBY, George (Snr)
British entertainer
(1877–1921)

**3**

Coughin' well, tonight.
 Catchphrase
*He had a convulsive cough which eventually killed him.*

**4**

John Willie, come on.
 Catchphrase, from a monologue

### FORSTER, E.M.
British novelist
(1879–1970)

**5**

A Room With a View.
 Title of novel (1908)
*Noel Coward's song with this title did not appear until* This Year of
Grace *(1928).*

**1**
Only connect! That was the whole of her sermon. Only connect the prose and the passion, and both will be exalted, and human love will be seen at its height.
*Howard's End* (1910)
*'Only connect' is also used as the novel's epigraph.*

**2**
Personal relations are the important thing for ever and ever, and not this outer life of telegrams and anger.
*Ib.*

**3**
It will generally be admitted that Beethoven's Fifth Symphony is the most sublime noise that has ever penetrated into the ear of man.
*Ib.*

**4**
If I had to choose between betraying my country and betraying my friend, I hope I should have the guts to betray my country.
'What I Believe', *Two Cheers for Democracy* (1938)

**5**
I belong to the fag-end of Victorian liberalism.
Broadcast talk, 1946

**FORSYTH, Bruce**
British entertainer
(1928–  )

**6**
I'm in charge!
Catchphrase in TV show, *Sunday Night at the London Palladium*, from *c.* 1958

**7**
Didn't he do well?
Catchphrase in TV show, *The Generation Game*, 1970s

**1**

Good game, good game!
   Catchphrase in *ib*.

**2**

Nice to see you, to see you, nice!
   Catchphrase in *ib*.

### FORTY-SECOND STREET

*US film 1933. Script by James Seymour and Rian James. With Warner Baxter as Julian Marsh, the theatre producer, and Ruby Keeler as Peggy Sawyer, the chorus girl.*

**3**

*Julian (to Peggy):* You're going out a youngster – but you've got to come back a star!
   Soundtrack

### FRASER, Malcolm
Australian Liberal Prime Minister
(1930–   )

**4**

Life is not meant to be easy.
   Deakin lecture, 20 July 1971
*Fraser related it to Shaw,* Back to Methuselah, *'Life is not meant to be easy, my child; but take courage: it can be delightful.'*

### FREED, Alan
US broadcaster
(1922–65)

**5**

Moondog's Rock 'n' Roll Party.
   Title of radio programme, 1951

*Freed is credited with taking the term 'rock 'n' roll' from black sexual slang and applying it to a type of music.*

### FRENCH, Marilyn
US novelist
(1929–  )

1

All men are rapists and that's all they are. They rape us with their eyes, their laws and their codes.
   *The Women's Room* (1978)
*Said by a character whose daughter has been raped.*

### FREUD, Sigmund
Austrian psychiatrist
(1856–1939)

2

The artist has won – through his fantasy – what before he could only win *in* his fantasy: honour, power, and the love of women.
   *Introductory Lectures on Psycho-Analysis*, No. 23 (1916)

3

*On phallic dream symbolism:*
Sometimes a cigar is just a cigar.
   Attrib.

### FRIEDMAN, Milton
US economist
(1912–  )

4

## There's no such thing as a free lunch.
*This is an old US expression, dating back to 1840 at least. Friedman gave it new life in the 1970s, using it in articles, lectures, and as the title of a book, to support his monetarist theories.*

## FROHMAN, Charles
US theatre producer
(1860–1915)

**1**

Why fear death? It is the most beautiful adventure in life.
  Quoted in A. Birkin, *J.M. Barrie and the Lost Boys*
*Last words before going down with the* Lusitania, *echoing the words from the play* Peter Pan *(see BARRIE 41:3) which he had produced.*

## THE FRONT PAGE
*US play 1928. Written by Charles MacArthur and Ben Hecht.*

**2**

The son of a bitch stole my watch!
*Last line.*

## FROST, David
British broadcaster
(1939–  )

**3**

*After satirical attack on a person:*
Seriously, though, he's doing a grand job.
  Catchphrase, TV show, *That Was The Week That Was* (1962)

**4**

Hello, good evening, and welcome.
  Catchphrase, from 1960s onwards

**5**

Sexual chemistry.
  News reports, 1982
*Endorsing a suggestion from a reporter as to what would be an important element in the on-screen relationship of presenters at the breakfast television station, TV-am.*

**1**

We have been on a working honeymoon.
Remark to reporters, March 1983
*Returning with his second wife from Venice.*

**FROST, Robert**
US poet
(1874–1963)

**2**

Something there is that doesn't love a wall.
'Mending Wall', *North of Boston* (1914)

**3**

Good fences make good neighbours.
*Ib.*

**4**

The woods are lovely, dark and deep.
But I have promises to keep,
And miles to go before I sleep,
And miles to go before I sleep.
'Stopping by Woods on a Snowy Evening' (1923)

**FRYE, David**
US impressionist and comedian
(1934– )

**5**

*On Gerald R. Ford:*
He looks like the guy in a science fiction movie who is the first to see
the Creature.
Attrib. 1975

### FUCHIDA, Mitsuo
Japanese pilot
(1902–   )

1
Tora-tora-tora.

> Radio message, 7 December 1941

*Fuchida was leading the Japanese attack on Pearl Harbor. This was the signal to confirm that the fleet was being taken by surprise. 'Tora' means 'tiger'.*

### FUNK, Walther
German Nazi minister
(1890–1960)

2
Kristallnacht ('Night of Broken Glass').

> Attrib.

*Euphemism to describe Nazi pogrom against Jews in Germany on the night of 9/10 November 1938.*

### FYLEMAN, Rose
British poetess
(1877–1957)

3
There are fairies at the bottom of our garden!

> 'The Fairies', first printed in *Punch*, 23 May 1917

# G

## GABOR, Zsa Zsa
Hungarian-born film actress
(1919–   )

1

*In answer to the question 'How many husbands have you had?':*
You mean apart from my own?
  Attrib.

## GAITSKELL, Hugh
British Labour politician
(1906–63)

2

*Attempting to persuade his party not to adopt a policy of unilateral disarmament:*
There are some of us . . . who will fight and fight and fight again to save the party we love.
  Speech, Labour Party Conference, 3 October 1960

3

*On Britain joining the European Community:*
It does mean, if this is the idea, the end of Britain as an independent European state . . . it means the end of a thousand years of history.
  Speech, Labour Party Conference, 3 October 1962

## GALBRAITH, John Kenneth
US economist
(1908–   )

4

The Affluent Society.
  Title of book (1958)

1
The conventional wisdom.
    In *ib.*
*Phrase devised to describe 'the beliefs that are at any time assiduously,*
*solemnly and mindlessly traded between the pretentiously wise.'*

2
The Great Wall, I've been told, is the only man-made structure on
earth that is visible from the moon. For the life of me I cannot see why
anyone would go to the moon to look at it, when, with almost the same
difficulty, it can be viewed in China.
    Article in the *Sunday Times Magazine*, 197?

## GALSWORTHY, John
British novelist
(1867–1933)

3
Nobody tells me anything.
    Stock phrase of 'James Forsyte' in *The Man of Property* (1906) and
    *In Chancery* (1920)

## GANDHI, Indira
Indian Prime Minister
(1917–84)

4
Even if I die in the service of this nation, I would be proud of it. Every
drop of my blood, I am sure, will contribute to the growth of this
nation and make it strong and dynamic.
    Speech, Bhubaneswar, Orissa, 31 October 1984
*Twenty-four hours later she was assassinated. The wording varied*
*from report to report.*

## GANDHI, Mahatma
Indian politician
(1869–1948)

1

*When asked what he thought of Western civilization:*
I think it would be a good idea.
    Attrib.

## GARBO, Greta
Swedish-born film actress
(1905–   )

2

## I think I go home.
    Attrib. remark
*Much beloved by Garbo imitators, this line is sometimes said to have been used as a negotiating ploy when Garbo was seeking a pay rise from Louis B. Mayer. However, her 'interpreter', Sven-Hugo Borg, stated that she said to him 'Borg, I think I shall go home now. It isn't worth it, is it?' after her fellow Swede, the director Mauritz Stiller, was fired (1926).*

3

## I want to be alone.
*She 'said' the line in the 1929 silent film* The Single Standard *and in later 'talkies', but when referring to herself she tended to say 'I like to be alone'.*

## GARNER, John Nance
US Democratic Vice-President
(1868–1937)

4

*On the Vice-Presidency:*
[It] isn't worth a pitcher of warm piss.
    Attrib.
*Usually bowdlerized to 'spit'. He also said the job 'didn't amount to a hill of beans'.*

## GEDDES, Sir Eric
British Conservative politician
(1875–1937)

1

I have personally no doubt we will get everything out of her [Germany] that you can squeeze out of a lemon and a bit more . . . I will squeeze her until you can hear the pips squeak . . . I would strip Germany as she has stripped Belgium.

Speech, Cambridge Guildhall, 9 December 1918

2

The Germans, if this Government is returned, are going to pay every penny; they are going to be squeezed as lemon is squeezed – until the pips squeak. My only doubt is not whether we can squeeze hard enough, but whether there is enough juice.

Speech, Beaconsfield Club, 10 December 1918

## GELDOF, Bob
Irish-born singer
(1952–    )

3

I'm into pop because I want to get rich, get famous and get laid.
Attrib.

## GEORGE V, HM King
British sovereign
(1865–1936)

4

## Wake up, England!
Speech, Guildhall, London, 5 December 1901
*On returning from an Empire tour, as Duke of York, he said: 'I venture to allude to the impression which seemed generally to prevail*

*among our brethren overseas, that the old country must wake up if she intends to maintain her old position of pre-eminence in her Colonial trade against foreign competitors.'*

1

Today, 23 years ago, dear Grandmama died. I wonder what she would have thought of a Labour Government.
Diary, 22 January 1924
*He had just asked Ramsay MacDonald to form the first Labour Government.*

2

After you've met one hundred and fifty Lord Mayors, they all begin to look the same.
Attrib.

3

My father was frightened of his mother. I was frightened of my father, and I'm damned well going to make sure that my children are frightened of me.
Quoted in R. Churchill, *Life of the Earl of Derby*

4

Never miss an opportunity to relieve yourself; never miss a chance to sit down and rest your feet.
Attrib.
*See also EDWARD VIII 150:1*

5

*On the pact between Sir Samuel Hoare, Foreign Secretary, and Pierre Laval over Abyssinia, 1935:*
No more coals to Newcastle, no more Hoares to Paris.
Quoted in K. Rose, *George V*

6

*To the suggestion that his favourite watering place be dubbed Bognor Regis:*
Bugger Bognor!
*Ib.*
*Not his last words, as often supposed.*

**1**
*To members of the Privy Council at Sandringham:*
Gentlemen. I am sorry for keeping you waiting like this – I am unable
to concentrate.
    20 January 1936. Quoted in H. Nicolson, *George V*
*Sometimes called his last words.*

**2**
*To his secretary, Lord Wigram:*
How is the Empire?
    Quoted by S. Baldwin in broadcast, 21 January 1936
*Sometimes quoted as his last words.*

## GEORGE VI, HM King
British sovereign
(1895–1952)

**3**
We're not a family: we're a firm.
    Attrib.

## 'GEORGE, Boy'
British singer
(1961–   )

**4**
I'd rather have a cup of tea than go to bed with someone – any day.
    Remark, variously expressed, 1983

## GEORGE, David Lloyd
(later Earl Lloyd George of Dwyfor)
British Liberal Prime Minister
(1863–1945)

**5**
*On Conservative use of a majority in the House of Lords to block
legislation:*
This is the leal and trusty mastiff which is to watch over our interests,

but which runs away at the first snarl of the trade unions? A mastiff? It is the right hon. gentleman's poodle. It fetches and carries for him. It barks for him. It bites anybody that he sets it on to.
　　Speech, House of Commons, 26 June 1907
*Summarized by the phrase 'Mr Balfour's poodle'. A.J. Balfour was the Conservative leader.*

1

Sporting terms are pretty well understood wherever English is spoken . . . Well, then. The British soldier is a good sportsman . . . Germany elected to make this a finish fight with England . . . The fight must be to a finish – to a knock out.
　　Interview, printed in *The Times*, 29 September 1915
*In his memoirs, Lloyd George entitled one chapter 'The Knock-out Blow' – which was how this notion was popularly expressed.*

2

What is our task? To make Britain a fit country for heroes to live in.
　　Speech, Wolverhampton, 24 November 1918
*This turned into the slogan 'A land fit for heroes' or 'A country fit for heroes'.*

3

The world is becoming like a lunatic asylum run by lunatics.
　　Attrib. in 1933
*See also STALLINGS 413:4.*

4

*On Neville Chamberlain:*
A good mayor of Birmingham in an off-year.
　　Attrib.
*Also attributed to Lord Hugh Cecil in the form 'No better than a Mayor of Birmingham, and in a lean year at that.'*

5

*On Sir John Simon:*
He has sat so long upon the fence that the iron has entered into his soul.
　　Attrib.

**1**
*On Herbert Samuel:*
When they circumcised Herbert Samuel they threw away the wrong bit.
    Attrib.

**2**
*On Sir Douglas Haig:*
He was brilliant to the top of his army boots.
    Attrib.

## GERSHWIN, George
US composer
(1898–1937)

**3**
*To Oscar Levant:*
If you had it all over again, would you fall in love with yourself?
    Attrib.
*See LEVANT 278:1 for his reply.*

## GERSHWIN, Ira
US lyricist
(1896–1983)

**4**
I got rhythm,
I got music,
I got my man—
Who could ask for anything more.
    Song, 'I Got Music', *Girl Crazy* (1930)

**5**
I Got Plenty o' Nuthin.
    Title of song, *Porgy and Bess* (1935)

1

It Ain't Necessarily So.
Title of song in *ib.*

2

Nice Work, If You Can Get It.
Title of song, *A Damsel in Distress* (1937)

3

So, if you like pajamas and I like pa-jah-mas . . .
Let's call the whole thing off!
Song, 'Let's Call the Whole Thing Off', *Shall We Dance* (1937)

4

They Can't Take That Away From Me.
Title of song in *ib.*

5

In time the Rockies may crumble,
Gibraltar may tumble
(They're only made of clay),
But our love is here to stay.
Song, 'Love Is Here to Stay', *The Goldwyn Follies* (1937)

**GETTY, J. Paul**
US oil tycoon
(1892–1976)

6

*Explaining why he refused to pay ransom money to secure the release
of his grandson:*
I have fourteen other grandchildren and if I pay one penny now, then
I'll have fourteen kipnapped grandchildren.
Attrib. 26 July 1973

7

The meek shall inherit the earth, but not the mineral rights.
Attrib.

**1**
*Last words:*
I want my lunch.
  Attrib.


### GIBBONS, Stella
British novelist
(1902–  )

**2**
Something nasty in the woodshed.
  *Passim* in *Cold Comfort Farm* (1933)


### GIBBS, Wolcott
US writer
(1902–58)

**3**
*Parody of* Time *magazine style:*
Backward ran sentences until reeled the mind.
  *More in Sorrow* (1958)

**4**
Where it will end, knows God.
  *Ib.*


### GILLIATT, Penelope
British writer and critic
(1933–  )

**5**
The characteristic sound of the English Sunday: Harold Hobson
barking up the wrong tree.
  Quoted in the *Guardian*, 2 August 1976
*Hobson was for many years drama critic of the* Sunday Times.

## GILMOUR, Sir Ian
British Conservative politician
(1926–   )

1

*On being sacked as Deputy Foreign Secretary by Margaret Thatcher:*
It does no harm to throw the occasional man overboard, but it does not
do much good if you are steering full speed ahead for the rocks.
   Quoted in *Time*, September 1981

## GINSBERG, Allen
US poet
(1926–   )

2

Liverpool is at the present moment the centre of the consciousness of
the human universe.
   Attrib. *c.*1964

## GIRAUDOUX, Jean
French playwright
(1882–1944)

3

Only the mediocre are always at their best.
   Attrib.
*This saying has also been credited to Max Beerbohm and W. Somerset
Maugham.*

## GLEASON, Jackie
US comedian
(1916–   )

4

And awa-a-aay we go.
   Catchphrase on TV show, from 1950s onwards

1
How sweet it is.
 Saying in *ib*.


### GODARD, Jean-Luc
French film director
(1930–   )

2
Every film should have a beginning, a middle and an end – but not
necessarily in that order.
 Quoted in L. Deighton, *Close Up*


### GOEBBELS, Joseph
German Nazi leader
(1897–1945)

3
We can do without butter, but, despite all our love of peace, not
without arms. One cannot shoot with butter, but with guns.
 Translation of speech, Berlin, 17 January 1936
*Possible origin of the phrase 'Guns or butter' or 'Guns before butter'.*
*See also GOERING below.*


### GOERING, Hermann
German Nazi leader
(1893–1946)

4
Guns will make us powerful; butter will only make us fat.
 Radio broadcast, late 1936

## GOGARTY, Oliver St John
Irish writer
(1878–1957)

1
If a queen bee were crossed with a Fresian bull, would not the land flow with milk and honey?
  Attrib.

## *GOLDFINGER*

*UK film 1964. Script by Richard Maibaum and Paul Dehn. With Sean Connery as James Bond.*

2
*Bond:* A martini, shaken, not stirred.
  Soundtrack
*His penchant for this drink had been mentioned in Ian Fleming's first novel,* Casino Royale *(1953) and in the first film,* Dr No (1962), *but this was the first time the line was used in this form.*

## GOLDMAN, William
US screenwriter
(1931–   )

3
*Dictum on Hollywood film-making:*
Nobody knows anything.
  *Adventures in the Screentrade* (1983)

## GOLDSMITH, Sir James
British businessman
(1933–   )

4
## If you pay peanuts, you get monkeys.

*This remark – used by him in connection with the pay given to journalists on his short-lived news magazine* Now! *(c.1980) – is not original. This modern proverb was in use by 1966.*

**1**
When you marry your mistress, you create a job vacancy.
Attrib.

## GOLDWATER, Barry M.
US Republican politician
(1909–    )

**2**
*Accepting his party's nomination for the Presidency:*
I would remind you that extremism in the defence of liberty is no vice. And let me remind you also that moderation in the pursuit of justice is no virtue.
Speech, San Francisco convention, 16 July 1964

**3**
In your heart you know I'm right.
Campaign slogan, 1964

## GOLDWYN, Samuel
Polish-American film producer
(1882–1974)

**4**
*On Louis B. Mayer's funeral:*
The reason so many people showed up at his funeral was because they wanted to make sure he was dead.
Quoted in B. Crowther, *Hollywood Rajah*
*Probably apocryphal, if only because the funeral was in fact sparsely attended.*

1

*To Jack L. Warner, when Goldwyn discovered that one of his directors was moonlighting for Warner Bros.:*
How can we sit together and deal with this industry if you're going to do things like that to me? If this is the way you do it, gentlemen, include me out!

Quoted by S. Goldwyn Jnr, *TV Times*, 13 November 1982
*One of the few genuine Goldwynisms.*

2

An oral contract is not worth the paper it's written on.
*Ib.*

3

## In two words – impossible.
*Ib.*
*Unlikely to be genuine, according to his son.*

4

The trouble with this business is the dearth of bad pictures.
Attrib. but probably apocryphal

5

They're always biting the hand that lays the golden egg.
Ditto.

6

We have all passed a lot of water since then.
Ditto.

7

Anyone who goes to a psychiatrist needs to have his head examined.
Ditto.

8

*Waving from liner to friends on the quayside:*
Bon Voyage!
Quoted in L. Hellman, *Pentimento*

1
*On films with a 'message':*
Messages are for Western Union.
  Attrib.


## *GONE WITH THE WIND*

*US film 1939. Script by Sidney Howard, based on the novel by Margaret Mitchell. With Vivien Leigh as Scarlett O'Hara and Clark Gable as Rhett Butler.*

2
*Scarlett:* Where shall I go? What shall I do?
*Rhett:* Frankly, my dear, I don't give a damn.
  Soundtrack

3
*Concluding words:*
*Scarlett:* After all, tomorrow is another day.

4
The Greatest Motion Picture Ever Made.
  Slogan

*See also BOOK TITLES 65:6.*


## *THE GOON SHOW*

*UK radio comedy series, from 1951. Also called THE GOONS. Script by Spike Milligan and Larry Stephens. With Spike Milligan as Little Jim, Harry Secombe as Seagoon, Peter Sellers as Bluebottle, and Wallace Greenslade (announcer).*

5
And there's more where that came from.
  Catchphrase

1
And this is where the story really begins.
  Catchphrase

2
Damn clever, these Chinese.
  Catchphrase

3
Q. Do you come here often?
A. Only in the mating season.
  Catchphrase

4
The dreaded lergy.
  Catchphrase
*Pronounced 'lurgy'.*

5
*Seagoon:* Hello folks, and what about the workers?
  Catchphrase

6
*Little Jim:* He's fallen in the water.
  Catchphrase

7
He's very good, you know.
  Catchphrase

8
*Greenslade:* It's all in the mind, you know.
  Catchphrase

9
I've been sponned!
  Catchphrase

1

Needle, nardle, noo.
    Catchphrase

2

Time for your OBE, Neddie!
    Catchphrase

3

You can't get the wood, you know.
    Catchphrase

4

*Bluebottle:* You dirty rotten swine, you.
    Catchphrase

5

You silly twisted boy.
    Catchphrase

## GRABLE, Betty
### US film actress
### (1916–73)

6

There are two reasons why I'm in show business, and I'm standing on
both of them.
    Attrib.

## GRADE, Lew
### (later Lord Grade)
### Russian-born media tycoon in Britain
### (1906–   )

7

All my shows are great. Some of them are bad. But they are all great.
    Quoted in the *Observer*, 14 September 1975

**1**

*To Franco Zeffirelli who explained that the high cost of the film* Jesus of Nazareth *was partly because there had to be twelve apostles:*
Twelve! So who needs *twelve?* Couldn't we make do with *six?*
  Quoted in *Radio Times*, October 1983

### GRAHAM, Dr Billy
US evangelist
(1918–   )

**2**

Decide for Christ.
  Slogan, from 1940s onwards

**3**

I want you to get up out of your seats.
  Frequent exhortation, current by 1966

### GRAHAME, Kenneth
British writer
(1859–1932)

**4**

There is *nothing* – absolutely nothing half so much worth doing as simply messing about in boats.
  *The Wind in the Willows* (1908)

**5**

O bliss! O poop-poop! O my! O my!
  *Ib.*
*'Toad' on the joys of motoring.*

**6**

The clever men at Oxford
  Know all there is to be knowed.
But they none of them know one half as much
  As intelligent Mr Toad.
  *Ib.*

## GRAVES, Robert
British poet
(1895–1985)

**1**
Goodbye To All That.
   Title of autobiography (1929)

**2**
The remarkable thing about Shakespeare is that he is really very good
– in spite of all the people who say he is very good.
   Quoted in the *Observer*, 6 December 1964

## GRAYSON, Larry
British comedian
(1930–   )

**3**
Shut that door!
   Catchphrase, from 1970 onwards

**4**
What a gay day!
   Catchphrase

**5**
He seems like a nice boy, doesn't he?
   Catchphrase, of contestants on TV show, *The Generation Game*,
   from 1978 onwards

## GRAYSON, Victor
British Labour politician
(1881–1920?)

**6**
Never explain: your friends don't need it and your enemies won't
believe it.
   Attrib.

### GREENE, Graham
British novelist
(1904–   )

1

Fame is a powerful aphrodisiac.
Quoted in *Radio Times*, 10 September 1964

### GREEN, Hughie
British broadcaster
(1920–   )

2

I mean that most sincerely, friends.
Stock phrase, TV shows, 1950s–70s

3

It's make your mind up time.
Stock phrase on TV show *Opportunity Knocks*, from 1960s onwards

### GREER, Germaine
Australian writer and feminist
(1939–   )

4

*When Ned Sherrin claimed that* Laugh-In *was a spin-off of* That Was
The Week That Was:
Like Concorde is a spin-off of the Tiger Moth, darling.
On *Quote . . . Unquote*, BBC Radio, 7 March 1976

5

No sex is better than bad sex.
Attrib.

## GRENFELL, Joyce
British entertainer
(1910–80)

1

George – don't do that.
'Nursery Sketches', (1953)

## GREY, Sir Edward
(later Viscount Grey of Fallodon)
British Liberal politician
(1862–1933)

2

*In his room at the Foreign Office, 3 August 1914:*
The lamps are going out all over Europe; we shall not see them lit
again in our life-time.
Recounted in *Twenty-five Years* (1925)

## GRIFFITH, D.W.
US film director
(1874–1948)

3

Out of the cradle endlessly rocking.
Film script, *Intolerance* (1916)
*This repeated sub-title quotes the title of a poem by Walt Whitman.*

4

*Directing an epic film:*
Move those ten thousand horses a trifle to the right. And that mob out
there, three feet forward.
Attrib.

## GRIFFITH-JONES, Mervyn
British lawyer
(1907–79)

5

*As prosecuting counsel to jury at trial of Penguin Books Ltd who were*

*accused of publishing an obscene work in D.H. Lawrence's* Lady
Chatterley's Lover, *October 1960:*
Is it a book that you would have lying around in your house? Is it a
book that you would even wish your wife or your servants to read?
  Quoted in C.H. Rolph, *The Trial of Lady Chatterley*

### GROMYKO, Andrei
Soviet politician
(1909–    )

1

*Proposing Mikhail Gorbachev as Soviet Communist Party leader:*
This man has a nice smile, but he has got iron teeth.
  Speech, 1985

### GUEDALLA, Philip
British writer
(1889–1944)

2

The cheerful clatter of Sir James Barrie's cans as he went round with
the milk of human kindness.
  *Some Critics*

3

History repeats itself; historians repeat each other.
  Attrib.
*Compare BALFOUR 39:3.*

### GUINAN, Texas
US nightclub hostess
(1884–1933)

4

*Greeting to clients:*
Hello, sucker!
  Quoted in W. & M. Morris, *Dictionary of Word and Phrase
  Origins*

1
*Description of small-town businessman trying to prove himself a big
shot in the city:*
Big butter-and-egg man.
   *Ib.*

2
*When refused entry to France with her troupe in 1931:*
It goes to show that fifty million Frenchmen *can* be wrong.
*See also ANONYMOUS 20:4.*

## GULBENKIAN, Nubar
British industrialist and philanthropist
(1896–1972)

3
The best number for a dinner party is two: myself and a damn good
head waiter.
   Quoted in the *Observer*, 19 December 1965

## GURNEY, Dorothy Frances
British poetess
(1858–1932)

4
The kiss of the sun for pardon,
   The song of the birds for mirth,
One is nearer God's Heart in a garden
   Than anywhere else on earth.
      'God's Garden'

## GWENN, Edmund
Britfish actor
(1875–1959)

1
*When someone said to him, on his deathbed, 'It must be very hard':*
It is. But not as hard as farce.
   Quoted in *Time*, 30 January 1984

# H

## HAIG, Alexander
US Republican politician
(1924– )

**1**

*After an assassination attempt on President Reagan:*
As of now, I am in charge at the White House.
Quoted in *The Times*, 1 April 1981

## HAIG, Sir Douglas
(later Earl Haig)
British soldier
(1861–1928)

**2**

*On Lord Derby:*
A very weak-minded fellow, I'm afraid, and, like the feather pillow, bears the marks of the last person who has sat on him!
Letter to wife, 14 January 1918

**3**

*To British troops on the Western Front:*
Every position must be held to the last man: there must be no retirement. With our backs to the wall, and believing in the justice of our cause, each one of us must fight on to the end.
Order, 12 April 1918

## HAILSHAM, Viscount
(later Quintin Hogg, later Lord Hailsham)
British Conservative politician
(1907– )

**4**

*On the Profumo affair:*
A great party is not to be brought down because of a squalid affair between a woman of easy virtue and a proved liar.
Interview, BBC TV, 13 June 1963

1

*On Labour policies during a General Election:*
If the British public falls for this, I say it will be stark, staring bonkers.
 Press conference, London, 12 October 1964

## HALDANE, J.B.S.
British scientist
(1892–1964)

2

My suspicion is that the universe is not only queerer than we suppose,
but queerer than we *can* suppose.
 *Possible Worlds* (1927)

## HALL, Archibald
British butler and murderer
(1924–  )

3

*On being convicted of five murders:*
It was easy after the first one. After that I was trying for the *Guinness
Book of Records.*
 Quoted in the *Observer*, 5 November 1978

## HALL, Henry
British band leader
(1899–  )

4

Here's to the next time.
 Stock phrase, from 1930s onwards.

5

This *is* Henry Hall speaking and tonight is my guest night.
 Stock phrase, from 1934 onwards.

## HAMMARSKJÖLD, Dag
Swedish UN official
(1905–61)

**1**

Never let success hide its emptiness from you, achievement its nothingness, toil its desolation. And so . . . keep alive the incentive to push on further, that pain in the soul which drives us beyond ourselves . . . Do not look back. And do not dream about the future, either. It will neither give you back the past, nor satisfy your other daydreams. Your duty, your reward – your destiny – are *here* and *now*.

   *Markings* (1965)

## HAMMERSTEIN II, Oscar
US lyricist
(1895–1960)

**2**

Ol' Man River
He just keeps rollin' along.
   'Ol Man River', *Show Boat* (1927)

**3**

The last time I saw Paris, her heart was warm and gay,
I heard the laughter of her heart in every street café.
   Song, 'The Last Time I Saw Paris', *Lady Be Good* (1941)

**4**

The corn is as high as an elephant's eye.
   Song, 'Oh, What a Beautiful Mornin'', *Oklahoma!* (1943)

**5**

June Is Bustin' Out All Over.
   Title of song, *Carousel* (1945)

1

You'll Never Walk Alone.
   Title of song in *ib.*

2

There Is Nothin' Like a Dame.
   Title of song, *South Pacific* (1949)

3

Some Enchanted Evening.
   Title of song in *ib.*

4

Fools give you reasons, wise men never try.
   Song, 'Some Enchanted Evening' in *ib.*

5

I'm Gonna Wash That Man Right Out of My Hair.
   Title of song in *ib.*

6

Hello, Young Lovers (Wherever You Are).
   Title of song, *The King and I* (1951)

7

The hills are alive with the sound of music.
   From title song, *The Sound of Music* (1959)

8

These are a few of my favourite things.
   Song, 'My Favourite Things', in *ib.*

## HAMMOND, Percy
(1873–1936)

9

I have knocked everything but the knees of the chorus-girls, and
Nature has anticipated me there.
   Quoted in *The Frank Muir Book*

## HAMPTON, Christopher
British playwright
(1946–    )

**1**
Masturbation is the thinking man's television.
  *The Philanthropist* (1970)

**2**
*Philip (bewildered):* I'm sorry. *(Pause.)* I suppose I am indecisive. *(Pause.)* My trouble is, I'm a man of no convictions. *(Longish pause.)* At least, I think I am.
  *Ib.*

**3**
Asking a working writer what he thinks about critics is like asking a lamp-post how it feels about dogs.
  Quoted in the *Sunday Times Magazine*, 16 October 1977


## HANCOCK'S HALF-HOUR
*UK radio and TV series, from 1954 onwards (also called simply HANCOCK on TV). Scripts by Alan Simpson and Ray Galton. With Tony Hancock (1924–68).*

**4**
Ha-harr, Jim, lad.
  Stock routine
*Impersonating Robert Newton as Long John Silver in the film* Treasure Island *(1950).*

**5**
Mis-ter *Chris*-tian . . . I'll have you *hung* from the *high*-est *yard*-arm in the *N*avy.
  Stock routine
*Impersonating Charles Laughton as Captain Bligh in the film* Mutiny on the Bounty *(1935).*

1

A man of my cal-i-bre.
  Stock phrase

2

I thought my mother was a bad cook but at least her gravy used to move about a bit.
  'A Sunday Afternoon at Home' (radio), 22 April 1958

3

A pint? That's very nearly an armful.
  'The Blood Donor' (TV), 23 June 1961

## HANFF, Minnie Maud
### US advertising copywriter
### (1880–1942)

4

Vigor, Vim, Perfect Trim;
Force made him, Sunny Jim.
  Jingle for Force breakfast cereal (1903)
*The name 'Sunny Jim' was invented by Miss Hanff and a Miss Ficken.*

5

High o'er the fence leaps Sunny Jim,
Force is the food that raises him.
  Ditto (1920)

## HANRAHAN, Brian
### British journalist
### (1949–  )

6

*Reporting British attack on airport at Port Stanley, during Falklands war:*
I'm not allowed to say how many planes joined the raid but I counted them all out and I counted them all back.
  Report broadcast by BBC, 1 May 1982

## HARBACH, Otto
US lyricist
(1873–1963)

**1**

She didn't say yes,
She didn't say no.
    Song, 'She Didn't Say Yes', *The Cat and the Fiddle* (1931)

**2**

Smoke Gets in Your Eyes.
    Title of song, *Roberta* (1933)

## HARBURG, E.Y.
US lyricist
(1898–1981)

**3**

It's only a paper moon,
Sailing over a cardboard sea,
But it wouldn't be make-believe
If you believed in me.
    Song, 'It's Only a Paper Moon', *The Great Magoo* (1932)
*Written with Billy Rose.*

**4**

Once I built a rail-road,
Now it's done.
Brother, can you spare a dime?
    Song, 'Brother Can You Spare a Dime', *New Americana* (1932)

**5**

Somewhere over the rainbow, skies are blue,
And the dreams that you dare to dream really do come true.
    Song, 'Over the Rainbow', *The Wizard of Oz* (1939)

1

Follow the Yellow Brick Road.
   Title of song in *ib*.

2

Happiness Is a Thing Called Joe.
   Title of song (1942)
*See also SCHULTZ 378:4.*


**HARDING, Gilbert**
British broadcaster
(1907–60)

3

*In answer to US immigration question, 'Is it your intention to overthrow the government of the United States by force?':*
Sole purpose of visit.
   Attrib.

4

*To Mae West's manager who had suggested he might sound a bit more 'sexy' when interviewing her for the BBC:*
If, sir, I possessed the power of conveying unlimited sexual attraction through the potency of my voice, I would not be reduced to accepting a miserable pittance from the BBC for interviewing a faded female in a damp basement.
   Quoted in *Gilbert Harding by His Friends*


**HARDING, Warren G.**
US Republican President
(1865–1923)

5

America's present need is not heroics but healing, not nostrums but normalcy.
   Speech, Boston, May 1920
*Giving rise to the slogans 'Back to Normalcy' and 'Return to Normalcy with Harding.'*

## HARDY, Oliver
US film comedian
(1892–1957)

1
*To Stan Laurel:*
Here's another fine mess you've gotten me into.
　　Catchphrase in films from the 1920s onwards
Another Fine Mess *was the title of their shorts in 1930.*

## HARE, Robertson
British comedy actor
(1891–1979)

2
Indubitably!
　　Catchphrase

3
Oh, calamity.
　　Catchphrase

## HARGREAVES, William
British songwriter
(1846–1919)

4
I'm Burlington Bertie
I rise at ten thirty and saunter along like a toff,
I walk down the Strand with my gloves on my hand,
Then I walk down again with them off.
　　Song, 'Burlington Bertie from Bow' (1915)
*Not to be confused with 'Burlington Bertie' (1900) by Harry B.
Norris.*

## HART, Lorenz
US lyricist
(1895–1943)

**1**

With a Song in My Heart.
Title of song (1930)

**2**

When love congeals
It soon reveals
The faint aroma of performing seals
The double-crossing of a pair of heels.
Song, 'I Wish I Were in Love Again', *Babes in Arms* (1937)

**3**

That's why the lady is a tramp.
Song, 'The Lady Is a Tramp', in *ib.*

**4**

Bewitched, Bothered and Bewildered.
Title of song, *Pal Joey* (1940)

**5**

I Didn't Know What Time It Was.
Title of song in *ib.*

**6**

My Funny Valentine.
Title of song in *ib.*


## HARTLEY, L.P.
British novelist
(1895–1972)

**7**

The past is a foreign country: they do things differently there.
*The Go-Between* (1953)

### HASKINS, Minnie Louise
British poetess
(1875–1957)

1

And I said to the man who stood at the Gate of the Year, 'Give me a light that I may tread safely into the unknown.' And he replied, 'Go out into the darkness, and put your hand into the hand of God. That shall be to you better than light, and safer than a known way.'

*The Desert* (Introduction) (1908)
*Quoted by King George VI in Christmas broadcast, 1939.*

### HASSALL, Christopher
British writer
(1912–63)

2

*On Edith Sitwell:*
She's genuinely bogus.
Attrib.

### HATTON, Will
British comedian

3

*To partner Ethel Manners:*
Don't you know there's a war on?
Catchphrase, 1940s

### HAVERS, Sir Michael
British lawyer and Conservative politician
(1923– )

4

*On the immunity from prosecution offered to the spy, Sir Anthony Blunt, in 1964:*
He maintained his denial. He was offered immunity from prosecution. He sat in silence for a while. He got up, looked out of the

window, poured himself a drink and after a few minutes confessed. Later he co-operated, and he continued to co-operate. That is how the immunity was given and how Blunt responded.

Speech, House of Commons, 21 November 1979
*As Attorney-General.*


## 'HAW-HAW, Lord'
(William Joyce)
US-born propagandist for German Nazis
(1906–46)

**1**
Germany calling, Germany calling.
   Radio broadcasts to Britain, during the Second World War


## HAY, Ian
British novelist and playwright
(1876–1952)

**2**
The First Hundred Thousand.
   Title of novel (1915)

**3**
What do you mean, funny? Funny-peculiar, or funny ha-ha?
   Play, *The Housemaster* (1936)


## HAYES, J. Milton
British writer
(1884–1940)

**4**
There's a one-eyed yellow idol to the North of Khatmandu.
   Poem, 'The Green Eye of the Yellow God'

## HEALEY, Denis
British Labour politician
(1917–   )

**1**

I warn you there are going to be howls of anguish from the 80,000 people who are rich enough to pay over 75% on the last slice of their income.

Speech, Labour Party Conference, 1 October 1973

**2**

*On being attacked by Sir Geoffrey Howe in parliamentary debate over his budget proposals:*

That part of his speech was rather like being savaged by a dead sheep.

Speech, House of Commons, 14 June 1978

*Earlier, Sir Roy Welensky had said of Iain Macleod that being attacked by him was like being 'bitten by a dead sheep'.*

**3**

I plan to be the Gromyko of the Labour party for the next thirty years.

Remark, on several occasions, 1984

**4**

Silly Billy!

Catchphrase

*Invented for him by the impressionist, Mike Yarwood, and then sometimes used by him.*

## HEATH, Edward
British Conservative Prime Minister
(1916–   )

**5**

Nor would it be in the interests of the [European] Community that its enlargement should take place except with the full-hearted consent of the Parliament and people of the new member countries.

Speech to the Franco-British Chamber of Commerce, Paris, 5 May 1970

1
*On tax cuts and a freeze on prices by nationalized industries:*
## This would, at a stroke, reduce the rise in prices, increase productivity and reduce unemployment.
Press release (No. G.E.228), from Conservative Central Office, 16 June 1970
*Never actually spoken by Heath.*

2
We were returned to office to change the course of history of this nation – nothing less. If we are to achieve this task we will have to embark on a change so radical, a revolution so quiet and yet so total, that it will go far beyond the programme for a parliament to which we are committed and on which we have already embarked, far beyond the decade and way into the 80s.
Speech, Conservative Party Conference, October 1970

3
*On the Lonrho affair (involving tax avoidance):*
It is the unpleasant and unacceptable face of capitalism, but one should not suggest that the whole of British industry consists of practices of this kind.
Speech, House of Commons, 15 May 1973


**'HEATHERTON, Fred'**
Pseudonym of British and US songwriters

4
Big ones, small ones, some as big as your head.
Song, 'I've Got a Lovely Bunch of Cocoanuts' (1944)


**HELLER, Joseph**
US novelist
(1923–    )

5
Orr was crazy and could be grounded. All he had to do was ask; and as

soon as he did, he would no longer be crazy and would have to fly more missions . . . Yossarian was moved very deeply by the absolute simplicity of this clause of Catch-22 and let out a respectful whistle.

    *Catch-22* (1961)


## HELLMAN, Lillian
US playwright and writer
(1905–84)

1

*Letter to Chairman, House Committee on Un-American Activities, Washington, 19 May 1952:*
To hurt innocent people whom I knew many years ago in order to save myself is, to me, inhuman and indecent and dishonorable. I cannot and will not cut my conscience to fit this year's fashions.

    Quoted in *Scoundrel Time* (1976)


## *HELL'S ANGELS*

*US film 1930. Script by Howard Estabrook and Harry Behn. With Jean Harlow as Helen.*

2

*About to exchange her fur wrap for a dressing gown:*
Helen: Would you be shocked if I put on something more comfortable?

    Soundtrack


## HELPMANN, Sir Robert
Australian dancer and choreographer
(1909–86)

3

*After the opening night of* Oh, Calcutta!:
The trouble with nude dancing is that not everything stops when the music stops.

    Quoted in *The Frank Muir Book*

# HEMINGWAY, Ernest
US novelist
(1899–1961)

1
The Sun Also Rises.
   Title of novel (1926)

2
*Definition of 'guts':*
Grace under pressure.
   Article in the *New Yorker*, 30 November 1929
   *Based on Latin 'fortiter in re, suaviter in modo', and later invoked by*
   *John F. Kennedy in his* Profiles in Courage.

3
*In response to the remark 'The very rich are different from you and*
*me':*
##   Yes, they have more money.
   Discussed in T. Burnam, *More Misinformation* (1980)
   *F. Scott Fitzgerald had written 'Let me tell you about the very rich.*
   *They are different from you and me' in 1926 and the exchange is*
   *sometimes given as having been between the two writers. In fact, the*
   *response came from the critic Mary Colum who told Hemingway in*
   *1936 'The only difference between the rich and other people is that the*
   *rich have more money.'*

4
Did thee feel the earth move?
   *For Whom the Bell Tolls* (1940)

5
Where do the noses go? I always wondered where the noses would go.
   *Ib.*

6
Across the River and Into the Trees.
   Title of novel (1950)

*Perhaps alluding to the last words of General Stonewall Jackson (killed in error by his own troops in 1863): 'Let us cross over the river, and rest under the trees.'*
*See also WHITE 451:2.*

1

If you are lucky enough to have lived in Paris as a young man, then wherever you go for the rest of your life, it stays with you, for Paris is a moveable feast.

Epigraph to *A Moveable Feast* (1964)

### HENDERSON, Leon
US economist
(1895–1986)

2

Having a little inflation is like being a little pregnant.
Attrib.

### HENDRIX, Jimi
US rock musician
(1942–70)

3

Once you're dead, you're made for life.
Attrib.

### 'HENRY, O.'
US writer
(1862–1910)

4

*Last words:*
Turn up the lights [*or:* Put up the shades], I don't want to go home in the dark.
Attrib.
*Quoting the song 'I'm Afraid to Go Home in the Dark'.*

## HEPBURN, Katherine
US film actress
(1909–  )

1

*In response to query, 'Hey, you used to be Joan Crawford, didn't you?'*
Not any more I'm not.
    Attrib.

*See also* STAGE DOOR *412:6.*

## HERBERT, A.P.
(later Sir Alan)
British writer and politician
(1890–1971)

2

Holy Deadlock.
    Title of novel on divorce (1934)

3

The critical period in matrimony is breakfast-time.
    *Uncommon Law* (1935)

## HEWART, Gordon
(later Lord Hewart)
British lawyer
(1870–1943)

4

*When taunted by F.E. Smith about the size of his stomach with, 'What's it to be – a boy or a girl?':*
If it's a boy I'll call him John. If it's a girl I'll call her Mary. But if, as I suspect, it's only wind, I'll call it F.E. Smith.
    Attrib.
*This story can also be found in US and Australian folklore involving other pairs.*

**1**
*In case of Rex v. Sussex Justices, 9 November 1923:*
A long list of cases shows that it is not merely of some importance but
is of fundamental importance that justice should not only be done, but
should manifestly be seen to be done.
King's Bench Reports (1924)


## HIGHWAY PATROL
*US TV police series, 1955–9. With Broderick Crawford.*

**2**
*Into radio-set, signifying agreement:*
Ten-four.
Catchphrase


## HILL, Joe
### Swedish-born songwriter
### and industrial organizer in US
### (1879–1915)

**3**
Work and pray, live on hay,
You'll get pie in the sky when you die.
'The Preacher and the Slave' (1911)


## HILLARY, Edmund
### (later Sir Edmund)
### New Zealand mountaineer
### (1919–   )

**4**
*On being (with Tenzing Norgay) the first person to climb Mount
Everest, 29 May 1953:*
Well, we knocked the bastard off!
Recounted in *Nothing Venture, Nothing Win* (1975)

## HILLINGDON, Alice, Lady
Wife of 2nd Baron Hillingdon
(1857–1940)

1

I am happy now that Charles calls on my bedchamber less frequently than of old. As it is, I now endure but two calls a week and when I hear his steps outside my door I lie down on my bed, close my eyes, open my legs and think of England.

> Journal (1912), cited in E. Partridge, *A Dictionary of Catch Phrases*

*It has not proved possible to check the accuracy of this source.*

## HILLS, Denis
British teacher
(1913–   )

2

*On President Amin of Uganda:*
A village tyrant . . . a black Nero.

> The White Pumpkin (1975)

*Hills was sentenced to death for treason on account of these words but was freed after the intervention of the Queen and the Foreign Secretary.*

## HIROHITO, Emperor
Japanese Head of State and former divinity
(1901–   )

3

The war situation has developed not necessarily to Japan's advantage.

> Announcing Japan's surrender, 15 August 1945

## HITCHCOCK, Alfred
British-born film director
(1899–1980)

**1**
Actors are cattle.
Attrib.
*He later denied this: 'What I said was actors should be treated like cattle.'*

## HITLER, Adolf
German Nazi leader
(1889–1945)

**2**
With a suitcase full of clothes and underwear in my hand and an indomitable will in my heart, I set out for Vienna . . . I too hoped to become 'something'.
*Mein Kampf* (1933)

**3**
The great masses of the people . . . will more easily fall victims to a big lie than to a small one.
*Ib.*

**4**
It was no secret that this time the revolution would have to be bloody . . . When we spoke of it, we called it 'The Night of the Long Knives' ('Die nacht der Langen Messer').
Speech to the Reichstag, 13 July 1934
*Referring to the events of 29 June/2 July when, aided by the SS, Hitler liquidated the leadership of the SA.*

**5**
I go the way that providence dictates with the assurance of a sleepwalker.
Speech, Munich, 15 March 1936

1

And now before us stands the last problem that must be solved and will be solved. It is the last territorial claim which I have to make in Europe, but it is the claim from which I will not recede and which, God willing, I will make good . . . With regard to the problem of the Sudeten Germans, my patience is now at an end.

    Speech, Berlin Sportpalast, 26 September 1938

2

*On Neville Chamberlain:*
Well, he seemed such a nice old gentleman, I thought I would give him my autograph as a souvenir.

    Attrib.

3

Nacht und Nebel ('Night and Fog').

    Title of decree, issued 1941
*Hitler's euphemism for the way in which people suspected of crimes against occupying forces would be dealt with. They would be spirited away into the night and fog.*

4

The Final Solution ('Endlösung') of the Jewish problem.

    Term used by Nazi officials from the summer of 1941 onwards
*G. Reitlinger in* The Final Solution *(1953), suggests that the choice of phrase was probably, though not certainly, Hitler's own.*

5

*To Jodl at Oberkommando der Wehrmacht, 25 August 1944, after the recapture of Paris by the Allies:*
Is Paris burning? ('Brennt Paris?')

    Quoted in A. Crawley, *De Gaulle*
*He received no reply.*

### HOFFNUNG, Gerard
British cartoonist and tuba player
(1925–1959)

6

There is a French widow in every bedroom (affording delightful prospects).

Speech, Oxford Union debating society, 4 December 1958
*In 'Letters from Tyrolean landlords' on the motion 'Life begins at 38'.*

## HOLLAND, Rev. Henry Scott
British Anglican clergyman
(1847–1918)

1
Death is nothing at all. I have only slipped away into the next room. I am I and you are you. Whatever we were to each other, that we are still. Call me by my old familiar name, speak to me in the easy way you always used. Put no difference into your tone, wear no forced air of solemnity or sorrow . . . What is death but negligible accident? Why should I be out of mind because I am out of sight? I am waiting for you, for an interval, somewhere very near just around the corner. All is well.
    Attrib.

## HOOVER, Herbert
US Republican President
(1874–1964)

2
When a great many people are unable to find work, unemployment results.
    Quoted in P.F. Boller, *Presidential Anecdotes*

3
We are challenged with a peace-time choice between the American system of rugged individualism and a European philosophy of diametrically opposed doctrines – doctrines of paternalism and state socialism.
    Campaign speech, New York City, 22 October 1928

1

*Describing what would happen if tariff protection were removed:*
The grass will grow in the streets of a hundred cities, a thousand towns; the weeds will overrun the fields of millions of farms if that protection is taken away.
   Campaign speech, 31 October 1932

## HOPE, Anthony
British novelist
(1863–1933)

2

*At the first night of J.M. Barrie's play* Peter Pan:
Oh, for an hour of Herod!
   Quoted in A. Birkin, *J.M. Barrie and the Lost Boys*

3

*On W.S. Gilbert:*
His foe was folly and his weapon wit.
   Inscription, London (1915)

## 'HOPE, Laurence'
British poetess
(1865–1904)

4

Pale hands I loved beside the Shalamar.
   *The Garden of Karma* (1901)

## HORNE, Kenneth
British entertainer
(1900–69)

5

Did I ever tell you about the time I was in Sidi Barrani?
   Catchphrase on radio show *Much Binding in the Marsh*, 1940s

1

Read any good books, lately?
    Catchphrase in *ib.*


## HOUSMAN, A.E.
### British poet
### (1859–1936)

2

If a line of poetry strays into my memory, my skin bristles so that the
razor ceases to act.
    Lecture, *The Name and Nature of Poetry*, Cambridge, 9 May 1933


3

This is for all ill-treated fellows
    Unborn and unbegot,
For them to read when they're in trouble
    And I am not.
    Epigraph, *More Poems* (1936)


## HUBBARD, 'Kin'
### US humorist
### (1868–1930)

4

Life is just one damned thing after another.
    *A Thousand and One Epigrams*
*Also attributed to Frank Ward O'Malley (1875–1932), though the
saying may pre-date them both.*


5

Editor: a person employed by a newspaper whose business it is to
separate the wheat from the chaff and to see that chaff is printed.
    *Ib.*


6

If there's one thing above all a vulture can't stand, it's a glass eye.
    Attrib.

## HUGHES, Ted
British Poet Laureate
(1930–   )

1

It took the whole of Creation
To produce my foot, each feather:
Now I hold creation in my foot.
'Hawk Roosting', *The Hawk in the Rain* (1957)


## HUMPHREY, Hubert H.
US Democratic Vice-President
(1911–78)

2

The Politics of Joy.
Campaign slogan, 1964


## HUMPHRIES, Barry
Australian entertainer
(1934–   )

3

*As 'Dame Edna Everage':*
Wave your gladdies, possums!
Stock phrase

4

*As 'Dame Edna Everage', on seeing a Morris Traveller in Stratford-upon-Avon:*
Why, even the cars are half-timbered here!
TV show, 1970s

## HUPFIELD, Herman
US songwriter
(1894–1951)

1
You must remember this, a kiss is still a kiss,
A sigh is just a sigh;
The fundamental things apply,
As time goes by.
   Song, 'As Time Goes By', *Everybody's Welcome* (1931)
*Also in the film* CASABLANCA *(1943).*

## HUTCHINS, Robert M.
US educator
(1899–1977)

2
Whenever I feel like exercise, I lie down until the feeling passes.
   Attrib.

# I

### IBARRURI, Dolores
'La Pasionaria'
Spanish communist
(1895– )

1
They shall not pass ('No pasaran').
   Translation of radio speech, Madrid, 18 July 1936
*Later used as a Republican slogan in the Spanish Civil War (1936–9).*
*Compare PETAIN 337:3.*

2
It is better to die on your feet than to live on your knees.
   Translation of radio speech, Paris, 3 September 1936
*According to her autobiography (1966), she had also used these words*
*on 18 July when broadcasting in Spain. Emilio Zapata, the Mexican*
*guerrilla leader, had used the expression before her in 1910.*


### *I COVER THE WATERFRONT*
*US film 1933. Written by Wells Root, Jack Jevne and Max Miller.*

3
## Not tonight, Josephine.
*This film has been credited with launching the phrase, though I*
*suspect it merely popularized it. A British film c. 1932 records Lupino*
*Lane and Beatrice Lillie using the phrase in a variety sketch about*
*Nápoleon and Josephine. It may well have become an established*
*catchphrase by the end of the previous century. (By way of*
*compensation, the title of this US film became a catchphrase in its own*
*right.)*

## INGRAMS, Richard
British writer and editor of *Private Eye*,
the satirical magazine
(1937– )

1

*On the prospect of having to go to gaol, 1976:*
The only thing I really mind about going to prison is the thought of
Lord Longford coming to visit me.

Attrib.
*Ingrams has no recollection of having made this remark but is happy
to accept authorship.*

2

*Suggested personal motto:*
Publish and be sued.

On *Quote . . . Unquote*, BBC Radio, 4 May 1977

## INNES, Hammond
British novelist
(1913– )

3

*On growing trees:*
I'm replacing some of the timber used up by my books. Books are just
trees with squiggles on them.

Interviewed in *Radio Times*, 18 August 1984

## INSCRIPTIONS

4

*In the forest of Compiègne, France, where the Armistice was signed
at the end of the First World War:*
Here on 11 November 1918 succumbed the criminal pride of the
German Reich, vanquished by the free peoples which it tried to
enslave.

1
Kilroy was here.
*The most widely-known piece of graffiti. The phrase may have originated with James J. Kilroy, a shipyard inspector in Quincy, Mass., who would chalk it up to indicate a check had been made. Brought to Europe by GIs, c.1942.*

2
*Plaque left on moon by crew of Apollo XI:*
HERE MEN FROM THE PLANET EARTH
FIRST SET FOOT UPON THE MOON
JULY 1969 AD
WE CAME IN PEACE FOR ALL MANKIND.

## IN TOWN TONIGHT
*UK radio magazine programme (BBC), from 1933–60.*

3
*Voice 1:* Stop!
*Voice 2:* Once again we stop the mighty roar of London's traffic and from the great crowds we bring you some of the interesting people who have come by land, sea and air to be In Town Tonight.
   Introductory announcement

4
Carry on, London!
   Concluding announcement

## IRISH REPUBLICAN ARMY

5
Our day will come ('Tiocfaidh Ar La')
   Slogan
*Also the title of a song by Ruby and the Romantics, 1963.*

1

Thatcher will now realize that Britain cannot occupy our country, torture our prisoners and shoot our people in their own streets and get away with it. Today we were unlucky. But remember, we have only to be lucky once. You will have to be lucky always.

Quoted in *Time*, 22 October 1984

*This message was contained in an anonymous telephone call to a Dublin radio station following the unsuccessful IRA attempt to blow up Margaret Thatcher and other government leaders at a Brighton hotel.*

## IRMA LA DOUCE

*UK stage musical 1958, adapted from the French original of Alexandre Breffort and Marguerite Monnot. (Later filmed in US.)*

2

*Opening words:*
Don't worry, it's quite suitable for the children. This is a story about passion, bloodshed, desire and death – everything in fact that makes life worth living.

Preamble to song 'Valse Milieu'

### ISHERWOOD, Christopher
British-born writer
(1904–86)

3

I am a camera with its shutter open, quite passive, recording, not thinking.

'A Berlin Diary', *Goodbye to Berlin* (1939)

## ITMA

*UK radio comedy show (1939–49). The title means 'It's that man again' – an exclamation caused by the frequent newspaper appear-*

*ances of Adolf Hitler in the 1930s. Script by Ted Kavanagh and Tommy Handley. With Tommy Handley; Clarence Wright; Horace Percival as Ali Oop, Cecil and the Diver; Jack Train as Claude, Colonel Chinstrap, Lefty and Funf; Hugh Morton as Sam Fairfechan; Sydney Keith as Sam Scram; Dorothy Summers as Mrs Mopp; Joan Harben as Mona Lott; and Fred Yule as George Gorge.*

1
*Cecil:* After you, Claude . . .
*Claude:* No, after you, Cecil.
   Catchphrase

2
*Sam Fairfechan:* As if I cared!
   Catchphrase

3
*Sam Scram:* Boss, boss, sumpin terrible's happened.
   Catchphrase

4
*Mrs Mopp:* Can I do you now, sir?
   Catchphrase

5
*The Diver:* Don't forget the diver.
   Catchphrase
*Based on the saying of an actual one-legged man who dived off New Brighton pier for pennies in the 1920s.*

6
*Wright:* Good morning . . . nice day.
   Catchphrase

7
*Colonel Chinstrap (accepting what he thought to be the offer of a drink):* I don't mind if I do.
   Catchphrase

**1**

*Ali Oop:* I go – I come back.
  Catchphrase

**2**

*The Diver:* I'm going down now, sir.
  Catchphrase

**3**

*Mono Lott:* It's being so cheerful as keeps me going.
  Catchphrase

**4**

*Lefty:* It's me noives.
  Catchphrase

**5**

*George Gorge:* Lovely grub, lovely grub.
  Catchphrase

**6**

*Ali Oop:* No likely, oh crikey!
  Catchphrase

**7**

*Funf (German spy):* This is Funf speaking.
  Catchphrase

# J

### JACOBS, Joe
US boxing manager
(1896–1940)

1

*Believing that his client, Max Schmeling, had been cheated of a*
*heavyweight title by Jack Sharkey, 21 June 1932:*
We wuz robbed!
   Attrib.

2

*Losing a bet on the World Baseball series, October 1935:*
I should have stood in bed.
   Quoted in J. Lardner, *Strong Cigars and Lovely Women*

### JAGGER, Mick and RICHARD, Keith
British rock musicians and songwriters
(1943– ) and (1943– )

3

I can't get no satisfaction.
   Song, 'Satisfaction' (1965)

4

It's Only Rock 'n' Roll.
   Title of song (1974)

### JAMES, Henry
US novelist
(1843–1916)

5

*After having a stroke (2 December 1915) he said he had heard a voice*
*saying:*
So here it is at last, the distinguished thing.
   Quoted in E. Wharton, *A Backward Glance*
*Not his dying words.*

## JAMES, William
US psychologist
(1842–1910)

**1**

The moral flabbiness born of the bitch-goddess Success.
  Letter to H.G. Wells, 11 September 1906

## JAY, Douglas
British Labour politician
(1907–   )

**2**

Fair Shares for All, is Labour's Call.
  Slogan, Battersea North by-election, June 1946

**3**

For in the case of nutrition and health, just as in the case of education, the gentleman in Whitehall really does know better what is good for people than the people know themselves.
  *The Socialist Case* (1947)

## JAY, Peter
British journalist and diplomat
(1937–   )

**4**

As we walked the White Cliffs overlooking the English Channel during the weekend he [James Callaghan] was taking over the Government . . . [he said] he saw his role as being like that of Moses – to lead the people away from the fleshpots of Egypt into the desert and in the direction of the promised land . . . even if it were never to be given to him to see that land . . . [It was] the language of realism and statesmanship.
  Speech, Washington, August 1977

1
A mission to explain.
   IBA public meeting, Croydon, 1980 and many times thereafter
*Phrase encapsulating his programme philosophy for the TV-am breakfast television station.*

2
Remember above all that together we can – being so nice and so talented – work it out.
   Pep-talk to TV-am staff, November 1982, quoted in M. Leapman, *Treachery*


**JENKIN, Patrick**
British Conservative politician
(1926–   )

3
*Advice to members of the public as Energy Minister, during the Three-Day Week, 1974:*
You don't even need to do your teeth with the light on. You can do it in the dark.
   Interviewed on BBC Radio *Newsbeat*, February 1974


**JENKINS, Roy**
British Labour, then Social Democrat, politician
(1920–   )

4
The permissive society has been allowed to become a dirty phrase. A better phrase is the civilized society.
   Speech, Abingdon, 19 July 1969

5
## Breaking the mould of British politics.
*When the Social Democratic Party was established in 1981, there was much talk of 'breaking the mould of British politics' – i.e. doing away*

with the traditional system of a Government party and one chief Opposition party. This was by no means a new way of describing political change and getting rid of an old system for good, in a way that prevents it being reconstituted. However, Jenkins had quoted Andrew Marvell's Horatian Ode Upon Cromwell's Return from Ireland (1650): 'And cast the kingdoms old,/Into another mould' in his book What Matters Now as early as 1972. The use of the expression in connection with the SDP was not restricted to Jenkins, if indeed he uttered the phrase at all after 1981.

## JENNINGS, Paul
British humorist
(1918– )

1

Wembley, adj. Suffering from a vague *malaise*. 'I feel a bit w. this morning.'

'Ware, Wye, Watford', *The Jenguin Pennings* (1963)

## JESSEL, George
US entertainer
(1898– )

2

*On the large number of mourners at Harry Cohn's funeral:*
Same old story: you give 'em what they want and they'll fill the theatre.

Quoted in L. Hellman, *Scoundrel Time*
*Also attributed to Red Skelton.*

## JOAD, C.E.M.
British broadcaster
(1891–1953)

3

It all depends what you mean by . . .

*Passim* in *Brains Trust*, BBC radio, 1940s

## JOFFRE, Joseph Jacques Césaire
French soldier
(1852–1931)

1

*Order for the start of the first battle of the Marne:*
We are about to engage in a battle on which the fate of our country depends and it is important to remind all ranks that the moment has passed for looking to the rear; all our efforts must be directed to attacking and driving back the enemy. Troops that can advance no farther must, at any price, hold on to the ground they have conquered and die on the spot rather than give way. Under the circumstances which face us, no act of weakness can be tolerated.

Recounted in *The Memoirs of Marshal Joffre* (1932)


## JOHN XXIII
Italian-born Pope
(1881–1963)

2

It often happens that I wake at night and begin to think about a serious problem and decide I must tell the Pope about it. Then I wake up completely and remember I am the Pope.

Attrib.

3

Anybody can be Pope; the proof of this is that I have become one.

Attrib.


## JOHN, Augustus
British artist
(1878–1961)

4

*To Nina Hamnet:*
We have become, Nina, the sort of people our parents warned us about.

Attrib.

## JOHNSON, Hiram
US all-party Senator
(1866–1945)

1

The first casualty when war comes is truth.
Speech, US Senate, 1917

## JOHNSON, Lyndon B.
US Democratic President
(1908–73)

2

Come now, let us reason together.
Frequent exhortation
*Based on Isaiah 1:18.*

3

*When Senate Majority leader:*
I've got his pecker in my pocket.
Quoted in D. Halberstam, *The Best and the Brightest*

4

*On becoming President following the assassination of John F. Kennedy:*
All I have, I would have given gladly not to be standing here today.
Speech to Congress, 27 November 1963

5

In your time we have the opportunity to move not only toward the rich society and the powerful society but upward to the Great Society.
Speech, University of Michigan, May 1964

6

We are not about to send American boys nine or ten thousand miles away from home to do what Asian boys ought to be doing for themselves.
Broadcast address, 21 October 1964

1
*On Vietnam:*
You let a bully come into your front yard, the next day he'll be on your porch.

Quoted in *Time*, 15 April 1984
*A remark he made on several occasions.*

2
That Gerald Ford. He can't fart and chew gum at the same time.

Quoted in J.K. Galbraith, *A Life in Our Times*
*Correct version of the oft-misquoted: 'He couldn't walk and chew gum at the same time.'*

3
*On why he kept J. Edgar Hoover at the FBI:*
I'd much rather have that fellow inside my tent pissing out, than outside my tent pissing in.

Quoted in *ib.*

4
Did y'ever think, Ken, that making a speech on ee-conomics is a lot like pissing down your leg? It seems hot to you, but it never does to anyone else.

Quoted in *ib.*

5
*When told by an officer that he was walking towards the wrong helicopter, with the words, 'That's your helicopter over there, sir':*
Son, they are all my helicopters.

Attrib.

6
I want *loyalty*. I want him to kiss my ass in Macy's window at high noon and tell me it smells like roses. I want his pecker in my pocket.

Quoted in D. Halberstam, *The Best and the Brightest*

7
*Announcing his intention not to stand again as President:*
It is true that a house divided against itself is a house that cannot stand. There is a division in the American house now and believing

this as I do, I have concluded that I should not permit the Presidency to become involved in the partisan divisions that are developing in this political year. Accordingly, I shall not seek, and I will not accept, the nomination of my party for another term as your President.

Broadcast address, 31 March 1968

## JOHST, Hanns
German Nazi playwright
(1890–1978)

1

*Storm-trooper:* When I hear the word 'culture', I reach for my revolver.

Translation from *Schlageter* (1933)
*A more accurate translation would be: '. . . I release the safety catch of my Browning' (automatic rifle). A saying often attributed to Hermann Goering.*

## JOLSON, Al
US entertainer
(1888–1950)

2

You ain't heard nothin' yet.

Soundtrack, *The Jazz Singer* (1927)
*Ad lib introduction to song. He did not add 'folks'.*

## JONES, Spike
US musician
(1911–1965)

3

*After eccentric rendering of classic theme:*
Thank-you, music-lovers.

Catchphrase, from 1940s

## JONG, Erica
US novelist
(1942–   )

**1**
The zipless fuck is the purest thing there is. And it is rarer than the unicorn. And I have never had one.
*Fear of Flying* (1973)

**2**
My response . . . was . . . to evolve my fantasy of the Zipless Fuck
. . . Zipless because when you come together zippers fell away like petals.
*Ib.*

## JOSEPH, Michael
British publisher
(1897–1958)

**3**
Authors are easy enough to get on with – if you are fond of children.
Quoted in the *Observer*, 29 May 1949

## JOYCE, James
Irish novelist
(1882–1941)

**4**
The snotgreen sea. The scrotumtightening sea.
*Ulysses* (1937)

**5**
riverrun, past Eve and Adam's, from swerve of shore to bend of bay.
*Finnegan's Wake* (1939)

1

*When a young man accosted him in Zurich and asked, 'May I kiss the hand that wrote* Ulysses?'
No, it did a lot of other things, too.
   Quoted in R. Ellman, *James Joyce*

2

Love me, love my umbrella.
   Attrib.

## *JUMBO*

*US film 1962. With Jimmy Durante. Joke specifically credited to Charles Lederer.*

3

*Sheriff:* Where are you going with that elephant?
*Durante: What* elephant?
   Soundtrack

## JUNG, Carl
### Swiss psychologist
### (1875–1961)

4

[Man's] psyche should be studied because we are the origin of all coming evil.
   Interview, *Face to Face*, BBC TV, 22 October 1959

5

Liverpool is the pool of life.
   Attrib. as having been said in 1927

# K

## KAEL, Pauline
### US film critic
### (1919–   )

**1**

Kiss Kiss Bang Bang
    Title of book (1968)
*From the wording on an Italian film poster seen by her, 'perhaps the briefest statement imaginable on the basic appeal of movies'.*

**2**

*Of Barbra Streisand in* What's Up, Doc?
She's playing herself – and it's awfully soon for that.
    *Deeper into Movies* (1973)

## KAUFMAN, George S.
### US playwright
### (1889–1961)

**3**

Everything I've ever said will be credited to Dorothy Parker.
    Quoted in S. Meredith, *George S. Kaufman and the Algonquin Round Table*

**4**

*At rehearsal for the Marx Brothers film* Animal Crackers *for which he wrote the script:*
Excuse me for interrupting but I actually thought I heard a line I wrote.
    *Ib.*

**1**

*Of Raymond Massey's off-stage interpretation of Abraham Lincoln:*
Massey won't be satisfied until somebody assassinates him.
   *Ib.*

**2**

*When stopped at the stage door and asked if he was 'with the show':*
Well, let's say I'm not against it . . .
   *Ib.*

**3**

*Of an actor called Guido Nadzo:*
Guido Nadzo is nadzo guido.
   *Ib.*

**4**

Satire is what closes Saturday night.
   *Ib.*

**5**

*Of a dead waiter:*
God finally caught his eye.
   *Ib.*
*Also attributed to D. McCord, among others.*

**6**

*When a poor bridge partner asked how he should have played a hand:*
Under an assumed name.
   *Ib.*

**7**

You Can't Take It With You.
   Title of play (written with Moss Hart) (1936)


### KEATS, John (C.)
US writer
(1920–   )

**8**

Americans have plenty of everything and the best of nothing.
   *You Might As Well Live* (1970)

## KENNEDY, Edward F.
US Democratic politician
(1932–   )

1

*Failing to win his party's nomination for the Presidency:*
For me, a few hours ago, this campaign came to an end. For all those
whose cares have been our concern, the work goes on, the cause
endures, the hope still lives, and the dream shall never die.
  Speech at Democratic Convention, 13 August 1980

## KENNEDY, Jimmy
Ulster songwriter
(1902–84)

2

If you go down in the woods today
You're sure of a big surprise . . .
For every bear that ever there was
Will gather there for certain because
Today's the day the teddy bears have their picnic.
  Song, 'The Teddy Bears' Picnic' (1932/3)
*Written to music by John W. Bratton.*

## KENNEDY, John F.
US Democratic President
(1917–63)

3

I just received the following wire from my generous Daddy – 'Dear
Jack. Don't buy a single vote more than necessary. I'll be damned if
I'm going to pay for a landslide.'
  Speech, Washington, 1958

4

*Accepting the Democratic nomination:*

We stand today on the edge of a New Frontier . . . But the New Frontier of which I speak is not a set of promises – it is a set of challenges. It sums up not what I intend to offer the American people, but what I intend to ask of them.

Speech, Los Angeles Convention, 1960

1

Do you realize the responsibility I carry? I'm the only person standing between Nixon and the White House.

Remark, 13 October 1960, quoted in A.M. Schlesinger Jr, *A Thousand Days*

2

*When asked how he became a war hero:*
They sank my boat.

*Ib.*

3

Let the word go forth from this time and place, to friend and foe alike, that the torch has been passed to a new generation of Americans, born in this century, tempered by war, disciplined by a hard and bitter peace, proud of our ancient heritage, and unwilling to witness or permit the slow undoing of those human rights to which this nation has always been committed, and to which we are committed today at home and around the world.

Let every nation know, whether it wishes us well or ill, that we shall pay any price, bear any burden, meet any hardship, support any friend, oppose any foe to assure the survival and the success of liberty.

Inaugural address, Washington, 20 January 1961

4

Let us never negotiate out of fear, but let us never fear to negotiate.

*Ib.*

5

Together let us explore the stars . . .

*Ib.*

**1**

All this will not be finished in the first one hundred days. Nor will it be finished in the first one thousand days, nor in the life of this Administration, nor even perhaps in our lifetime on this planet. But let us begin.

   *Ib.*

**2**

Now the trumpet summons us again – not as a call to bear arms, though arms we need; not as a call to battle, though embattled we are; but a call to bear the burden of a long twilight struggle, year in and year out, 'rejoicing in hope, patient in tribulation', a struggle against the common enemies of man: tyranny, poverty, disease and war itself.

   *Ib.*

**3**

And so, my fellow Americans, ask not what your country can do for you; ask what you can do for your country.

   *Ib.*

**4**

I believe that this nation should commit itself to achieving the goal, before this decade is out, of landing a man on the moon and returning him safely to earth.

   Supplementary State of the Union message to Congress, 25 May 1961

**5**

We don't see the end of the tunnel, but I must say I don't think it is darker than it was a year ago, and in some ways lighter.

   Press conference, 12 December 1962

*Numerous politicians have used the expression 'The light at the end of the tunnel', but it later became a catchphrase of the Vietnam War.*

**6**

I think it's the most extraordinary collection of talent, of human knowledge, that has ever been gathered together at the White House – with the possible exception of when Thomas Jefferson dined alone.

   Speech at dinner for Nobel Prizewinners, 29 April 1962

1

Some men are killed in a war and some men are wounded, and some men never leave the country . . . Life is unfair.

   Quoted in A.M. Schlesinger Jr, *Robert Kennedy and His Times*

2

*Conferring honorary US citizenship on Winston Churchill:*
He mobilized the English language and sent it into battle.

   Speech, 9 April 1963
*See also MURROW 318:4.*

3

All free men, wherever they may live, are citizens of Berlin, and, therefore, as a free man, I take pride in the words 'Ich bin ein Berliner'.

   Speech, Berlin City Hall, 26 June 1963
*If he had said 'Ich bin Berliner' that would have been sufficient. 'Ein Berliner' is a doughnut.*

4

*On the Test Ban Treaty:*
Yesterday, a shaft of light cut into the darkness . . . For the first time, an agreement has been reached on bringing the forces of nuclear destruction under international control.

   Broadcast address, 26 July 1963

5

Forgive but never forget.

   Remark attributed to him by Ted Sorensen in 1968 TV interview

### KENNEDY, Joseph P.
US politician, businessman, and father of JFK
(1888–1969)

6

When the going gets tough, the tough get going.

   Quoted in J.H. Cutler, *Honey Fitz*
*Possibly not original.*

1

Don't get mad, get even.
   Quoted in B. Bradlee, *Conversations with Kennedy*
*Attributed to 'the Boston Irish political jungle'.*


2

If you want to make money, go where the money is.
   Quoted in A.M. Schlesinger Jr, *Robert Kennedy and his Times*


3

Kennedys don't cry.
   *Ib.*
*Family rendering of his 'We don't want any crying in this house.'*


## KENNEDY, Robert F.
### US Democratic politician
### (1925–68)

4

One-fifth of the people are against everything all the time.
   Quoted in the *Observer*, 10 May 1964


5

*After winning California primary:*
My thanks to all of you. And now it's on to Chicago and let's win
there.
   Speech, Los Angeles, 4 June 1968
*His last public remark before being murdered.*


See also SHAW 383:4.


## KEPPEL, Mrs Alice
### British mistress of King Edward VII

6

*On the day of King Edward VIII's abdication:*
Things were done better in my day.
   Attrib.
*Also attributed to Maxine Elliott.*

## KEROUAC, Jack
US writer
(1922–1969)

1

You know, this is really a beat generation.
  Recalled in *The Origins of the Beat Generation*
*Phrase borrowed from a broken-down drug addict called Herbert Huncke.*

## KEYNES, John Maynard
British economist
(1883–1946)

2

In the long run we are all dead.
  Attrib.

3

*On being asked what happened when David Lloyd George was alone in a room:*
When he's alone in a room, there's nobody there.
  Quoted by Baroness Asquith, *As I Remember,* BBC TV, 30 April 1967

## KHRUSCHEV, Nikita S.
Soviet Communist Party leader
(1894–1971)

4

*On the likelihood of the Soviet Union rejecting communism:*
Those who wait for that must wait until a shrimp learns to whistle.
  Attrib. 1955

5

*Denouncing Stalin:*
[He promoted a] cult of personality.
  Speech to 20th Party Congress, 25 February 1956

1
*To Western diplomats at Moscow reception:*
Whether you like it or not, history is on our side. We will bury you.
   Reported in *The Times*, 19 November 1956
*Khruschev later attempted to explain that he meant 'we will outlive you' in the sense of 'outstrip' economically rather than anything more threatening.*

2
If you start throwing hedgehogs under me, I shall throw two porcupines under you.
   Quoted in the *Observer*, 10 November 1963

3
If you cannot catch a bird of paradise, better take a wet hen.
   Attrib.

## KILMER, Joyce
US poet and journalist
(1886–1918)

4
I think that I shall never see
A poem lovely as a tree.
   'Trees' (1913)

## KING, Rev. Dr Martin Luther, Jnr
US civil rights leader
(1929–68)

5
I have a dream.
   Speech, Washington civil rights demonstration, 28 August 1963
*He had used this theme in other speeches that summer.*

1

Free at last, free at last, thank God Almighty, we are free at last!
  *Ib.*
*Quoting an old Negro spiritual.*

2

I've been to the mountain top . . . I've looked over and I've seen the
promised land. I may not get there with you, but I want you to know
tonight that we as a people will get to the promised land. So, I'm
happy tonight. Mine eyes have seen the glory of the coming of the
Lord.
  Speech, Memphis, 3 April 1968
*The next day he was assassinated.*


### KING, Philip
British playwright
(1904–79)

3

*To policeman confronting a horde of vicars:*
Sergeant, arrest most of these people!
  *See How They Run* (1944)
*Sometimes misquoted as 'Arrest several of these vicars!'*


### *KING KONG*

*US film 1933. Script by James Creelman and Ruth Rose. With Robert
Armstrong.*

4

*Last line:*
Oh no, it wasn't the airplanes. It was beauty killed the beast.
  Soundtrack

### KING KONG

*US film 1976. Script by Lorenzo Semple Jnr. With Jeff Bridges as Jack Prescott and Jessica Lange as Dwan.*

1
*Jack (to Dwan) about King Kong:* He's bigger than both of us, know what I mean?
   Soundtrack

### KING'S ROW

*US film 1941. Script by Casey Robinson. With Ronald Reagan as Drake McHugh and Ann Sheridan as Randy Monaghan.*

2
*Drake:* Randy – where's the rest of me?
*On waking to find that his legs have been amputated by a sadistic doctor. Used by Reagan as the title of an early autobiography.*

### KINGSMILL, Hugh
British writer
(1889–1949)

3
It is difficult to love mankind unless one has a reasonable private income and when one has a reasonable private income one has better things to do than loving mankind.
   Quoted in R. Ingrams' *God's Apology*

4
Friends are God's apology for relations.
   *Ib.*

## KINNOCK, Neil
British Labour politician
(1942–   )

1

*In reply to heckler's comment, 'At least Mrs Thatcher has got guts':*
And it's a pity that people had to leave theirs on the ground at Goose
Green in order to prove it.
   TV election programme, 5 June 1983

## KIPLING, Rudyard
British poet and novelist
(1865–1936)

2

The flannelled fools at the wicket or the muddied oafs at the goals.
   'The Islanders' (1902)

3

I keep six honest serving men
(They taught me all I knew):
Their names are What and Why and When
And How and Where and Who.
   'The Elephant's Child', *The Just-So Stories* (1902)

4

The Cat That Walked By Himself.
   Title of story in *ib.*

5

Watch the wall, my darling, while the Gentlemen go by!
   'A Smuggler's Song'

6

If you can keep your head when all about you
Are losing theirs and blaming it on you . . .
   'If', *Rewards and Fairies* (1910)

1

If you can meet with Triumph and Disaster
And treat those two impostors just the same . . .
  *Ib.*

2

If you can talk with crowds and keep your virtue,
Or walk with Kings – nor lose the common touch . . .
  *Ib.*

3

If you can fill the unforgiving minute
With sixty seconds' worth of distance run,
Yours is the Earth and everything that's in it,
And – which is more – you'll be a Man, my son!
  *Ib.*

4

For the female of the species is more deadly than the male.
  'The Female of the Species' (1911)

5

Our England is a garden, and such gardens are not made
By singing: – 'Oh, how beautiful!' and sitting in the shade.
  'The Glory of the Garden' (1911)

6

So when the world is asleep, and there seems no hope of her waking
  Out of the long, bad dream that makes her mutter and moan,
Suddenly, all men arise to the noise of fetters breaking,
  And every one smiles at his neighbour and tells him his soul is his
own!
  'The Dawn Wind' (1911)

*See also BALDWIN 37:3.*


**KISSINGER, Henry**
US Republican Secretary of State
(1923–   )

7

*Diagnosing his success as a 'swinger':*

Power is the ultimate aphrodisiac.
    Attrib.
*Also in the form 'great aphrodisiac', quoted in the* New York Times,
*19 January 1971.*

1
There cannot be a crisis next week. My schedule is already full.
    Quoted in *Time*, 24 January 1977

*See also BOOK TITLES 63:4.*


**KITCHEN, Fred**
British entertainer
(1872–1950)


2
Meredith, we're in!
    Sketch, 'The Bailiff' (1907)


**KNOX, Father Ronald**
British priest and writer
(1888–1957)

3
*Definition of a baby:*
A loud noise at one end and no sense of responsibility at the other.
    Attrib.


## *KNUTE ROCKNE – ALL AMERICAN*

*US film 1940. Script by Robert Buckner, based on reminiscences.
With Pat O'Brien as Knute Rockne and Ronald Reagan as George
Gipp.*

4
*Rockne:* 'Rock,' he said, 'some time when the team is up against it and

the breaks are beating the boys, tell them to go out there with all they got and win just one for the Gipper.'
Soundtrack
*Based on the words of the real Rockne at half-time in a 1928 army game, recalling what the real Gipp (a football star who died young) had said to him: 'Rock, someday when things look real tough for Notre Dame, ask the boys to go out there and win one for me.' 'Win this one for the Gipper' became a slogan of Ronald Reagan's supporters when he went into politics.*

## KOCH, Ed
### US politician and Mayor of New York City
### (1924–  )

1
How'm I doing?
  Catchphrase from *c.*1977

## *KOJAK*

*US TV police drama series, from 1973–7. With Telly Savalas as Kojak.*

2
Who loves ya, baby?
  Stock phrase

## KOVACS, Ernie
### US entertainer
### (1919–62)

3
*On television:*
A medium, so called because it is neither rare nor well done.
  Attrib.
*See also ACE 9:1.*

# L

## LABOUR PARTY
British political organization

**1**

To secure for the workers by hand or by brain the full fruits of their industry and the most equitable distribution thereof that may be possible upon the basis of the common ownership of the means of production, distribution, and exchange.

  Clause 4 of the party's Constitution (Party Objects), adopted 1918/1926

*The words 'socialization of the means of production etc.' appeared in the 1900 Labour Party manifesto.*

## LANCASTER, Osbert
(later Sir Osbert)
British cartoonist
(1908–86)

**2**

*'Maudie Littlehampton' (on the Lady Chatterley trial):* It's an odd thing, but now one knows it's profoundly moral and packed with deep spiritual significance a lot of the old charm seems to have gone.

  Caption to cartoon in the *Daily Express* (1961)

## LANCHESTER, Elsa
British film actress
(1902–86)

**3**

*On Maureen O'Hara:*
She looked as though butter wouldn't melt in her mouth. Or anywhere else.

  Attrib.

## LANDOWSKA, Wanda
Hungarian harpsichordist
(1877–1959)

1
*Remark to fellow musician:*
Oh, well, you play Bach *your* way. I'll play him *his*.
  Attrib.


## LANG, Andrew
British poet
(1844–1912)

2
He uses statistics as a drunken man uses lamp-posts – for support rather than illumination.
  Attrib.


## LANG, Julia
British broadcaster
(1921–   )

3
*As prelude to telling a story:*
Are you sitting comfortably? Then I'll begin.
  *Passim* in *Listen with Mother*, BBC Radio, from 1950 onwards


## LARKIN, Philip
British librarian and poet
(1922–85)

4
Nothing, like something, happens anywhere.
  'I Remember, I Remember', *The Less Deceived* (1955)

1
Why should I let the toad *work*
   Squat on my life?
Can't I use my wit as a pitchfork
   And drive the brute off?
     'Toads' in *ib.*

2
Give me your arm, old Toad;
Help me down Cemetery Road.
   'Toads Revisited', *The Whitsun Weddings* (1964)

3
Get stewed:
Books are a load of crap.
   'A study of Reading Habits' in *ib.*

4
What will survive of us is love.
   'An Arundel Tomb', in *ib.*

5
Perhaps being old is having lighted rooms
Inside your head, and people in them, acting.
People you know, yet can't quite name.
   'The Old Fools', *High Windows* (1974)

6
Sexual intercourse began
In nineteen sixty-three
(Which was rather late for me) –
Between the end of the *Chatterley* ban
And the Beatles' first LP.
   'Annus Mirabilis', in *ib.*

7
They fuck you up, your mum and dad.
   They may not mean to, but they do.

They fill you up with the faults they had
   And add some extra, just for you.
   'This Be the Verse' in *ib*.

1
Man hands on misery to man.
   It deepens like a coastal shelf.
Get out as early as you can,
   And don't have any kids yourself.
   *Ib*.

2
Deprivation is for me what daffodils were for Wordsworth.
   Interview in the *Observer*, 1979

## THE LAST FLIGHT
*US film 1931. Script by John Monk Saunders. With Richard Barthelmess.*

3
*On why some American airmen in Europe had gone bull-fighting, with the result that one was gored to death:*
*RB:* It seemed like a good idea at the time.
   Soundtrack
*L. Halliwell in* The Filmgoer's Book of Quotes *(1978) suggests that this was the first time the catchphrase was used on film.*

## THE LAST REMAKE OF BEAU GESTE
*US film 1977. Script by Marty Feldman and Chris J. Allen. With Terry-Thomas and Ann-Margret.*

4
*Prison governor (T-T) to woman (A-M) who has slept with him in order to secure an escape:*
Delighted you came, my dear, and I'd like you to know that you made a happy man feel very old.
   Soundtrack

# LAUDER, Sir Harry
Scots entertainer
(1870–1950)

1

I Love a Lassie.
   Title of song

2

Keep Right On to the End of the Road.
   Title of song

3

Roamin' in the gloamin',
By the bonny banks of Clyde.
   Song, 'Roamin' in the Gloamin''

4

It's a Braw Brecht Moonlecht Night.
   Title of song (1904)
*Written by Tobias/Field/Ormont.*

5

## Bang went saxpence.
*Joke repopularized by Lauder. Originated by Charles Keene in
Punch (1868) – 'Mun, a had na' been the-erre abune two hours when
– bang – went saxpence!!!'*

6

Oh, it's nice to get up in the mornin'
But it's nicer to lie in bed.
   Song, 'It's Nice to Be in Bed'


## LAUGH-IN, ROWAN AND MARTIN'S
*US television comedy series 1967–73. Script by various. With Dan
Rowan, Dick Martin, Judy Carne, Goldie Hawn, Arte Johnson, Gary
Owens, Lily Tomlin, and Dewey 'Pigmeat' Markham.*

1

The Flying Fickle Finger of Fate.
    Stock phrase
*Based on an armed forces expression, 'Fucked by the fickle finger of fate', from the 1930s.*

2

Here come de judge!
    Catchphrase
*An old vaudeville catchphrase of Dewey 'Pigmeat' Markham's. He was brought along to utter it again.*

3

*Tomlin (as telephone operator):* Is this the party to whom I am speaking?
    Catchphrase

4

Look that up in your Funk and Wagnalls.
    Catchphrase

5

*Carne:* Sock it to me!
    Catchphrase
*Derived from Aretha Franklin song, 'Respect' (1968).*

6

*Owens (announcer):* This is beautiful downtown Burbank.
    Catchphrase

7

You bet your sweet bippy!
    Catchphrase

8

*Johnson (as German soldier):* Verry interesting . . . (but stupid)!
    Catchphrase

## LAW, Andrew Bonar
### British Conservative Prime Minister
### (1858–1923)

1

I must follow them; I am their leader.

Quoted in E. Raymond, *Mr Balfour*

*Usually this is ascribed to Alexandre Auguste Ledru-Rollin who said it as a mob passed by in the 1848 Paris revolution ('Eh, je suis leur chef, il fallait bien les suivre').*

## LAWRENCE, D.H.
### British novelist
### (1885–1930)

2

*On a publisher's rejection of* Sons and Lovers:

Curse the blasted, jelly-boned swines, the slimy, the belly-wriggling invertebrates, the miserable sodding rotters, the flaming sods, the snivelling, dribbling, dithering, palsied, pulseless lot that make up England today.

Letter to Edward Garnett, 3 July 1912

3

*On James Joyce:*

Nothing but old fags and cabbage-stumps of quotations from the Bible and the rest, stewed in the juice of deliberate, journalistic dirty-mindedness.

Letter to Aldous Huxley, 15 August 1928

4

Some things can't be ravished. You can't ravish a tin of sardines.

*Lady Chatterley's Lover* (1928)

5

John Thomas says good-night to Lady Jane, a little droopingly, but with a hopeful heart.

*Ib.*

*Closing words.*

1
How beastly the bourgeois is
especially the male of the species.
   'How Beastly the Bourgeois Is' (1929)


## LAWRENCE, T.E.
### British soldier and writer
### (1888–1935)

2
I loved you, so I drew these tides of men into my hands
   and wrote my will across the sky in stars
to earn you freedom, the seven pillared worthy house,
   that your eyes might be shining for me
when we came.
   Epigraph 'To S.A.', *The Seven Pillars of Wisdom* (1926)


## LEACOCK, Stephen
### US writer
### (1869–1944)

3
He flung himself from the room, flung himself upon his horse and
rode madly off in all directions.
   'Gertrude the Governess', *Nonsense Novels* (1911)


## LEARY, Dr Timothy
### Hippie guru
### (1920–   )

4
Turn on, tune in, drop out.
   Title of lecture, 1967

## 'LE CARRE, John'
### British novelist
### (1931–  )

1

The Spy Who Came In From the Cold.
  Title of novel (1963)

## 'LE CORBUSIER'
### French architect
### (1887–1965)

2

A house is a machine for living in ('Une maison est une machine-à-habiter').
  *Vers une architecture* (1923)

## LEHMAN, Ernest
### US writer
### (1920–  )

3

Sweet Smell of Success.
  Title of novel and film (1957)

## LEHMANN, Rosamond
### British writer
### (1901–  )

4

*On Ian Fleming:*
The trouble with Ian is that he gets off with women because he can't get on with them.
  Quoted in J. Pearson, *The Life of Ian Fleming*
  *Borrowing a line from Elizabeth Bowen.*

### LEHRER, Tom
US songwriter and entertainer
(1928–   )

1

Life is like a sewer. What you get out of it depends on what you put in.
   Record album, 'An Evening Wasted with Tom Lehrer' (1953)

2

He was into animal husbandry – until they caught him at it.
   *Ib.*

3

It is sobering to consider that when Mozart was my age he had already
been dead for a year.
   Attrib.

### LEIBER, Jerry and STOLLER, Mike
US songwriters
(1933–   ) and (1933–   )

4

You ain't nothin' but a hound dog,
Cryin' all the time.
   Song, 'Hound Dog' (1956)

5

I (Who Have Nothing).
   Title of song (*c.*1963)
*Credited to 'Donida; Leiber, Stoller, Mogol'.*

### LEMAY, Curtis E.
US general and air force chief
(1906–   )

6

*On the North Vietnamese:*
My solution to the problem would be to tell [them] . . . they've got to
draw in their horns or we're going to bomb them into the Stone Age.
   *Mission with LeMay* (1965)

## LE MESURIER, John
British actor
(1912–83)

**1**

*His death announcement in a newspaper personal column:*
John Le Mesurier wishes it to be known that he conked out on
November 15th. He sadly misses family and friends.
   *The Times*, 15 November 1983

**2**

It's all been rather lovely.
   Last words, quoted in *ib.*

## 'LENIN, N.'
Russian revolutionary and Soviet leader
(1870–1924)

**3**

One Step Forward, Two Steps Back.
   Translation of book title (1904)

**4**

It is true that liberty is precious – so precious that it must be rationed.
   Quoted in S. & B. Webb, *Soviet Communism* (1936)

**5**

*Question to show that there are two categories of people – those who
do and those to whom it is done:*
Who, whom? We or they?
   Quoted in F. Maclean, *Disputed Barricade*

**6**

*On Bernard Shaw:*
A good man fallen among Fabians.
   Quoted in A. Ransome, *Six Weeks in Russia in 1919*

## LENNON, John
British singer and songwriter
(1940–80)

1
Those in the cheaper seats clap. The rest of you rattle your jewellery.
  Remark, Royal Variety Performance, 15 November 1963

2
Christianity will go. It will vanish and shrink. I needn't argue about that. I'm right and I'll be proved right. We're more popular than Jesus now.
  Interview with the London *Evening Standard*, March 1966

3
Imagine there's no heaven
It's easy if you try
No help below us
Above us only sky
Imagine all the people
Living for today.
  Song 'Imagine' (1975)

4
## Life is what happens to us while we are making other plans.
  Song, 'Beautiful Boy' (1980)
*This is a quotation which Laurence J. Peter in* Quotations for Our Time *ascribes to 'Thomas La Mance' – but I have been unable to trace him.*

## LENNON, John and McCARTNEY, Paul
British songwriters
(1940–80) and (1942–   )

5
Yeh-yeh-yeh.
  Song 'She Loves You' (1963)

1

It's been a hard day's night.
  Song 'A Hard Day's Night' (1964)
*The phrase is said to have been suggested by Ringo Starr, though Lennon may have used it first.*

2

Yesterday, all my troubles seemed so far away.
  Song, 'Yesterday' (1965)

3

Waits at the window, wearing the face that she keeps in a jar by
  the door
Who is it for?
All the lonely people, where do they all come from?
  Song 'Eleanor Rigby' (1967)

4

Will you still need me, will you still feed me
When I'm sixty-four?
  Song, 'When I'm Sixty-Four' (1967)

5

I get by with a little help from my friends.
  Song, 'With a Little Help from My Friends' (1967)

6

All You Need Is Love.
  Title of song (1967)

7

Let It Be.
  Title of song (1970)

**LERNER, Alan Jay**
US lyricist and playwright
(1918–86)

8

Why Can't a Woman Be More Like a Man?
  Title of song, *My Fair Lady* (1956)

1
Oh, yes, I remember it well.
 Song, 'I Remember It Well', *Gigi* (1958)

2
Thank heaven for little girls,
For little girls get bigger every day.
 Song, 'Thank Heaven for Little Girls' in *ib*.

3
Don't let it be forgot
That once there was a spot
For one brief shining moment that was known
As Camelot . . .
 Title song, *Camelot* (1960)

4
You write a hit the same way you write a flop.
 Attrib.

5
There is no greater fan of the opposite sex than me, and I have the bills
to prove it.
 Attrib.

### THE LETTER
*US film 1940. Script by Howard Koch, from the story by W. Somerset Maugham. With Bette Davis.*

6
Yes, I killed him. And I'm glad, I tell you. Glad, glad, glad!
 Attrib.
*Although associated with Bette Davis in the film, it is not uttered in it.*

## LEVANT, Oscar
US pianist and actor
(1906–72)

7
Strip the phoney tinsel off Hollywood and you'll find the real tinsel
underneath.
 Attrib.

1

*In reply to George Gershwin's barb (see 188:3):*
Play us a medley of your hit.
    Attrib.

2

*Romance on the High Seas* was Doris Day's first picture; that was
before she became a virgin.
    *Memoirs of an Amnesiac* (1965)
*Compare G. MARX 297:6.*


## LEVERHULME, Viscount
### British industrialist
### (1851–1925)

3

Half the money I spend on advertising is wasted, and the trouble is I
don't know which half.
    Quoted in D. Ogilvy, *Confessions of an Advertising Man*


## 'LIBERACE'
### US pianist
### (1919–87)

4

When the reviews are bad I tell my staff that they can join me as I cry
all the way to the bank.
    *Liberace: An Autobiography* (1973)


## *LITTLE CAESAR*
*US film 1930. Script by various. With Edward G. Robinson as Rico.*

5

*Rico (dying words):* Mother of Mercy, is this the end of Rico?
    Soundtrack

## LITVINOV, Maxim
Soviet politician
(1876–1951)

1
Peace is indivisible.
    Said on several occasions and at League of Nations, Geneva, 1 July 1936

## *LIVES OF A BENGAL LANCER*
*US film 1935. Script by various. Douglass Dumbrille as Mohammed Khan.*

2
*Khan:* We have ways of making men talk.
*An early example of a film catchphrase also rendered as 'We have ways (and means) of making you talk.'*

## LOESSER, Frank
US songwriter
(1910–69)

3
See What the Boys in the Back Room Will Have.
    Title of song, *Destry Rides Again* (1939)
*See also BEAVERBROOK 46:3.*

4
Finally found a fellow
He says 'Murder!' – he says!
Every time we kiss he says 'Murder!' – he says!
Is that the language of love?
    Song, '"Murder" He Says', *Happy Go Lucky* (1943)
Murder He Says *was the title of a film (US, 1945).*

**1**

Yes, time heals all things,
So I needn't cling to this fear,
It's merely that Spring
Will be a little late this year.
Song, 'Spring Will Be a Little Late This Year', *Christmas Holiday* (1944)

**2**

I'd like to get you on a slow boat to China
All to myself alone.
Song, 'On a Slow Boat to China' (1948)

**3**

How To Succeed in Business Without Really Trying.
Title of musical (1961)
*Taken from Shepherd Meade's non-fiction guidebook of that title.*

### LOMBARDI, Vince
US football coach
(1913–70)

**4**

Winning isn't everything. It's the only thing.
Attrib.
*Various versions of this oft-repeated statement exist.*

### THE LONE RANGER
*US radio, film and TV Western series, from 1933.*

**5**

Return with us now to those thrilling days of yesteryear . . . the Lone
Ranger rides again!
Introductory announcement

1

*Lone Ranger (to horse):* Hi-yo, Silver!
  Catchphrase

2

*Tonto:* Him bad man, kemo sabe.
  Stock phrase


# LONG, Huey
US demagogue
(1893–1935)

3

I looked around at the little fishes present and said, 'I'm the Kingfish.'
  Quoted in A. Schlesinger Jr, *The Politics of Upheaval*

4

Every man a king but no man wears a crown.
  Slogan, 1928
*Quoting William Jennings Bryan.*


# LONGWORTH, Alice Roosevelt
US political hostess
(1884–1980)

5

*Embroidered on a cushion at her Washington home:*
If you haven't anything nice to say about anyone, come and sit by me.
  Quoted in the *New York Times*, 25 February 1980

6

*Of Calvin Coolidge:*
\#\#   Looked as if he had been weaned on a pickle.
  *Ib.*
*She heard this at the dentist.*

1

*Of Thomas E. Dewey:*

\#\#    Dewey looks like the bridegroom on the wedding cake.

   *Ib.*

*She heard this from Grace Hodgson Flandrau.*

2

*On Dewey's nomination, in 1948:*

You can't make a soufflé rise twice.

   Attrib.

### LOOS, Anita
US novelist
(1893–    )

3

Gentlemen Prefer Blondes.

   Title of novel (1925)

*To which a sequel was added: 'But they marry brunettes.'*

4

A girl like I.

   *Passim* in *ib.*

5

Kissing your hand may make you feel very good but a diamond and safire bracelet lasts forever.

   *Ib.*

*This was the inspiration for the Jule Styne/Leo Robin song 'Diamonds Are a Girl's Best Friend' in the 1953 film based on the book.*

### LOTHIAN, 11th Marquess of
British Conservative politician
(1882–1940)

6

The only lasting solution is that Europe itself should gradually find its way to an internal equilibrium and a limitation of armaments by political appeasement.

   Letter to *The Times*, 4 May 1934

## LOUIS, Joe
US boxer
(1914–81)

1

*On his fight with the quick-moving Billy Conn (whom he beat by a knock-out, 19 June 1946):*
He can run, but he can't hide.
   Attrib.
*Alluded to by President Reagan (1985) in a warning to terrorists:*
*'You can run, but you can't hide.'*


## LOVE STORY
*US film 1970. Script (also novel) by Erich Segal. With Ryan O'Neal as Oliver.*

2

*Oliver:* What can you say about a 25-year-old girl who died? That she was beautiful? And brilliant. That she loved Mozart and Bach. And the Beatles. And me.
   Soundtrack


3

*Oliver:* Love means never having to say you're sorry.
   Soundtrack
*In the book it appears as 'Love means not ever . . .' A graffito 'A vasectomy means never having to say you're sorry' was current by 1974.*


## LOVELL, James
US astronaut
(1928– )

4

*After explosion on board Apollo XIII, seriously endangering the crew:*
OK, Houston, we have had a problem here . . . Houston, we have a problem.
   Radio message, 11 April 1970

*It is hard to decipher precisely what was being said and the words have
also been attributed to John L. Swigert Jr.*

## LOW, David
British cartoonist
(1891–1963)

1
Very well, alone.
    Caption to his cartoon, *Evening Standard*, 18 June 1940
*The cartoon showed a British soldier confronting a hostile sea and a
sky full of bombers.*

## LOWELL, Robert
US poet
(1917–77)

2
If we see light at the end of the tunnel,
It's the light of the oncoming train.
    'Day by Day' (1977)
*Probably not original.*

## LOWRY, L.S.
British painter
(1887–1976)

3
A bachelor lives like a king and dies like a beggar.
    Attrib.

## LUDENDORFF, Erich
German general
(1865–1937)

1

*On British troops in the First World War:*
\#\#    Lions led by donkeys.
   Attrib.
*In fact, Field Marshal von Falkenhayn in his memoirs records the following exchange: Ludendorff: 'The English fight like lions.' Hoffman: 'True. But don't we know that they are lions led by donkeys?'*

## LUTYENS, Sir Edwin
British architect
(1869–1944)

2

*Before a Royal Commission:*
The answer is in the plural and they bounce.
   Attrib.

3

This piece of cod passeth all understanding.
   Quoted in R. Lutyens, *Sir Edwin Lutyens*

## LYNCH, Jack
Irish Taoiseach (Head of Government)
(1917–   )

4

I would not like to leave contraception on the long finger too long.
   Quoted in the *Irish Times*, 23 May 1971

# M

## McALPINE, Sir Alfred
### British civil engineer
### (1881–1944)

**1**

Keep Paddy behind the big mixer.
   Attrib.
*Last words.*

## MacARTHUR, Douglas
### US general
### (1880–1964)

**2**

The President of the United States ordered me to break through the
Japanese lines and proceed from Corregidor to Australia for the
purpose, as I understand it, of organizing the American offensive
against Japan, a primary object of which is the relief of the
Philippines. I came through and I shall return.
   Statement, Adelaide, 20 March 1942

**3**

People of the Philippines, I have returned.
   Statement, Leyte, 20 October 1944

**4**

In war there is no substitute for victory.
   Speech to Congress, 19 April 1951

**5**

*On his dismissal by President Truman:*
The world has turned over many times since I took the oath on the
Plain at West Point, and the hopes and dreams have long since

vanished. But I still remember the refrain of one of the most popular barrack ballads of that day, which proclaimed, most proudly, that old soldiers never die. They just fade away. And like the old soldier of that ballad, I now close my military career and just fade away – an old soldier who tried to do his duty as God gave him the light to see that duty. Goodbye.

*Ib.*

## MACARTHY, Sir Desmond
### British writer and critic
### (1887–1952)

1

[Journalists are] more attentive to the minute hand of history than to the hour hand.

Quoted in K. Tynan, *Curtains*

## MACAULAY, Rose
### British novelist
### (1881–1958)

2

'Take my camel, dear', said my aunt Dot, as she climbed down from this animal on her return from High Mass.

*The Towers of Trebizond* (1956)
*Opening words.*

## McAULIFFE, Anthony C.
### US general
### (1898–1975)

3

*When asked to surrender by the Germans at the Battle of Bastogne:*
Nuts!

Message, 23 December 1944
*His message may have been worded more strongly.*

## McCARTHY, Senator Joseph
US politician and witch-hunter
(1908–57)

1

*Of an alleged communist sympathizer:*
It makes me sick, sick, sick way down inside.
  Quoted in P. Lewis, *The Fifties*

2

*On how you can spot a communist:*
It looks like a duck, walks like a duck, and quacks like a duck.
  Attrib.

## McCARTNEY, Paul
see LENNON, John and McCARTNEY, Paul

## McCOY, Horace
US writer
(1897–1955)

3

They Shoot Horses, Don't They?
  Title of novel (1935)

## McCRAE, John
Canadian poet
(1872–1918)

4

In Flanders fields the poppies blow
Between the crosses, row on row,
That mark our place.
  'In Flanders Fields' (1915)

1
If ye break faith with us who die
We shall not sleep, though poppies grow
On Flanders fields.
   *Ib.*


### McCULLOCH, Derek
British broadcaster
(1897–1967)

2
Goodbye, children . . . everywhere.
   Stock phrase, *Children's Hour*, BBC Radio, from 1940s onwards


### McENROE, John
US tennis player
(1959–   )

3
*To umpire at Wimbledon 1981:*
You are the pits of the world.
   Quoted in the *Sunday Times*, 24 June 1984


4
*To umpire:*
You cannot be serious.
   Attrib.
*This remark achieved catchphrase status in the early 1980s.*


### McGOVERN, George
US Democratic politician
(1922–   )

5
*On his Vice-Presidential running mate:*
I am one thousand per cent for Tom Eagleton and I have no intention
of dropping him from the ticket.
   Attrib. 1972
*He dropped him shortly afterwards.*

## McKINNEY, Joyce
US former beauty queen
(1950–   )

1

*On Mormon ex-lover she had kidnapped:*
I loved Kirk so much, I would have skied down Mount Everest in the nude with a carnation up my nose.

   In British court, 1977


## MACLEOD, Iain
British Conservative politician
(1913–70)

2

We now have the worst of both worlds – not just inflation on the one side or stagnation on the other side, but both of them together. We have a sort of 'stagflation' situation.

   Speech, House of Commons, 17 November 1965


## McLUHAN, Marshall
Canadian writer
(1911–80)

3

The new electronic interdependence recreates the world in the image of a global village.

   *The Gutenberg Galaxy* (1962)


4

The medium is the message.

   *Understanding Media* (1964)


5

Television brought the brutality of war into the comfort of the living room. Vietnam was lost in the living rooms of America – not on the battlefields of Vietnam.

   Quoted in the Montreal *Gazette*, 16 May 1975

# MACMILLAN, Harold
(later 1st Earl of Stockton)
British Conservative Prime Minister
(1894–1986)

**1**

The Middle Way.
   Title of book (1938)

**2**

*After a summit conference at Geneva:*
There ain't gonna be no war.
   Press conference, London, 24 July 1955
*Possibly an allusion to M. Twain,* Tom Sawyer Abroad, *Ch. 1 (1894):
'There's plenty of boys that will come hankering . . . when you've got
an apple . . . but when they've got one . . . they . . . say thank you
'most to death, but there ain't a-going to be no core.' But almost
certainly a direct quote from the c.1910 music hall song 'There ain't
going to be no war/So long as we've a king like good King Edward
[VII].'*

**3**

*Of a Foreign Secretary's life:*
Forever poised between a cliché and an indiscretion.
   Quoted in *Newsweek*, 30 April 1956

**4**

*After the resignation of his Chancellor of the Exchequer and others:*
I thought the best thing to do was to settle up these little local
difficulties, and then turn to the wider vision of the Commonwealth.
   Statement, London airport, 7 January 1958

**5**

Jaw-jaw is better than war-war.
   Remark, Canberra, 30 January 1958
*See CHURCHILL 108:5.*

1

Let's be frank about it. Most of our people have never had it so good.
  Speech, Bedford, 20 July 1957
*'You Never Had It So Good' was a slogan used by the Democrats in
the 1952 US Presidential election.*

2

## Exporting is fun.
  Speech to businessmen, 1960
*He never actually said the words contained in an advance text for the
press.*

3

The wind of change is blowing through this continent.
  Speech, Parliament, Cape Town, 3 February 1960

4

Power? It's like a dead sea fruit; when you achieve it, there's nothing
there.
  Attrib.

5

I was determined that no British Government should be brought
down by the action of two tarts.
  Attrib. 13 July 1963

6

*On his resignation as Prime Minister:*
I hope that it will soon be possible for the customary processes of
consultation to be carried on within the party about its future
leadership.
  Statement (read by R.A. Butler) to Conservative Party Conference,
  10 October 1963

7

If people want a sense of purpose they should get it from their
archbishop. They should certainly not get it from their politicians.
  Quoted in H. Fairlie, *The Life of Politics*

## MACNEICE, Louis
British poet
(1907–63)

1

It's no go the merrygoround, it's no go the rickshaw,
All we want is a limousine and a ticket for the peepshow.
  'Bagpipe Music' (1937)


## MAETERLINCK, Maurice
Belgian poet and playwright
(1862–1949)

2

The living are just the dead on holiday.
  Attrib.


## MAGEE, John Gillespie
US-born air force pilot and poet
(1922–41)

3

Oh! I have slipped the surly bonds of earth,
And danced the skies on laughter-silvered wings;
Sunward I've climbed and joined the tumbling mirth
Of sun-split clouds – and done a hundred things
You have not dreamed of – wheeled and soared and swung
High in the sunlit silence. Hov'ring there
I've chased the shouting wind along and flung
My eager craft through footless halls of air.
Up, up the long, delirious, burning blue
I've topped the wind-swept heights with easy grace,
Where never lark, or even eagle, flew;
And, while with silent lifting mind I've trod
The high, untrespassed sanctity of space,
Put out my hand, and touched the face of God.
  'High Flight', *More Poems from the Forces* (pub. 1943)

*Magee was killed while fighting in Europe with the Royal Canadian Air Force. President Reagan quoted the poem in a TV address following the space shuttle* Challenger *disaster in January 1986.*

### MALLORY, George Leigh
British mountaineer
(1886–1924)

1

*When asked why he wanted to climb Mount Everest:*
Because it's there.
　　Attrib. reply during US lecture tour, 1923

### MANKIEWICZ, Herman J.
US screenwriter
(1897–1953)

2

*When a Hollywood agent told him he had been swimming unscathed in shark-infested waters:*
I think that's what they call professional courtesy.
　　Attrib.

3

*After vomiting at the table of a fastidious host:*
It's all right, Arthur. The white wine came up with the fish.
　　Attrib.

*See also* CITIZEN KANE *pp. 109–10.*

### MANSFIELD, Katherine
New Zealand-born writer
(1888–1923)

4

Better to write twaddle, anything, than nothing at all.
　　Attrib.

## MAO TSE-TUNG
Chinese revolutionary and communist leader
(1893–1976)

1

Every Communist must grasp the truth, political power grows out of the barrel of a gun.

(6 November 1938) Included in *Quotations from Chairman Mao Tse-tung*

2

All reactionaries are paper tigers.

(Interview, 1946) *Ib.*

3

We must let a hundred flowers bloom and a hundred schools of thought contend.

Statement, May 1956

*Outlining a period of self-criticism which was launched, briefly, in May 1957.*

4

The Great Leap Forward

Name for enforced industrialization, 1958

5

People of the world, unite and defeat the US aggressors and all their running dogs!

Statement, 28 November 1964

6

*To his wife and her colleagues in conspiratorial group:*
Don't be a gang of four.

Attrib.

## MARKS, Leo
British intelligence expert and bookseller
(1920–   )

7

The life that I have is all that I have,
And the life that I have is yours.

The love that I have of the life that I have
Is yours and yours and yours.
   'Code Poem for the French Resistance'
*The poem was written to be used as the basis for codes used by Special
Operations Executive agents in the Second World War.*

## MARQUIS, Don
US writer
(1878–1937)

1

well archy the world is full of ups and downs but toujours gai is my
motto.
   *archy and mehitabel* (1927)

## MARSHALL, Arthur
British writer and entertainer
(1910–  )

2

It's all part of life's rich pageant.
   'The Games Mistress' (gramophone record), 1930s
*Suggested as the origin of this phrase.*

## MARSHALL, Thomas R.
US Democratic Vice-President
(1854–1925)

3

*To the chief clerk of the Senate during a tedious debate, 1917:*
What this country needs is a good five cent cigar.
   Attrib.

## MARX, Chico
US film comedian
(1886–1961)

1

*When his wife had caught him kissing a chorus girl:*
But I wasn't kissing her. I was whispering in her mouth.

 Quoted in G. Marx and R. Anobile, *The Marx Brothers Scrapbook*

## MARX, Groucho
US entertainer
(1895–1977)

2

*To the Friars Club, Beverly Hills:*
Please accept my resignation. I don't care to belong to any club that will have me as a member.

 Quoted in *The Groucho Letters*
*Various versions of this statement exist.*

3

I eat like a vulture. Unfortunately the resemblance doesn't end there.
 Attrib.

4

*When excluded from a beach club on racial grounds:*
Since my daughter is only half-Jewish, could she go in the water up to her knees?

 Quoted in the *Observer*, 21 August 1977

5

Many years ago I chased a woman for almost two years, only to discover her tastes were exactly like mine: we were both crazy about girls.

 Attrib.

6

I've been around so long, I knew Doris Day before she was a virgin.
 Attrib.

*See also LEVANT 278:2.*

1

We in this industry know that behind every successful screenwriter stands a woman. And behind her stands his wife.

    Attrib.

2

Show me a rose and I'll show you a girl called Sam.

    Song, 'Show me a Rose'

*Written by Ruby Kalmar.*

3

Hello, I must be going.

    Title of song.

*Written by Ruby Kalmar.*

4

I never forget a face, but I'll make an exception in your case.

    Attrib.

5

*On the films of Victor Mature:*

I never go to movies where the hero's bust is bigger than the heroine's.

    Attrib.

6

They say a man is as old as the woman he feels. In that case I'm eighty-five . . . I want it known here and now that this is what I want on my tombstone. Here lies Groucho Marx, and Lies and Lies and Lies. P.S. He never kissed an ugly girl.

    *The Secret Word is Groucho* (1976)

*See also* ANIMAL CRACKERS *p. 17,* THE COCOANUTS *p. 112,* A DAY AT THE RACES *p. 133, and* DUCK SOUP *p. 143.*

## MARY, HM Queen
British Royal, wife of George V
(1867–1953)

7

*To soldier who had exclaimed 'No more bloody wars for me':*

No more bloody wars, no more bloody medals.

    Attrib.

1

*To Stanley Baldwin on the Abdication:*
Well, Prime Minister, here's a pretty kettle of fish.
   Quoted in F. Donaldson, *Edward VIII*

## MASCHWITZ, Eric
### British songwriter
### (1901–69)

2

The sigh of midnight trains in empty stations . . .
The smile of Garbo and the scent of roses . . .
These foolish things
Remind me of you.
   Song, 'These Foolish Things' (1936)

3

A Nightingale Sang in Berkeley Square.
   Title of song, *New Faces* (1940)

## MASEFIELD, John
### British Poet Laureate
### (1878–1967)

4

I must down to the seas again.
   'Sea Fever' (1902)
*Although it appears to have been the poet's original intention to omit
the word 'go' from this line, it has been included in several editions of
his work.*

5

Dirty British coaster with a salt-caked smoke-stack
Butting through the Channel in the mad March days.
   'Cargoes' (1910)

## MASON, Donald
US Navy pilot
(1913–   )

**1**

Sighted sub, sank same.

Radio message, 28 January 1942

*On sinking a Japanese submarine in the South Pacific.*

## *MASTERMIND*

*UK TV general knowledge quiz (BBC) from 1970s onwards. With Magnus Magnusson as the chairman.*

**2**

*Magnusson (when time runs out halfway through question):*
I've started so I'll finish.

Stock phrase

**3**

*Contestant (not knowing answer):*
Pass.

Stock phrase

## MATHEW, Sir James
British lawyer
(1830–1908)

**4**

In England, justice is open to all, like the Ritz hotel.

Attrib.

## MAUGHAM, W. Somerset
British novelist and short story writer
(1874–1965)

**5**

*Of state-aided undergraduates:*
They are scum.

Quoted in E. Morgan, *Somerset Maugham*

1
*When a friend said he hated the food in England:*
What rubbish. All you have to do is eat breakfast three times a day.
  *Ib.*

2
At a dinner party one should eat wisely but not too well, and talk well
but not too wisely.
  *A Writer's Notebook* (1949)

3
I've always been interested in people, but I've never liked them.
  Quoted in the *Observer*, 28 August 1949

## MAXTON, Jimmy
Independent Labour Party MP
(1855–1946)

4
*On a man who had proposed disaffiliation of the ILP from the Labour
Party:*
If my friend cannot ride two horses – what's he doing in the bloody
circus?
  Quoted in G. McAllister, *James Maxton*

## MAYS, Willie
US baseball player
(1931–  )

5
Say hey!
  Characteristic expression

# MENCKEN, H.L.
## US journalist
## (1880–1956)

**1**

No one ever went broke underestimating the intelligence of the American people.

Attrib.

**2**

*Standard reply to readers' letters when he was editor of the* American Mercury:

Dear Reader, You may be right.

Attrib.

**3**

*Suggested epitaph:*

If after I depart this vale, you remember me and have thought to please my ghost, forgive some sinner and wink your eye at a homely girl.

*The Smart Set* (1921)

**4**

The only really happy people are married women and single men.

Attrib.

**5**

*On President Coolidge:*

Here, indeed, was his one really notable talent. He slept more than any other President, whether by day or by night . . . Nero fiddled, but Coolidge only snored . . . He had no ideas, and he was not a nuisance.

In the *American Mercury* (1933)

**6**

Opera in English is, in the main, just about as sensible as baseball in Italian.

Attrib.

1

I've made it a rule never to drink by daylight and never to refuse a drink after dark.

Quoted in the *New York Post,* 18 September 1945

2

Conscience is the inner voice that warns us somebody may be looking.

*A Mencken Chrestomathy* (1949)

3

When women kiss, it always reminds me of prize-fighters shaking hands.

Attrib.


## MENZIES, Sir Robert
### Australian Liberal Prime Minister
### (1894–1978)

4

*When accused by a member of Parliament of harbouring a superiority complex:*
Considering the company I keep in this place, that is hardly surprising.

Quoted *Time,* 29 May 1978

5

*In answer to heckler who cried, 'I wouldn't vote for you if you were the Archangel Gabriel':*
If I were the Archangel Gabriel, madam, I'm afraid you would not be in my constituency.

Quoted in R. Robinson, *The Wit of Sir Robert Menzies*


## MERCER, Johnny
### US lyricist
### (1909–76)

6

You're just too marvellous,
Too marvellous for words.

Song, 'Too Marvellous for Words', *Ready, Willing and Able* (1937)

1
You're much too much and just too very very
To ever be in Webster's dictionary.
    *Ib.*

2
That Old Black Magic (Has Me In Its Spell).
    Title of song, *Star Spangled Rhythm* (1942)

3
We're drinking my friend,
To the end of a brief episode,
Make it one for my baby
And one for the road.
    Song, 'One For My Baby', *The Sky's the Limit* (1943)

4
*On seeing a British musical (1975):*
I could eat alphabet soup and *shit* better lyrics.
    Attrib.


## MERMAN, Ethel
### US entertainer
### (1908–84)

5
*To Irving Berlin when he wanted to change a song lyric:*
Call me Miss Birdseye. This show is frozen.
    Quoted in *The Times*, 13 July 1985


## MICHAELIS, John H.
### US general
### (1912–85)

6
*To 27th Infantry (Wolfhound) Regiment during the Korean War:*
You're not here to die for your country. You're here to make those
———— die for theirs.
    Attrib.

## MIES VAN DER ROHE, Ludwig
### German-born architect
### (1886–1969)

1

Less is more.

Quoted in the *New York Herald Tribune*, 1959

## MILLER, Arthur
### US playwright
### (1915–   )

2

A good newspaper, I suppose, is a nation talking to itself.

Quoted in the *Observer*, 26 November 1961

## MILLER, Jonathan
### British entertainer
### (1936–   )

3

'Gentlemen, lift the seat' . . . perhaps it's a loyal toast?

'The Heat-Death of the Universe', *Beyond the Fringe* (1961)

4

I'm not really a Jew; just Jew-ish, not the whole hog, you know.

'Real Class' in *ib*.

## MILLER, Max
### British comedian
### (1895–1963)

5

I've got a million of 'em.

Stock phrase, after delivering joke

**1**

There'll never be another.
   Catchphrase

**2**

When I'm dead and gone, the game's finished.
   Catchphrase

### MILLIGAN, Spike
Irish entertainer
(1918–   )

**3**

I'm Walking Backwards to Christmas.
   Title of song (1956)

**4**

The Army works like this: if a man dies when you hang him, keep
hanging until he gets used to it.
   Attrib.

**5**

Q. Are you Jewish?
A. No, a tree fell on me.
   Quoted in *Private Eye*, 1973

*See also* THE GOON SHOW *pp. 196–8.*

### MILNE, A.A.
British writer
(1882–1956)

**6**

They're changing guard at Buckingham Palace –
Christopher Robin went down with Alice.
Alice is marrying one of the guard.
'A soldier's life is terribly hard,'
                Says Alice.
   'Buckingham Palace', *When We Were Very Young* (1924)

1
The King asked
The Queen, and
The Queen asked
The Dairymaid:
'Could we have some butter for
the Royal slice of bread?'
   'The King's Breakfast' in *ib*.

2
Little boy kneels at the foot of the bed,
Droops on the little hands, little gold head.
Hush! Hush! Whisper who dares!
Christopher Robin is saying his prayers.
   'Vespers' in *ib*.

3
When Rabbit said, 'Honey or condensed milk with your bread?'
[Pooh] was so excited he said, 'Both,' and then, so as not to seem
greedy, he added, 'But don't bother about the bread, please.'
   *Winnie-The-Pooh* (1926)

4
Time for a little something.
   *Ib*.

5
*Pooh:* 'I am a Bear of Very Little Brain, and long words Bother me.'
   *Ib*.

6
The more it snows
   (Tiddely pom),
The more it goes
   (Tiddely pom),
The more it goes
   (Tiddely pom),
On snowing.
   *The House at Pooh Corner* (1928)

**1**
Worraworraworraworraworra. (Tigger)
*Ib.*

### MILNER, Alfred 1st Viscount
British imperialist
(1854–1925)

**2**
*On the peers and the budget:*
If we believe a thing to be bad, and if we have a right to prevent it, it is
our duty to try to prevent it, and to damn the consequences.
Speech, Glasgow, 26 November 1909

### *MINDER*
*UK TV drama series (Thames TV), 1979–85. Created by Leon Griffiths. With George Cole as Arthur Daley.*

**3**
*Daley (referring to his wife):*
'Er indoors.
Stock phrase

**4**
*Daley:* A nice little earner.
Stock phrase

### MINNOW, Newton
US government official
(1926–   )

**5**
*On American TV watched from morn till night:*
I can assure you that you will observe a vast wasteland.
Speech, National Association of Broadcasters, 1961

### THE MISFITS
*US film 1961. Script by Arthur Miller. With Marilyn Monroe and Clark Gable.*

**1**
*Last words:*
*MM:* How do you find your way back in the dark?
*CG:* Just head for that big star straight on. The highway's under it. It'll take us right home.
  Soundtrack

### MITFORD, Nancy
British author
(1904–73)

**2**
Love in a Cold Climate.
  Title of novel (1949)

**3**
I love children – especially when they cry, for then someone takes them away.
  Attrib.

### MIZNER, Wilson
US playwright
(1876–1933)

**4**
[Always] be nice to people on your way up, because you'll meet 'em on your way down.
  Attrib.
*Also attrib. to Jimmy Durante and others.*

**1**

Working for Warner Bros is like fucking a porcupine; it's a hundred pricks against one.

Quoted in D. Niven, *Bring on the Empty Horses*

**2**

*On Hollywood:*

A trip through a sewer in a glass-bottomed boat.

Attrib.

**3**

When you steal from one author, it's plagiarism; if you steal from many, it's research.

Attrib.

## MOLA, Emilio
Spanish Nationalist general
(1887–1937)

**4**

*When asked which of his four army columns would capture Madrid from the Republicans:*

The fifth column ('La quinta columna').

Remark to reporter, October 1936

*Referring to civilian help.*

## MONKHOUSE, Bob
British comedian
(1928–   )

**5**

Bernie, the bolt!

Catchphrase, TV show *The Golden Shot*, 1967–75

### 'MONOLULU, Ras Prince'
Racing tipster in UK
(fl. 1930s/50s)

1
I gotta horse!
   Stock phrase

### *MONOPOLY*
*US board game devised by Charles Darrow in 1929*

2
GO TO JAIL
MOVE DIRECTLY TO JAIL
DO NOT PASS 'GO'
DO NOT COLLECT £200.
   'Chance' card (UK version)

### MONROE, Marilyn
US film actress
(1926–62)

3
*When asked if she had really posed for a calendar with nothing on:*
I had the radio on.
   Attrib.

4
*On having matzo balls for supper at Arthur Miller's parents:*
Isn't there another part of the matzo you can eat?
   Attrib.

## MONTEFIORE, Hugh
### British Anglican clergyman
### (later Bishop)
### (1920–   )

1

Why did He not marry? Could the answer be that Jesus was not by nature the marrying sort?

At conference, Oxford, 26 July 1967


## MONTGOMERY, Bernard
### (later Viscount Montgomery of Alamein)
### British soldier
### (1887–1976)

2

*Address to officers, when taking command of the Eighth Army, 13 August 1942:*

Here we will stand and fight; there will be no further withdrawal . . . We are going to finish with this chap Rommel once and for all. It will be quite easy. There is no doubt about it. He is definitely a nuisance. Therefore we will hit him a crack and finish with him.

Soundtrack of post-war recording of speech


## MONTY PYTHON'S FLYING CIRCUS
*British TV comedy series (BBC), from 1969–74. Written and performed by Graham Chapman, John Cleese, Terry Gilliam, Eric Idle, Michael Jones and Michael Palin.*

3

I'm a lumberjack
And I'm OK
I sleep all night
And I work all day.

Song

1

*Cleese:* It's not pining, it's passed on. This parrot is no more. It's ceased to be. It's expired. It's gone to meet its maker. This is a late parrot. It's a stiff. Bereft of life it rests in peace. It would be pushing up the daisies if you hadn't nailed it to the perch. It's rung down the curtain and joined the choir invisible. It's an ex-parrot.

'Parrot sketch', 14 December 1969

2

*Idle:* Nudge, nudge, wink, wink. Say no more. Know what I mean?
   Catchphrase of prurient character

3

*Cleese:* And now for something completely different.
   Catchphrase

## MORECAMBE, Eric and WISE, Ernie
British entertainers
(1926–84) and (1925–   )

4

*Eric:* [Ernie's] Short, fat, hairy legs.
   Catchphrase

5

*Eric:* A touch of hello folks and what about the workers?
   Catchphrase

6

*Eric:* What do you think of the show so far?
*Audience:* Rubbish!
   Catchphrase

7

*Eric on Ernie's supposed hair-piece:*
You can't see the join.
   Catchphrase

**1**

*Ernie:* This play what I have wrote.
  Catchphrase

## MORGANFIELD, McKinley
('Muddy Waters')
US lyricist and blues singer
(1915–83)

**2**

Got My Mojo Workin'.
  Title of song

## MORRIS, Desmond
British zoologist and anthropologist
(1928–   )

**3**

The Naked Ape.
  Title of book (1967)

**4**

The city is not a concrete jungle, it is a human zoo.
  *The Human Zoo* (1969)

## MORRIS, James
(later Jan Morris)
British writer
(1926–   )

**5**

There's romance for you! There's the lust and dark wine of Venice!
No wonder George Eliot's husband fell into the Grand Canal.
  *Venice* (1960)
  *Closing words.*

**1**

DEDICATED GRATEFULLY TO THE WARDEN AND FEL-
LOWS OF ST ANTONY'S COLLEGE, OXFORD. EXCEPT
ONE.

*The Oxford Book of Oxford* (1978)

**MORRISON, Herbert**
(later Lord Morrison of Lambeth)
British Labour politician
(1888–1965)

**2**

*Calling for a voluntary labour force as Minister of Supply in wartime:*
Go to it.

Radio broadcast, 22 May 1940

**MORRISON, Herbert**
US broadcaster

**3**

*On the* Hindenburg *airship disaster:*
It is in smoke and flames now! Oh, the humanity!

Radio commentary, Lakehurst, New Jersey, 1937

**MORTON, Rogers**
US government official
(1914–79)

**4**

*Refusing any last-ditch attempts to rescue President Ford's re-
election campaign, 1976:*
I'm not going to re-arrange the furniture on the deck of the *Titanic.*

Attrib.

## MOUNTBATTEN OF BURMA, 1st Earl
British Viceroy and admiral
(1900–79)

1
Edwina and I spent all our married lives getting into other people's beds.

Remark quoted in P. Ziegler, *Mountbatten*

2
In my experience, I have always found that you cannot have an efficient ship unless you have a happy ship, and you cannot have a happy ship unless you have an efficient ship. That is the way I intend to start this commission, and that is the way I intend to go on – with a happy and an efficient ship.

Initial address to crew of *HMS Kelly*, 1939
*Adopted* verbatim *by Noel Coward in the script of the film* In Which We Serve.

3
The nuclear arms race has no military purpose. Wars cannot be fought with nuclear weapons . . . The world now stands on the brink of the final abyss. Let us all resolve to take all possible practicable steps to ensure that we do not, through our own folly, go over the edge.

Speech, Strasbourg, 1979

4
I can't think of a more wonderful thanksgiving for the life I have had than that everyone should be jolly at my funeral.

TV interview, shown after his death in August 1979

## *MRS DALE'S DIARY*
*UK radio soap opera (BBC), from 1948–69 (latterly* THE DALES*).
With Ellis Powell and Jessie Matthews as Mrs Dale.*

5
*Mrs Dale (on her husband):* I'm worried about Jim.
Stock phrase

## MUGGERIDGE, Kitty
British writer and wife of Malcolm M.

1

*On David Frost:*
He rose without a trace.
   Attrib. in 1960s

## MUGGERIDGE, Malcolm
British writer and broadcaster
(1903–   )

2

*On Evelyn Waugh:*
He looked, I decided, like a letter delivered to the wrong address.
   'My Fair Gentleman', *Tread Softly For You Tread on My Jokes*
   (1966)

3

*On Anthony Eden:*
He was not only a bore; he bored for England.
   'Boring for England' in *ib.*

4

*On Queen Elizabeth II:*
Frumpish and banal.
   Magazine article, October 1957

5

*On* Punch *(which he once edited):*
Very much like the Church of England. It is doctrinally inexplicable
but it goes on.
   Attrib.

6

I have had my [TV] aerials removed – it's the moral equivalent of a
prostate operation.
   Quoted in *Radio Times*, April 1981

**1**

Twilight of empire . . . a phrase which occurred to me long ago.
  *Diaries* (entry for 21 December 1947)

**MURROW, Edward R.**
US broadcaster
(1908–65)

**2**

This . . . is . . . London.
  Standard beginning to his wartime reports, 1940s

**3**

Goodnight . . . and good luck.
  Stock phrase

**4**

He [Churchill] mobilized the English language and sent it into battle
to steady his fellow countrymen and hearten those Europeans upon
whom the long dark night of tyranny had descended.
  Broadcast, 30 November 1954
*See KENNEDY 254:2.*

**MUSSOLINI, Benito**
Italian fascist leader
(1883–1945)

**5**

*On Hitler:*
That garrulous monk.
  Quoted in W. Churchill, *The Second World War* (1948)

## MUSSOLINI, Vittorio
Italian air force pilot and son of Benito

1
*On a bombing raid in Abyssinia:*
I dropped an aerial torpedo right in the centre, and the group opened up like a flowering rose. It was most entertaining.
*Voli sulle Ambe* (1937)

# N

### NABOKOV, Vladimir
Russian-born novelist
(1899–1977)

1
Lolita, light of my life, fire of my loins. My sin, my soul.
  *Lolita* (1955)
*Opening words.*


### THE NAKED CITY
*US film 1948. Script by Malvin Wald and Albert Matz.*

2
*Last lines:*
*Narrator:* There are eight million stories in the naked city. This has
been one of them.
  Soundtrack
*Also used in TV series of the same name.*


### NASH, Ogden
US poet
(1902–71)

3
Candy
Is dandy
But liquor
Is quicker.
  'Reflection on Ice-Breaking', *Hard Lines* (1931)

1
I think that I shall never see
A billboard lovely as a tree.
Perhaps unless the billboards fall,
I'll never see a tree at all.
  'Song of the Open Road', *Happy Days* (1933)


## THE NAVY LARK
*UK radio comedy series (BBC), 1960s/70s. Script by Lawrie Wyman.*
*With Leslie Phillips and Jon Pertwee.*

2
*LP:* Left hand down a bit.
*JP:* Left hand down a bit, it is, sir.
  Stock phrase when docking ship or similar


## NETWORK
*US film 1976. Script by Paddy Chayevsky. With Peter Finch.*

3
*PF:* I'm as mad as hell, and I'm not going to take this anymore!
  Soundtrack
*Also used by US politician Howard Jarvis as a slogan for his*
*tax-pegging campaign in California, 1978.*


## NEVINS, Allan
US writer and teacher
(1890–1971)

4
The former allies had blundered in the past by offering Germany too
little and offering even that too late, until finally Nazi Germany had
become a menace to all mankind.
  Article in *Current History*, May 1935

## JANICE NICHOLLS
British clerk/telephonist
(c.1947– )

1

*When judging new record releases:*
I'll give it foive.
Stock phrase, TV show, *Thank Your Lucky Stars, c.*1963

## NICHOLSON, Vivian
British football pools winner
(1936– )

2

*On winning £152,000 in 1961:*
I'm going to spend, spend, spend, that's what I'm going to do.
Recounted in V. Nicholson and S. Smith, *I'm Going to Spend, Spend, Spend.*

## NICOLSON, Sir Harold
British writer and politician
(1886–1968)

3

The gift of broadcasting is, without question, the lowest human capacity to which any man could attain.
Quoted in the *Observer*, 5 January 1947

## NIGHTINGALE, Florence
British nurse
(1820–1910)

4

*When given the Order of Merit on her deathbed:*
Too kind, too kind.
Attrib.

## NIXON, Richard M.
US Republican President
(1913–    )

1

*On 'Checkers', a dog given to his daughters:*
Regardless of what they say about it, we are going to keep it.
   TV address, 23 September 1952
*He was defending himself, when running as Vice-President candidate, against charges that he had a secret fund.*

2

I don't believe I ought to quit because I am not a quitter.
   *Ib.*

3

*To the press, on losing a California Governorship election:*
Just think about how much you're going to be missing. You won't have Nixon to kick around any more, because, gentlemen, this is my last press conference.
   7 November 1962

4

And this certainly has to be the most historic phone call ever made.
   Telephone call to astronauts on moon, 20 July 1969

5

*On USS* Hornet *welcoming astronauts home:*
This is the greatest week in the history of the world since the Creation.
   24 July 1969

6

*On a plan for a Vietnam peace:*
And so, tonight – to you, the great silent majority of my fellow Americans – I ask for your support.
   Broadcast address, 3 November 1969

7

I don't give a shit about the lira.
   In conversation, 23 June 1972, revealed in tape transcript

1

*On the Watergate cover-up:*
I don't give a shit what happens. I want you all to stonewall it, let them plead the Fifth Amendment, cover-up or anything else, if it'll save it, save the plan.

In conversation, 22 March 1973, revealed in tape transcript

2

There will be no whitewash in the White House.

Speech, 17 April 1973

3

*On a charge of tax avoidance:*
People have got to know whether or not their President is a crook. Well, I am not a crook. I have earned everything I have got.

Press conference, 11 November 1973

4

*To General Alexander Haig:*
You fellows, in your business, you have a way of handling problems like this. Somebody leaves a pistol in the drawer. I don't have a pistol.

(7 August 1974) Quoted in R. Woodward and C. Bernstein, *The Final Days*

5

This country needs good farmers, good businessmen, good plumbers . . .

Farewell address at White House, 9 August 1974

6

You can't put the toothpaste back in the tube.

Attrib.

*His aide, John D. Erhlichman, was also quoted, in 1975, as having said to John Dean, 'Once the toothpaste is out of the tube, it is awfully hard to get it back again.'*

7

When the President does it, that means it is not illegal.

TV interview with D. Frost, 19 May 1977

1

I brought myself down. I gave them a sword and they stuck it in and they twisted it with relish. And I guess if I'd been in their position I'd have done the same thing.
   *Ib.*


### NOVELLO, Ivor
British composer and actor
(1893–1951)


2

Keep the Home Fires Burning.
   Title of song (written with Lena Guilbert Ford) (1915)


3

And Her Mother Came Too.
   Title of song, *A to Z* (1922)

*See also* TARZAN THE APE MAN *p. 419.*


### *NOW VOYAGER*
*US film 1942. Based on the novel by Olive Higgins Prouty. With Bette Davis as Charlotte Vale.*

4

*Charlotte:* Let's not ask for the moon – we have stars.
   Soundtrack
*Closing words.*

# O

## OATES, Capt. Lawrence 'Titus'
### British explorer
### (1880–1912)

**1**

*Leaving companions in tent on return from South Pole, 16 March 1912:*
I am just going outside, and I may be some time.
Quoted in R.F. Scott, *Scott's Last Expedition*

*See also EPITAPHS 158:4.*

## O'CASEY, Sean
### Irish playwright
### (1884–1964)

**2**

The whole worl' is in a state o' chassis.
*Juno and the Paycock* (1924)

**3**

*On P.G. Wodehouse:*
English literature's performing flea.
Quoted in P.G. Wodehouse, *Performing Flea*

## O'CONNOR, Edwin
### US writer
### (1918–68)

**4**

The Last Hurrah.
Title of novel (1956)

## O'MALLEY, Frank Ward
US writer
(1875–1932)

1

Life is just one damned thing after another.
    Attrib.
*See also HUBBARD 230:4.*

## ONE MILLION YEARS BC
*UK film 1966*

2

The characters and incidents portrayed and the names used herein are
fictitious and any similarity to the names, character or history of any
person is entirely accidental and unintentional.
    Caption on film
*Standard disclaimer – at the start of a film in which the dialogue
consists entirely of cavemen's grunts.*

## OPPENHEIMER, J. Robert
US physicist
(1904–67)

3

*Quoting Vishnu from the* Gita, *at explosion of first atomic bomb, New
Mexico, 16 July 1945:*
I am become death, the destroyer of worlds.
    Attrib.

## ORCZY, Baroness
Hungarian-born novelist
(1865–1947)

4

We seek him here, we seek him there,
Those Frenchies seek him everywhere.
Is he in heaven? – Is he in hell?
That demmed, elusive Pimpernel?
    *The Scarlet Pimpernel* (1905)

## 'ORWELL, George'
British novelist and journalist
(1903–50)

**1**

I'm fat, but I'm thin inside. Has it ever struck you that there's a thin man inside every fat man, just as they say there's a statue inside every block of stone?

*Coming Up for Air* (1939)

*See also CONNOLLY 114:4 and WHITEHORN 452:1.*

**2**

Four legs good, two legs bad.

*Animal Farm* (1945)

**3**

All animals are equal, but some are more equal than others.

*Ib.*

**4**

Comrade Napoleon is always right.

*Ib.*

**5**

It was a bright cold day in April, and the clocks were striking thirteen.

*Nineteen Eighty-Four* (1949)

**6**

Big Brother is watching you.

*Ib.*

**7**

If you want a picture of the future, imagine a boot stamping on a human face – for ever.

*Ib.*

**8**

There can hardly be a town in the South of England where you could throw a brick without hitting the niece of a bishop.

Attrib.

**1**

[Attlee] reminds me of nothing so much as a recently dead fish before it has had time to stiffen.

   Diary, entry for 19 May 1942

**2**

*Reviewing a book by Edmund Blunden:*
Mr Blunden is no more able to resist a quotation than some people are to refuse a drink.

   *Manchester Evening News,* 20 April 1944

### OSBORNE, John
British playwright
(1929–   )

**3**

There aren't any good brave causes left.

   *Look Back in Anger* (1956)

**4**

Damn you, England. You're rotting now, and quite soon you'll disappear.

   Letter in *Tribune,* August 1961

**5**

Don't clap too hard – it's a very old building.

   *The Entertainer* (1957)

**6**

She's not going to walk in here . . . and turn it into a Golden Sanitary Towel Award Presentation.

   *Hotel in Amsterdam* (1968)

### OWEN, Dr David
British Labour, then SDP, politician
(1938–   )

**7**

We are fed up with fudging and nudging, with mush and slush.

   Speech, Labour Party Conference, Blackpool, 2 October 1980

## OWEN, Wilfred
British poet
(1893–1918)

**1**

Above all, this book is not concerned with Poetry. The subject of it is War, and the pity of War. The Poetry is the pity.

'Preface', *Poems* (1920)

## OXFORD UNION SOCIETY

**2**

That this House will in no circumstances fight for its King and Country.

Motion debated 9 February 1933
*It was carried by 275 votes to 153.*

# P

### PACKARD, Vance
US writer
(1914–   )

1
The Hidden Persuaders.
   Title of book (1957)


### PAINE, Albert Bigelow
US writer
(1861–1937)

2
The Great White Way.
   Title of novel (1901)
*Later used as a name for Broadway.*


### PARKER, Dorothy
US writer
(1893–1967)

3
*When told that Calvin Coolidge had died:*
How can they tell?
   Attrib. 1933

4
*On A.A. Milne's* The House at Pooh Corner *in her column 'Constant Reader':*
Tonstant Weader fwowed up.
   Attrib.

1

*When told that she was 'very outspoken':*
Outspoken by whom?
  Attrib.

2

Guns aren't lawful;
Nooses give;
Gas smells awful;
You might as well live.
  'Resume', *Enough Rope* (1927)

3

Men seldom makes passes
At girls who wear glasses.
  'News Item' in *ib.*

4

Scratch an actor and you'll find an actress.
  Attrib.

5

*In reply to comment, 'Anyway, she's always very nice to her inferiors':*
Where does she find them?
  Quoted in *Lyttelton Hart-Davis Letters*

6

*Reviewing Katherine Hepburn:*
She ran the whole gamut of emotions from A to B.
  Attrib.

7

One more drink and I'd be under the host.
  Quoted in J. Keats, *You Might As Well Live*

8

Brevity is the soul of lingerie – as the Petticoat said to the Chemise.
  *Ib.*

1
*Suggested epitaphs:*
This is on me. Excuse my dust. If you can read this you are standing too close.
    *Ib.*

2
You know, that woman speaks eighteen languages? And she can't say 'no' in any of them.
    *Ib.*

3
*When a man asked to be excused to go to the men's room:*
He really needs to telephone, but he's too embarrassed to say so.
    *Ib.*

4
Tell him I've been too fucking busy – or vice versa.
    *Ib.*

5
*When Clare Booth Luce, going through a swing-door with her, said, 'Age before beauty':*
Pearls before swine.
    *Ib.*

6
*When someone said, 'They're ducking for apples' at a Hallowe'en party:*
There, but for a typographical error, is the story of my life.
    *Ib.*

7
*On her requirements for an apartment:*
[Enough space] to lay a hat – and a few friends.
    *Ib.*

8
*On naming her canary 'Onan':*
Because he spills his seed on the ground.
    *Ib.*

**1**

*Telegram to Mrs Robert Sherwood, when delivered of a baby:*
DEAR MARY, WE ALL KNEW YOU HAD IT IN YOU.
   *Ib.*

**2**

*When pregnant herself:*
It serves me right for putting all my eggs in one bastard.
   *Ib.*

**3**

*Challenged to compose a sentence including the word 'horticulture':*
You can lead a horticulture but you can't make her think.
   *Ib.*

**4**

If all the young girls at the Yale Prom were laid end to end, I wouldn't
be at all surprised.
   Attrib.

**5**

Oh, life is a glorious cycle of song,
A medley of extemporanea;
And love is a thing that can never go wrong
And I am Marie of Roumania.
   'Comment', *Enough Rope*


### PARKER, Johnny
British naval lieutenant

**6**

*On helping to free British seamen held captive on the German ship*
Altmark:
The Navy's here!
   Quoted in *The Times*, 19 February 1940
*Precisely who said the words is in doubt, but Parker has emerged as*
*the most likely person – and he claimed that he did.*

## PARKINSON, C. Northcote
British professor
(1909– )

1

It is a commonplace observation that work expands so as to fill the time available for its completion.
*Economist*, 19 November 1955
*Later known as 'Parkinson's Law'.*

## PATERSON, Banjo
Australian writer
(1864–1941)

2

Oh! there once was a swagman camped in a Billabong,
  Under the shade of a Coolabah tree;
And he sang as he looked at his old billy boiling,
  'Who'll come a-waltzing Matilda with me?'
  Song, 'Waltzing Matilda'
*Written in 1894, the song was first published in 1903.*

## PAUL, Leslie
British social philosopher
(1905–85)

3

Angry Young Man.
  Title of autobiographical book (1951)
*Use of the phrase to describe a group of writers in the fifties can be traced to publicity material for John Osborne's play* Look Back in Anger, *first produced at the Royal Court Theatre, London, May 1956.*

## PEALE, Norman Vincent
US clergyman and writer
(1899–   )

**1**

The Power of Positive Thinking.
   Title of book (1952)

## PEARSON, Hesketh
British biographer
(1887–1964)

**2**

A widely-read man never quotes accurately . . . Misquotation is the pride and privilege of the learned.
   *Common Misquotations* (1937)

**3**

Misquotations are the only quotations that are never misquoted.
   *Ib.*

## *THE PEOPLE*
*London Sunday newspaper*

**4**

Our reporter made an excuse and left.
   Quoted in *The Times*, 17 October 1981
*Standard exit line after a reporter had set up a compromising situation – e.g. provoking prostitutes or pimps to reveal their game. From the 1920s onwards?*

## PERELMAN, S.J.
US writer
(1904–79)

**5**

I've got Bright's disease and he's got mine.
   Attrib.

## PERKINS, Carl
US singer/songwriter
(1932–   )

1
It's a-one for the money
Two for the show
Three to get ready
Now go, cat, go,
But don't you step on my blue suede shoes.
  Song, 'Blue Suede Shoes' (1956)

## PERKINS, Frances
US politician
(1882–1965)

2
\#\#   Call me madam.
  Discussed in G. Martin, *Madam Secretary – Frances Perkins* (1976)
*Said to have been her reply when asked – as the first woman to hold US Cabinet rank – how she wished to be addressed. In fact, a man's words to the effect that 'Madam Secretary' would be in order were put into her mouth.*

## PETAIN, Henri Philippe
French soldier and politician
(1856–1951)

3
*Defending Verdun:*
\#\#   They shall not pass.
  Attrib. 26 February 1916
*Although associated with Pétain, 'The Hero of Verdun', this slogan appears to have been said first by General Robert Nivelle (1856–1924) in the form 'Vous ne les laisserez pas passer'.*
*See also IBARRURI 233:1.*

## PETER, Dr Laurence J.
Canadian-born writer
(1919– )

1

In a hierarchy every employee tends to rise to his level of incompetence.
*The Peter Principle – Why Things Always Go Wrong* (with R. Hull) (1969)

2

The noblest of all dogs is the hot-dog; it feeds the hand that bites it.
*Quotations for Our Time* (1977)


## PHILIP, HRH the Prince
Greek-born British Royal
(1921– )

3

Just at this moment we are suffering a national defeat comparable to any lost military campaign, and what is more it is self-inflicted . . . I think it is about time we pulled our finger out.
Speech to businessmen, 17 October 1961

4

Dentopedology is the science of opening your mouth and putting your foot in it. I've been practising it for years.
Attrib.


## PICKLES, Wilfred
British broadcaster
(1904–78)

5

Welcome to a spot of homely fun, presenting the people to the people . . . with Mable at the table and Harry Hudson at the piano.
Introductory material, *Have a Go*, BBC radio, 1946–67

**1**

Are yer courtin'?
> Stock question to young participants in *ib.*

**2**

'Ave you ever 'ad any embarrassing moments?
> Stock question in *ib.*

**3**

Give 'im/'er the money, Barney.
> Stock remark to winners in *ib.*
> *Barney Colehan was the producer of the show.*

**4**

What's on the table, Mable?
> Stock remark to his wife, presiding over the prizes in *ib.*


## PINTER, Harold
British playwright
(1930–   )

**5**

*(Pause.)*
> Frequent stage direction, *passim*

**6**

If only I could get down to Sidcup! I've been waiting for the weather to break. He's got my papers, this man I left them with, it's got it all down there, I could prove everything.
> *The Caretaker* (1960)

**7**

*Asked what his plays were about:*
The weasel under the cocktail cabinet.
> Quoted in J. Russell Taylor, *Anger and After*

**1**

I tend to believe that cricket is the greatest thing that God ever created on earth . . . certainly greater than sex, although sex isn't too bad either.

Interview in the *Observer*, 5 October 1980

### PIRSIG, Robert M.
US writer
(1929–   )

**2**

Zen and the Art of Motorcycle Maintenance.

Title of book (1974)

### PITKIN, William B.
US professor in journalism
(1878–1953)

**3**

Life Begins at Forty.

Title of book (1932)

### PLATT, Ken
British comedian
(1922–   )

**4**

*Of a person:*
Daft as a brush.

Catchphrase, from 1940s onwards

*Adapted from the northern saying, 'Soft as a brush'.*

**5**

I won't take me coat off – I'm not stopping.

Catchphrase, from 1951 onwards

# PLAY TITLES

**1**

Another Country (Julian Mitchell)
*From the second verse of 'I vow to thee my country' by Sir C. A. Spring-Rice (q.v.) – 'There is another country . . .' (i.e. heaven).*

**2**

Cat on a Hot Tin Roof (Tennessee Williams)
*From the US expression, to be 'as nervous as a cat on a hot tin roof'.*

**3**

Conduct Unbecoming (Barry England)
*From British military regulations dating from the nineteenth century: 'conduct unbecoming the character of an officer and a gentleman' (whence also the final phrase).*

**4**

Fings Ain't Wot They Used T'be (Lionel Bart)
*After song, 'Things Ain't What They Used To Be', by Mercer Ellington and Ted Persons (1939).*

**5**

Journey's End (R.C. Sherriff)
*Not from Shakespeare or Dryden, but from a book Sherriff declined to name in his autobiography.*

**6**

The Long and the Short and Tall (Willis Hall)
*From the song 'Bless 'em All' (by Jimmy Hughes and Frank Lake, 1940) – or the parody, 'Sod 'em All.'*

**7**

Oh, Calcutta! (revue devised by Kenneth Tynan)
*From the French expression, 'Oh, quel cul t'as' ('what a lovely arse you've got'), possibly late 19th century.*

**8**

A Patriot for Me (John Osborne)

*When a servant of the Habsburg Empire was being recommended as a
sterling patriot to Franz II, he asked, 'But is he a patriot for me?'*

1
Stop the World, I Want to Get Off (Anthony Newley and Leslie
Bricusse)
*From a graffito.*

2
Who's Afraid of Virginia Woolf? (Edward Albee)
*From a graffito.*

## PLOMER, William
### British writer and poet
### (1903–73)

3
Patriotism is the last refuge of the sculptor.
Attrib.

## POPEYE
*US cartoon strip and film cartoon series, 1933–50*

4
I yam what I yam and that's all that I yam.
Stock phrase
*Original character created by Elzie Crisler.*

## PORTER, Cole
### US composer and lyricist
### (1891–1964)

5
And when they ask us, how dangerous it was,
We never will tell them, we never will tell them:

How we fought in some café
With wild women night and day,
'Twas the wonderfulest war you ever knew.'
  'War Song' included in the *Complete Lyrics of Cole Porter*
*Usually ascribed to Anon., this parody of the Jerome Kern/Herbert*
*Reynolds song 'They Didn't Believe Me' is now believed to have*
*originated with Porter during the First World War.*


1
Birds do it, bees do it
Even educated fleas do it
Let's do it, let's fall in love.
  Song, 'Let's Do It, Let's Fall in Love', *Paris* (1928)


2
Goldfish in the privacy of bowls do it.
  *Ib.*


3
Night and day you are the one.
  Song, 'Night and Day', *Gay Divorce* (1932)


4
Miss Otis regrets she's unable to lunch today.
  Song, 'Miss Otis Regrets', *Hi Diddle Diddle* (1934)


5
Anything Goes.
  Title of song and musical (1934)


6
I get no kick from champagne.
Mere alcohol doesn't thrill me at all,
So tell me why should it be true
That I get a kick out of you?
  Song, 'I Get a Kick Out of You' in *ib.*

1

You're the Top!
  Title of song in *ib.*


2

When they begin the beguine.
  'Begin the Beguine', *Jubilee* (1935)


3

A trip to the moon on gossamer wings.
  'Just One of Those Things' in *ib.*


4

So goodbye, dear, and amen.
  *Ib.*


5

It was great fun,
But it was just one of those things.
  *Ib.*


6

I've Got You Under My Skin.
  Title of song, *Born to Dance* (1936)


7

While the crowds in all the night clubs punish the parquet.
  Song, 'Down in the Depths', *Red, Hot and Blue* (1936)


8

It's delightful, it's delicious, it's de-lovely.
  Song, 'It's De-Lovely', in *ib.*


9

My Heart Belongs to Daddy.
  Title of song, *Leave It to Me* (1938)

1

He may have hair upon his chest
But, sister, so has Lassie.
'I Hate Men', *Kiss Me Kate* (1948)

2

Brush Up Your Shakespeare.
Title of song in *ib*.

3

Always True to You in My Fashion.
Title of song in *ib*.
*Derived from 'I have been faithful to thee, Cynara! in my fashion' –*
*Ernest Dowson*, Non Sum Qualis Eram *(1896).*

4

Paris Loves Lovers.
Title of song, *Silk Stockings* (1955)

5

Who Wants to Be a Millionaire?
Title of song, *High Society* (1956)

### POTTER, Beatrix
British author and artist
(1866–1943)

6

You may go into the field or down the lane, but don't go into Mr
McGregor's garden: your Father had an accident there; he was put in
a pie by Mrs McGregor.
*The Tale of Peter Rabbit* (1902)

### POTTER, Gillie
British entertainer
(1887–1975)

7

Good evening, England. This is Gillie Potter speaking to you in
English.
Greeting in radio broadcasts, 1940s/50s

## POTTER, Stephen
British writer
(1900–69)

**1**

*Defining 'One-Upmanship':*
How to be one up – how to make the other man feel that something has
gone wrong, however slightly.
*Lifemanship* (1950)

**2**

*·A blocking phrase for conversation:*
'Yes, but not in the South', with slight adjustments will do for any
argument about any place, if not about any person.
*Ib.*

**3**

*How to promote a Cockburn '97, clearly past its best:*
Talk of the 'imperial decay' of your invalid port. 'Its gracious
withdrawal from perfection, keeping a hint of former majesty, withal,
as it hovers between oblivion and the divine *Untergang* of infinite
recession.'
*One-Upmanship* (1952)

## POWELL, Enoch
British Conservative, then Ulster Unionist politician
(1912–    )

**4**

*On the prospect for race relations in Britain:*
As I look ahead, I am filled with foreboding. Like the Roman, I seem
to see 'the River Tiber foaming with much blood'.
Speech, Birmingham, 20 April 1968
*Alluding to Virgil, Aeneid, Bk. VI: 'Thybrim multo spumantem
sanguine cerno.'*

1

All political lives, unless they are cut off in mid-stream at a happy juncture, end in failure, because that is the nature of politics and of human affairs.

*Joseph Chamberlain* (1977)


**POWELL, Sandy**
British entertainer
(1900–82)

2

Can you hear me, mother?
Catchphrase, from mid-1930s


**PRIESTLEY, J.B.**
British novelist and playwright
(1894–1984)

3

*On the 'little holiday steamers' used in the rescue from Dunkirk:*
[They] made an excursion to hell and came back glorious.
'Postscript to the News', BBC Radio, 5 June 1940

4

God can stand being told by Professor Ayer and Marghanita Laski that he doesn't exist.
Quoted in the *Listener*, 1 July 1965

5

I have always been a grumbler. I am designed for the part – sagging face, weighty underlip, rumbling, resonant voice. Money couldn't buy a better grumbling outfit.
Quoted in the *Guardian*, 15 August 1984

## THE PRISONER

*British TV series (1967). Written by George Markstein et al. With Patrick Magoohan as Political Prisoner Number Six.*

1

*Number Six:* I'm not a number, I'm a free man.
 Stock phrase

## PRIVATE EYE

*British satirical magazine (founded 1962)*

2

Tired and emotional.
*Euphemism for 'drunk' derived from spoof Foreign Office memo, dating from the time when George Brown was Foreign Secretary, 1966–8.*

3

Shock, horror, probe, sensation.
*Stock sensational newspaper headline.*

4

(Cont. page 94)
*Standard way of finishing an article.*

5

Phew! What a scorcher.
*Stock popular newspaper weather headline.*

6

This one will run and run.
*Stock quote from theatre critic – originally from Fergus Cashin in the Sun.*

7

Talking about Uganda.
*This euphemism first appeared in the edition of 9 March 1973 to denote sexual intercourse at a party between a woman and a Ugandan*

diplomat. *It is said to have been coined by James Fenton, the poet and critic. Later, 'Ugandan practices', 'Ugandan discussions' or 'discussing Ugandan affairs' were also employed.*

1
Pass the sick-bag, Alice.
*In parodies of newspaper style of Sir John Junor from c.1979. Junor himself confirmed (1985) that he had used the phrase once.*

2
I think we should be told.
   *Ib.*
*Junor denied (1985) that he had ever used the phrase.*

3
Shome mishtake (here) shurely?
*Alluding to speech style of William Deedes, newspaper editor.*

4
I wonder if, by any chance, they are related?
*Stock remark about lookalikes.*

5
Takes out onion.
*Stock phrase to denote phoney emotion, from c.1984.*


## THE PRIVATE LIFE OF HENRY VIII

*UK film 1934. Script by Lajos Biro and Frederick Lonsdale. With Charles Laughton as Henry VIII.*

6
*Before getting into bed with one of his brides:*
The things I've done for England . . .
   Soundtrack

## PROFUMO, John
British Conservative politician
(1915–  )

**1**
There was no impropriety whatsoever in my acquaintanceship with
Miss [Christine] Keeler.
Speech, House of Commons, 22 March 1963
*It later became clear that there had been.*

**2**
I shall not hesitate to issue writs for libel and slander if scandalous
allegations are made or repeated outside the House.
*Ib.*

## PROUST, Marcel
French novelist
(1871–1922)

**3**
I raised to my lips a spoonful of the tea in which I had soaked a morsel
of the cake . . . suddenly the memory returns. The taste was of the
little crumb of madeleine which on Sunday mornings at Combray . . .
my aunt Leonie used to give me, dipping it first in her own cup of real
or of lime-flower tea.
'Du Cote du chez Swann', *A La Recherche du Temps Perdu* (1913)
*In the C.K. Scott Moncrieff translation.*

## PROVERBS
(of probable twentieth-century origin)

**4**
All publicity is good publicity.
*Untraced.*

**1**

Better the cold blast of winter than the hot breath of a pursuing
elephant.
*Suggested Chinese origin.*

**2**

Do not remove a fly from your friend's forehead with a hatchet.
*Suggested Chinese origin.*

**3**

Every man likes the smell of his own farts.
    Quoted in *Faber Book of Aphorisms* (ed. Auden and Kronen-
    berger)
*Described as of Icelandic origin. See also AUDEN 33:2.*

**4**

Garbage in, garbage out.
*Computerese, current by 1964, meaning 'If it's not right going in, it
won't come out right'.*

**5**

If you're not part of the solution, you're part of the problem.
*Current from 1970s.*

**6**

It takes two to tango.
*From the song with this title by Hoffman and Manning (1952).*

**7**

One does not insult the river god while crossing the river.
*Suggested Chinese origin.*

**8**

One picture is worth ten thousand words.
*Created by Frederick R. Barnard for* Printer's Ink *8 December 1921
but ascribed to Chinese origin.*

**1**

The opera isn't over till the fat lady sings.
    Quoted in the *Washington Post*, 13 June 1978
*Dan Cook, a Texan journalist, is said to have invented this saying in 1975.*

### PRYDE, James
### British artist
### (1866–1941)

**2**

*At the unveiling of a statue to Nurse Edith Cavell:*
My god, they've shot the wrong person!
    Attrib.

### PUDNEY, John
### British poet
### (1909–77)

**3**

Do not despair
For Johnny head-in-air;
He sleeps as sound
As Johnny underground.
    'For Johnny' (1945)
*Lines used in film* The Way to the Stars.

### *PUNCH*
### *British humorous weekly*

**4**

Look here, Steward, if this is coffee, I want tea; but if this is tea, then I wish for coffee.
    Cartoon caption, vol. cxxiii (1902)

1
*Vicar's wife (sympathizingly):* Now that you can't get about, and are not able to read, how do you manage to occupy the time?
*Old Man:* Well, mum, sometimes I sits and thinks; and then again I just sits.

Caption to cartoon by Gunning-King, vol. cxxxi, 24 October 1906

### PUZO, Mario
US novelist
(1920–   )

2
He's a businessman. I'll make him an offer he can't refuse.
*The Godfather* (1969)

3
A lawyer with his briefcase can steal more than a thousand men with guns.
*Ib.*

### PYM, Barbara
British novelist
(1928–80)

4
*On having a novel rejected:*
What is the future of my kind of writing? . . . Perhaps in retirement . . . a quieter, narrower kind of life can be worked out and adopted. Bounded by English literature and the Anglican Church and small pleasures like sewing and choosing dress material for this uncertain summer.

Diary, entry for 6 March 1972

# R

### RALEIGH, Sir Walter
British academic
(1861–1922)

1
I wish I loved the Human Race;
I wish I loved its silly face;
I wish I liked the way it walks;
I wish I liked the way it talks;
And when I'm introduced to one
I wish I thought *What Jolly Fun!*
  'Wishes of an Elderly Man', *Laughter from a Cloud* (1923)

### *RAMBO*
US film 1985. With Sylvester Stallone as Rambo, a hunk bringing home American prisoners left behind after the Vietnam War.

2
*Rambo:* Do we get to win this time?
  Soundtrack

### RANDOLPH, David

3
*On* Parsifal:
The kind of opera that starts at six o'clock and after it has been going three hours, you look at your watch and it says 6.20.
  Quoted in *The Frank Muir Book*

### RANSOME, Arthur
British novelist and journalist
(1884–1967)

1

BETTER DROWNED THAN DUFFERS IF NOT DUFFERS WON'T DROWN.
*Swallows and Amazons* (1930)

### RATTIGAN, Sir Terence
British playwright
(1911–77)

2

French Without Tears.
Title of play (1937)

3

She has ideas above her station . . . How would you say that in French? . . . you can't say au-dessus de sa gare. It isn't that sort of station.
*Ib.*

4

A nice, respectable, middle-class, middle-aged maiden lady, with time on her hands and the money to help her pass it . . . Let us call her Aunt Edna . . . Aunt Edna is universal, and to those who may feel that all the problems of the modern theatre might be solved by her liquidation, let me add that . . . she is also immortal.
Preface, *Collected Plays*, Vol. II (1953)

### *RAY'S A LAUGH*
*UK radio comedy series (BBC) from 1949–60. Written by Ted Ray and various. With Ted Ray as Ivy, Bob Pearson as Mrs Hoskin, Graham Stark as Tommy Trafford, etc.*

5

*Mrs Hoskin:* Ee, it was agony, Ivy.
Catchphrase

1

*Ivy:* He's loo-vely, Mrs Hardcastle, he's loo-oo-vely!
   Catchphrase

2

*Tommy Trafford:* If you haven't been to Manchester, you haven't
lived.
   Catchphrase

## READ, Al
### British comedian

3

Cheeky monkey!
   Catchphrase, 1950s radio shows

4

Right, monkey!
   Catchphrase, 1950s

## REAGAN, Ronald
### US President and film actor
### (1911–   )

5

*To President Carter during 1980 election:*
There you go again!
   TV debate, 29 October 1980

6

You can tell a lot about a fellow's character by the way he eats jelly
beans.
   Quoted in the *Daily Mail*, 22 January 1981

**1**

*To surgeons, as he entered the operating room after attempted assassination:*
Please tell me you're Republicans.
   Quoted in *Time*, 13 April 1981

**2**

*When told by an aide that the Government was running normally, on the same occasion:*
What makes you think I'd be happy about that?
   *Ib.*

**3**

*During microphone test prior to radio broadcast:*
My fellow Americans, I am pleased to tell you that I have signed legislation to outlaw Russia for ever. We begin bombing in five minutes.
   Audio recording, 13 August 1984

**4**

*On his challenger, Walter Mondale, during 1984 election:*
I will not make age an issue of this campaign. I am not going to exploit for political purposes my opponent's youth and inexperience.
   TV debate, 22 October 1984

**5**

A shining city on a hill.
   Quoted in *Time*, 5 November 1984
*Evocation of the US as a land of security and success, frequently used in speeches during 1984 re-election campaign. Possibly derived from the Puritan, John Winthrop (1588–1649): 'We must consider that we shall be a city upon a hill.'*

**6**

*In victory speech on re-election:*
This is not the end of anything, this is the beginning of everything.
   Quoted in *The Times*, 8 November 1984

1

*On the same occasion, and during the preceding campaign:*
You ain't seen nothing yet!
    Quoted in the *Daily Express*, 8 November 1984
*See also JOLSON 246:2.*

2

*To the American Business Conference:*
I have my veto pen drawn and ready for any tax increase that Congress
might even think of sending up. And I have only one thing to say to
the tax increasers. Go ahead – make my day.
    Quoted in *Time*, 25 March 1985
*The last sentence was originally spoken by Clint Eastwood to a
gunman he was holding at bay in the film* Sudden Impact *(1983). It
reappeared in 1984 in a parody of the New York* Post *put together by
editors, most of them anti-Reagan, who imagined the President
starting a nuclear war by throwing down that dare to the Kremlin.*

3

*After hi-jack of a US plane by Shi'ite Muslims:*
We are not going to tolerate these attacks from outlaw states run by
the strangest collection of misfits, looney tunes and squalid criminals
since the advent of the Third Reich.
    Speech, 8 July 1985

*See also* BRIDGES AT TOKO-RI *p. 71,* KING'S ROW *p. 259, and*
LOUIS *283:1.*

**REED, Henry**
British poet and playwright
(1914–86)

4

*In parody of T.S. Eliot:*
As we get older we do not get any younger.
Seasons return, and today I am fifty-five,
And this time last year I was fifty-four,
And this time next year I shall be sixty-two.
    'Chard Whitlow', *A Map of Verona* (1946)

1
To-day we have naming of parts.
Yesterday
We had daily cleaning.
And tomorrow morning,
We shall have what to do after firing. But to-day,
Today we have naming of parts.
   'Lessons of the War' in *ib*.


### REED, John
US writer
(1887–1920)

2
Ten Days That Shook the World.
   Title of book (on Russian Revolution) (1919)
*Also used as the alternative, English, title of Sergei Eisenstein's 1927 film* October.


### REED, Rex
US critic
(1938–   )

3
Cannes is where you lie on the beach and stare at the stars – or vice versa.
   Attrib.


### REID, Beryl
British actress
(1918–   )

4
As the art mistress said to the gardener . . .
   Catchphrase as 'Monica' in *Educating Archie*, BBC Radio, 1950s

**1**

Jolly hockey-sticks.

Catchphrase in *ib.*

**2**

Good evening, each!

Catchphrase as 'Marlene' in *ib.*

## REITH, John
### (later Lord Reith)
### British broadcasting administrator
### (1889–1971)

**3**

It was in fact the combination of public service motive, sense of moral obligation, assured finance and the brute force of monopoly which enabled the BBC to make of broadcasting what no other country has made of it.

*Into the Wind* (1949)

**4**

I hear ye.

Stock retort

*A Scotticism meaning 'I have heard what you said but don't consider it worth commenting upon.' (Revealed in TV interview with Malcolm Muggeridge, August 1970.)*

## REMARQUE, Erich Maria
### German novelist
### (1897–1970)

**5**

All Quiet on the Western Front.

English translation of book title, 1929

*Remarque's original title was* Im Westen Nichts Neues *('Nothing New in the West'). The translation echoes the title of 'All Quiet Along the Potomac', an American song derived from a poem about the Civil War.*

## REPINGTON, Lieut-Col. Charles A'Court
British soldier and journalist
(1858–1925)

1
I saw Major Johnstone, who is here to lay the bases of an American History. We discussed the right name of the war. I said that we called it now *The War*, but that this could not last. The Napoleonic War was *The Great War*. To call it *The German War* was too much flattery for the Boche. I suggested *The World War* as a shade better title, and finally we mutually agreed to call it *The First World War* in order to prevent the millennium folk from forgetting that the history of the world was the history of war.

Diary entry for 10 September 1918 published in *The First World War 1914–18* (1920)

## *THE RETURN OF SHERLOCK HOLMES*
*UK film 1929. With Clive Brook as Holmes and H. Reeves-Smith as Watson.*

2
*Watson:* Amazing, Holmes.
*Holmes:* Elementary, my dear Watson, elementary.
*Nowhere in the writings of Sir Arthur Conan Doyle (1859–1930) does the great detective say this phrase. These were the last lines of dialogue of the first sound film version.*

## REUBEN, David
US doctor and author
(1933–   )

3
Everything You Always Wanted to Know About Sex But Were Afraid to Ask.
Title of book (1970)

# RHODES, Cecil
British-born colonialist
(1853–1902)

1

Remember that you are an Englishman and have consequently won first prize in the lottery of life.
Quoted in P. Ustinov, *Dear Me*

2

*Near to his death:*
So little done, so much to do.
Attrib.
*Echoing Tennyson, 'So many worlds, so much to do,/So little done, such things to be' – In memoriam A.H.H. (1850).*

3

*Last words:*
Turn me over, Jack.
Attrib.

# RIBBLESDALE, Lord
British aristocrat
(1854–1925)

4

It [is] gentlemanly to get one's quotations very slightly wrong. In that way one unprigs oneself and allows the company to correct one.
Recounted in Lady D. Cooper, *The Light of Common Day*

# RICE, Grantland
US sports journalist and poet
(1880–1954)

5

For when the One Great Scorer comes
To write against your name,
He marks – not that you won or lost –
But how you played the game.
'Alumnus Football'

## RICE, Tim
British lyricist
(1944–   )

1

Jesus Christ Superstar!
   Title of musical (with A. Lloyd Webber) (1970)
*Based on a 1960s Las Vegas billing, 'Tom Jones – Superstar'* . . .

2

*Herod to Christ:*
Prove to me that you're no fool,
Walk across my swimming pool.
   Song, 'King Herod's Song' in *ib.*

3

Don't Cry for Me, Argentina.
   Title of song, *Evita* (1976)

## RICE-DAVIES, Mandy
British woman
(1944–   )

4

*When told that Lord Astor had denied her allegations of some amorous involvement:*
Well, he would, wouldn't he?
   Magistrates' Court hearing, London, 28 June 1963

## RICHARD, Keith
see JAGGER, Mick and RICHARD, Keith

## 'RICHARDS, Frank'
British writer
(1875–1961)

5

*Cries of 'Billy Bunter':*
Yarooh! . . . I say you fellows! . . . You beast!
   *Passim* in Billy Bunter stories (1908–40)

**1**

The rottenfulness is terrific!
   Story in *The Magnet* No. 400 but *passim* in *ib.*
*Said by Hurree Jamset Ram, the basic formula was 'the —fulness is terrific'.*


### RIPLEY, Robert L.
US strip creator and illustrator
(1893–1949)

**2**

Believe It or Not.
   Title of syndicated newspaper feature, from 1918 onwards
*Popularizing a phrase already in existence.*


### RIVERS, Joan
US comedienne
(1937–   )

**3**

Can we talk?
   Stock phrase


### THE ROAD TO MOROCCO
*US film 1942. With Bob Hope and Bing Crosby.*

**4**

Like Webster's Dictionary
We're Morocco bound.
   Song, 'Road to Morocco'
*Written by Johnny Burke.*

## ROBERTS, Tommy Rhys, QC
Welsh lawyer
(1910–75)

1
Lloyd George knew my father.
*Sung to the tune of 'Onward Christian Soldiers', this was his party piece at legal dinners, from the 1940s on. His father had once shared a legal practice with Lloyd George. This is but one suggested source for the popular song.*

## ROBEY, Sir George
British comedian
(1869–1954)

2
The Prime Minister of Mirth.
  Bill matter

3
Desist!
  Catchphrase

## ROBSON, Bobby
British football manager
(1933–  )

4
The first ninety minutes are the most important.
  Quoted as title of TV documentary, 1983

## ROCKEFELLER, Nelson
US Republican politician and Vice-President
(1908–79)

5
The brotherhood of man under the fatherhood of God.
  Quoted in *Time*, 1 March 1982

*The words came originally from a saying of his father, John D. Rockefeller Jr (1874–1960) – 'These are the principles upon which alone a new world recognizing the brotherhood of man and the fatherhood of God can be established.' Rendered by others by the acronym 'BOMFOG'.*

### ROCKNE, Knute
US football coach
(1888–1931)

1
Show me a good and gracious loser and I'll show you a failure.
   Attrib. 1920s.

*See also* KNUTE ROCKNE *p. 262.*

### ROGERS, Will
US humorist
(1879–1935)

2
Dear Mr Coolidge: Well all I know is just what I read in the papers.
   *The Letters of a Self-Made Diplomat to His President* (1927)

3
*On the Venus de Milo:*
See what'll happen if you don't stop biting your finger-nails.
   Quoted in B. Cerf, *Shake Well Before Using*

### ROONEY, Mickey
US film actor
(1920–　)

4
Had I been brighter, the ladies been gentler, the Scotch been weaker, had the gods been kinder, had the dice been hotter, this could have been a one-sentence story: Once upon a time I lived happily ever after.
   Attrib. in 1965

**1**

*In films as 'Andy Handy' and with Judy Garland, 1930s/40s:*
Let's put on a show! . . . Let's do the show right here in the barn!
  Stock phrase

## ROOSEVELT, Franklin D.
US Democratic President
(1882–1945)

**2**

I pledge you, I pledge myself to a New Deal for the American people.
  Speech to the Democratic Convention, 1932

**3**

First of all, let me assert my belief that the only thing we have to fear is
fear itself – nameless, unreasoning, unjustified terror which paralyzes
needed efforts to convert retreat into advance.
  Inaugural address, Washington, 4 March 1933

**4**

A radical is a man with both feet firmly planted in the air.
  Radio broadcast, 26 October 1939

**5**

I have told you once and I will tell you again – your boys will not be
sent into any foreign wars.
  Election speech, 1940

**6**

And who voted against the appropriations for an adequate national
defense? MARTIN, BARTON and FISH.
  Election speeches, 1940

**7**

We must be the great arsenal of democracy.
  Fireside chat, 29 December 1940

**1**

*On the Japanese attack at Pearl Harbor:*
Yesterday, December 7 1941, a date which will live in infamy, the
United States of America was suddenly and deliberately attacked by
naval and air forces of the Empire of Japan.

Speech to Congress, 8 December 1941

## ROOSEVELT, Theodore
US Republican President
(1858–1919)

**2**

I am as strong as a bull moose and you can use me to the limit.

Letter to Mark Hanna, 1900

*When standing as Vice-President. He later tried to make a Presidential comeback as a 'Bull Moose' candidate in 1912.*

**3**

There is a homely adage which runs, 'Speak softly and carry a big stick
– and you will go far.' If the American nation will speak softly and yet
build and keep at a pitch of the highest training a thoroughly efficient
navy, the Monroe Doctrine will go far.

Speech (as Vice-President), Minnesota State Fair, 2 September
1901

**4**

*On Maxwell House coffee:*
Good . . . to the last drop.

Attrib. remark

*Visiting Joel Cheek, the perfector of the blend, 1907. The line was
used as the brand's slogan for many years.*

**5**

The lunatic fringe.

*Autobiography* (1913)

*Referring to elements in reform movements.*

## ROSE, Billy
US impresario and songwriter
(1899–1966)

1

Does the Spearmint Lose Its Flavour on the Bedpost Overnight?
  Title of song

*See also HARBURG 212:3.*


## ROSEBERY, Earl of
British Liberal Prime Minister
(1847–1929)

2

*On breaking away from his Liberal Party colleagues:*
For the present, at any rate, I must proceed alone. I must plough my
own furrow alone, but before I get to the end of that furrow it is
possible that I may not find myself alone.
  Speech, 19 July 1901


## ROSS, Alan S.C.
British academic
(1907–   )

3

U and Non-U. An Essay in Sociological Linguistics.
  Title of essay in *Noblesse Oblige* (1956)


## ROSS, Harold
US editor of the *New Yorker*
(1892–1951)

4

Who he?
  Quoted in J. Thurber, *The Years With Ross*
*Customary query on finding a name he did not know in an article.*

**1**
*Upon founding the* New Yorker *in 1925:*
The *New Yorker* will not be edited for the old lady from Dubuque.
  Remark
*Later she became known as 'the little old lady from Dubuque'.*

### ROTH, Philip
US novelist
(1933–   )

**2**
So (said the doctor). Now vee may perhaps to begin. Yes?
  *Portnoy's Complaint* (1969)
*Last words.*

### 'ROTTEN, Johnny'
British pop singer
(1957–   )

**3**
Love is two minutes fifty-two seconds of squishing noises. It shows your mind isn't clicking right.
  Attrib.
*In 1983 Rotten was quoted in the* Daily Mirror *as saying that it had become more like five minutes as he had acquired a new technique.*

### *ROUND THE HORNE*
*UK radio comedy series (BBC), from 1964–9. Script by Marty Feldman and Barry Took. With Kenneth Horne, Betty Marsden as Lady Beatrice Counterblast and Kenneth Williams as Sandy.*

**4**
*Sandy:* That's yer actual French.
  Catchphrase

**5**
*Counterblast:* Many, many times!
  Catchphrase

## ROWAN AND MARTIN'S LAUGH-IN see LAUGH-IN

### ROWLAND, Richard
US film executive

1
*When United Artists was established:*
The lunatics have taken over the asylum.
   Attrib.
*See also STALLINGS 413:4 and GEORGE, David Lloyd 187:3.*

### RUBIN, Jerry
US 'yippie' leader
(1938–   )

2
##   Don't trust anyone over thirty.
   Quoted in S.B. Flexner, *Listening to America*
*Actually first uttered by Jack Weinberg at Berkeley in 1964 during a*
*free speech demonstration.*

### RUNCIE, Robert
British Archbishop of Canterbury
(1921–   )

3
*On discussions with the Prince and Princess of Wales prior to*
*marrying them:*
My advice was delicately poised between the cliché and the
indiscretion.
   Quoted in *The Times*, 14 July 1981
*See also MACMILLAN 291:3.*

## RUNCIE, Rosalind
### Wife of the Archbishop of Canterbury
### (1932–    )

**1**

Too much religion makes me go pop.

    Quoted in M. Duggan, *Runcie: The Making of an Archbishop*

## RUNYON, Damon
### US writer
### (1884–1946)

**2**

Strictly a Hurrah Henry.

  'Tight Shoes'

*Jim Godbolt adapted this to 'Hooray Henry' in 1951 to describe a species of British upper-class twit.*

## RUSK, Dean
### US Democratic politician
### (1909–    )

**3**

*In conversation with journalist during Cuban Missile Crisis, 24 October 1962:*

We're eyeball to eyeball and I think the other fellow just blinked.

    Quoted in W. Safire, *Political Dictionary*

## RUSSELL, Bertrand
### (3rd Earl Russell)
### British philosopher and mathematician
### (1872–1970)

**4**

Drunkenness is temporary suicide: the happiness that it brings is merely negative, a momentary cessation of unhappiness.

    *The Conquest of Happiness* (1930)

1

Three passions, simple but overwhelmingly strong, have governed my life: the longing for love, the search for knowledge, and unbearable pity for the suffering of mankind . . .

I have sought love, first, because it brings ecstasy – ecstasy so great that I would often have sacrificed all the rest of life for a few hours of this joy. I have sought it, next, because it relieves loneliness – that terrible loneliness in which one shivering consciousness looks over the rim of the world into the cold unfathomable lifeless abyss. I have sought it, finally, because in the union of love I have seen, in a mystic miniature, the prefiguring vision of the heaven that saints and poets have imagined. This is what I sought, and though it might seem too good for human life, this is what – at last – I have found.

'What I have lived for', Prologue to Vol. 1, *The Autobiography of Bertrand Russell* (1967)

2

I have never but once succeeded in making [George Moore] tell a lie, that was by a subterfuge. 'Moore,' I said, 'do you *always* speak the truth?' 'No,' he replied. I believe this to be the only lie he had ever told.

*Ib.*

# S

### SABATINI, Rafael
Italian-born novelist
(1875–1950)

1

Born with the gift of laughter and a sense that the world was mad.
  *Scaramouche* (1921)

### SACKVILLE-WEST, V.
British novelist and poet
(1892–1962)

2

They rustle, they brustle, they crackle, and if you can crush beech nuts under foot at the same time, so much the better. But beech nuts aren't essential. The essential is that you should tramp through very dry, very crisp, brown leaves – a thick drift of them in the Autumn woods, shuffling through them, kicking them up . . . walking in fact 'through leaves'.
  Broadcast talk, 1950
*Explaining a family expression 'Through leaves' to express pure happiness as shown by young children shuffling through drifts of dry autumn leaves.*

### SAHL, Mort
US satirist
(1926–  )

3

*During viewing of lengthy film, Exodus:*
Let my people go!
  As told on LP album *The New Frontier* (1961)
*Another version is that Sahl, invited by the director, Otto Preminger, to a preview, stood up after three hours and said, 'Otto – let my people go!'*

## 'SAKI'
### (H.H. Munro)
### British short-story writer
### (1870–1916)

1

The cook was a good cook, as cooks go; and as cooks go she went.

'Reginald on Besetting Sins', *Reginald* (1904)

2

Waldo is one of those people who would be enormously improved by death.

'The Feast of Nemesis', *Beasts and Super-Beasts* (1914)

3

*Last words:*
Put that bloody cigarette out!

Quoted in A.J. Langguth, *Life of Saki*
*Said by Corporal Munro to one of his men who had lit up. He was killed by a German sniper.*


## SALINGER, J.D.
### US novelist
### (1919– )

4

If you really want to hear about it, the first thing you'll probably want to know is where I was born and what my lousy childhood was like, and how my parents were occupied and all before they had me, and all that David Copperfield kind of crap.

*The Catcher in the Rye* (1951)
*Opening words.*

## SALISBURY, 5th Marquess of
British Conservative politician
(1893–1972)

1

*On Iain Macleod:*
The present Colonial Secretary has been too clever by half. I believe
he is a very fine bridge player. It is not considered immoral, or even
bad form to outwit one's opponent at bridge. It almost seems to me as
if the Colonial Secretary, when he abandoned the sphere of bridge for
the sphere of politics, brought his bridge technique with him.

Speech, House of Lords, 1961

## SANDBURG, Carl
US poet
(1878–1967)

2

Sometime they'll give a war and nobody will come.

*The People, Yes* (1936)

*Charlotte Keyes (1914–   ) wrote an article in* McCall's *(October
1966) which was given the title 'Suppose They Gave a War, and No
One Came?' A US film (1969) was called* Suppose They Gave a War
and Nobody Came?

## SARONY, Leslie
British entertainer and writer
(1897–1985)

3

He sits among the cabbages and peas.

Song, 'Mucking About the Garden', (1920s)
*Using the pen name, 'Q. Cumber'.*

4

Ain't It Grand to Be Bloomin' Well Dead?

Title of song

### SARTRE, Jean-Paul
French philosopher and writer
(1905–80)

1

Hell is other people.
*Huis Clos* (1944)

### SAVILE, Jimmy
British entertainer
(1926–   )

2

As it happens.
Stock phrase

3

How's about that, then, guys and gals?
Stock phrase

### SAYERS, Dorothy L.
British detective novelist
(1893–1957)

4

*Lord Peter Wimsey proposing to Harriet Vane:* Placetne, magistra?
Gaudy Night (1936)
*She replies: 'Placet.'*

### SCHACHT, Hjalmar
German banker
(1877–1970)

5

I wouldn't believe Hitler was dead, even if he told me so himself.
Attrib. remark on 8 May 1945

## SCHOENBERG, Arnold
German composer
(1874–1951)

1
*When told his violin concerto needed a soloist with six fingers:*
Very well, I can wait.
    Attrib.


## SCHULTZ, Charles M.
US cartoonist and creator of
'Peanuts' strip
(1922–   )

2
Good grief, Charlie Brown!
    Stock phrase
*The behaviour of 'Charlie Brown' frequently elicits this exclamation
from other characters.*


3
It Was a Dark and Stormy Night . . .
    Title of book
*Derived from a children's 'circular' story-telling game.*


4
Happiness is a warm puppy.
    From strip *c.*1957
*This gave rise to numerous other 'Happiness is . . .' slogans.
Compare HARBURG 213:2.*


## SCHUMACHER, E.F.
German-born British economist
(1911–77)

5
Small Is Beautiful.
    Title of book (1973)

## SCOTT, C.P.
### British newspaper editor
### (1846–1932)

**1**

Comment is free, but facts are sacred.
  *Manchester Guardian*, 5 May 1921
*In a signed editorial marking the paper's centenary.*

**2**

Television? No good will come of this device. The word is half Greek and half Latin.
  Attrib.

## SCOTT, Captain R.F.
### British explorer
### (1868–1912)

**3**

*On the South Pole:*
Great God! This is an awful place and terrible enough for us to have laboured without the reward of priority.
  *Scott's Last Expedition: Journals* (1913)

**4**

Had we lived, I should have had a tale to tell of the hardihood, endurance, and courage of my companions which would have stirred the hearts of every Englishman. These rough notes and our dead bodies must tell the tale.
  (Message to the Public) *Ib.*

**5**

For God's sake look after our people.
  *Ib.* Last entry (29 March 1912)

## SELFRIDGE, H. Gordon
US store owner
(1856–1947)

1

There are . . . shopping days to Christmas
Quoted in A.H. Williams, *No Name on the Door*

2

Complete satisfaction or money cheerfully refunded.
Slogan in *ib.*

3

The customer is always right.
Slogan in *ib.*

4

'Business as usual' must be the order of the day.
Speech, 26 August 1914
*In the context of the early days of the First World War, the traditional store-keeper's slogan (as might be used after a fire, or similar) was first used by H.E. Morgan, an associate of Selfridge's. Winston Churchill also took up the cry.*

5

This famous store needs no name on the door.
Slogan.
*His Oxford Street store in London opened in 1909.*


## SELLAR, W.C. and YEATMAN, R.J.
British humorists
(1898–1951) and (1897–1968)

6

[The Roman Conquest was, however,] a *Good Thing*.
*Passim* in *1066 and All That* (1930)

1

Honi soie qui mal y pense ('Honey, your silk stocking's hanging down').
   *Ib.*

2

Shortly after this the cruel Queen died and a post-mortem examination revealed the word 'CALLOUS' engraved on her heart.
   *Ib.*

3

[Gladstone] spent his declining years trying to guess the answer to the Irish Question; unfortunately, whenever he was getting warm, the Irish secretly changed the question.
   *Ib.*

4

Do not on any account attempt to write on both sides of the paper at once.
   *Ib.*

### SELLERS, Peter
British actor
(1925–80)

5

*As Indian:*
Goodness, gracious me.
   Recording of song, 'Goodness Gracious Me' (1960)
*The song, written by Herbert Kretzmer, was recorded with Sophia Loren and based on characters in the film of Shaw's* The Million-airess.

## SERVICE, Robert W.
Canadian poet
(1874–1958)

**1**

Ah! the clock is always slow;
It is later than you think.
 'Spring'

**2**

And watching his luck was his light-o'-love, the lady that's known as Lou.
 'The Shooting of Dan McGrew' (1917)
*Written with Cuthbert Clarke.*

## SHANE
*US film 1953. Script by A.B. Guthrie Jnr, from a novel by Jack Shaeffer.*

**3**

## A man's gotta do what a man's gotta do.
*This line accords with the spirit of the book and the film, but occurs in neither (although this has been suggested). Used in promotion?*

## SHANKLY, Bill
British football manager
(1914–81)

**4**

Some people think football is a matter of life and death. I don't like that attitude. I can assure them it is much more serious than that.
 Attrib. in 1973

## SHAW, George Bernard
Irish playwright and critic
(1856–1950)

1

*On the song, 'The Red Flag':*
The funeral march of a fried eel.
   Quoted in W.S. Churchill, *Great Contemporaries*

2

*On Lord Rosebery:*
A man who never missed an occasion to let slip an opportunity.
   Attrib.

3

England and America are two countries separated by the same
language.
   Quoted in *Treasury of Humorous Quotations*
*Compare O. Wilde* The Canterville Ghost *(1887): 'We have really
everything in common with America nowadays except, of course,
language.'*

4

You see things; and you say 'Why?' But I dream things that never
were; and I say 'Why not?' *The Serpent*
   *Back to Methusaleh* (1921)
*Quoted by John F. Kennedy and Robert F. Kennedy many times – to
the extent that it is sometimes ascribed to them.*

5

I am Millionaire. That is my religion.
   *Major Barbara* (1907)

6

Wot prawce Selvytion nah?
   *Ib.*

7

Hell is full of musical amateurs: music is the brandy of the damned.
   *Man and Superman* (1903)

**1**

Titles distinguish the mediocre, embarrrass the superior, and are disgraced by the inferior.

*Ib.*

**2**

There are two tragedies in life. One is to lose your heart's desire. The other is to gain it.

*Ib.*

**3**

Do not do unto others as you would they should do unto you. Their tastes may not be the same.

*Ib.* 'Maxims for Revolutionists'

**4**

The golden rule is that there are no golden rules.

*Ib.*

**5**

He who can does. He who cannot, teaches.

*Ib.*

**6**

Marriage is popular because it combines the maximum of temptation with the maximum of opportunity.

*Ib.*

**7**

Assassination is the extreme form of censorship.

*The Shewing-Up of Blanco Posnett* (1909)

**8**

He's a gentleman: look at his boots.

*Pygmalion* (1914)

**9**

I'll make a duchess of that draggle-tailed guttersnipe.

*Ib.*

1
Remember that you are a human being with a soul and the divine gift
of articulate speech: that your native language is the language of
Shakespeare and Milton and the Bible; and don't sit there crooning
like a bilious pigeon.
   *Ib.*

2
My aunt died of influenza: so they said . . . But it's my belief (as how)
they done the old woman in.
   *Ib.*
*The words 'as how' were inserted by Mrs Patrick Campbell in her*
*performances as Eliza. Also incorporated in the film.*

3
*Freddy:* Are you walking across the Park, Miss Doolittle? If so—
*Liza:* Walk! Not bloody likely. I am going in a taxi.
   *Ib.*

4
Where the devil are my slippers?
   *Ib.*
*Last words.*

5
*To Helen Keller:*
I wish all Americans were as blind as you.
   Quoted in H. Pearson, *Bernard Shaw*
*Sometimes misquoted as 'All Americans are deaf, dumb, and blind'.*

6
*To a Swiss woman who had written, 'You have the greatest brain in*
*the world and I have the most beautiful body; so we ought to produce*
*the most perfect child':*
Yes, but fancy if it were born with my beauty and your brains?
   Quoted in *ib.*

1

*To Alfred Hitchcock who had said: 'One look at you, Mr Shaw, and I know there's famine in the land':*
One look at you, Mr Hitchcock, and I know who caused it.
  Quoted in B. Patch, *Thirty Years with GBS*

2

*When Samuel Goldwyn asked him if he would sell the film rights to his plays:*
The trouble is, Mr Goldwyn, that you are only interested in art and I am only interested in money.
  Quoted in P. French, *The Movie Moguls*

3

*On dancing:*
A perpendicular expression of a horizontal desire.
  Quoted G. Melly, *Revolt into Style*

4

With the single exception of Homer, there is no eminent writer, not even Sir Walter Scott, whom I can despise so entirely as I despise Shakespeare when I measure my mind against his . . . It would positively be a relief to me to dig him up and throw stones at him.
  *Dramatic Opinions and Essays*, Vol. 2 (1907)
*Quoting a view stated 1895–8.*


### SHAWCROSS, Sir Hartley
(later Lord Shawcross)
British Labour Attorney-General
(1902–   )

5

\#\#   We are the masters now.
  Speech, House of Commons, 2 April 1946
*In fact, he said: 'We are the masters at the moment, and not only at the moment, but for a very long time to come.'*

## SHINWELL, Emanuel
(later Lord Shinwell)
British Labour politician
(1884–1986)

1

We know that you, the organized workers of the country, are our friends . . . As for the rest, they do not matter a tinker's curse.
ETU Conference, Margate, 7 May 1947

## SIBELIUS, Jean
Finnish composer
(1865–1957)

2

Pay no attention to what the critics say. No statue has ever been put up to a critic.
Attrib.

## SICKERT, Walter
British painter
(1860–1942)

3

*To Denton Welch:*
Come again when you can't stay so long.
Quoted in D. Welch, 'Sickert at St Peter's', *Horizon*, Vol. vi No. 32 (1942)

## SIMENON, Georges
Belgian novelist
(1903–  )

4

I have made love to ten thousand women.
Interview with *Die Tat*, Zurich, 1977
*Later his wife said: 'The true figure is no more than twelve hundred.'*

## SIMON, Carly
US singer/songwriter
(1945–   )

**1**
You're so vain, you probably think this song is about you.
  Song, 'You're So Vain' (1972)

## SIMON, Guy
British writer
(1944–   )

**2**
Jimmy Carter had the air of a man who had never taken any decisions
in his life. They had always taken him.
  Quoted in the *Sunday Times*, 5 June 1978

## SIMON, Neil
US playwright
(1927–   )

**3**
New York . . . is not Mecca. It justs smells like it.
  *California Suite* (1976)

## SIMON, Paul
US singer/songwriter
(1941–   )

**4**
Like a bridge over troubled water,
I will ease your mind.
  Song, 'Bridge Over Troubled Water' (1970)

1
The words of the prophet are written
On the subway halls and tenement walls.
   Song, 'Sound of Silence' (1970)

**'SIMPLE, Peter'**
(Michael Wharton)
British columnist
(1913–   )

2
Rentacrowd Ltd, the enterprising firm which supplies crowds for all
occasions and has done so much to keep progressive causes in the
public eye.
   In 'The Way of the World', the *Daily Telegraph*, 1962 and *passim*

**SIMS, George R.**
British writer
(1847–1922)

3
It is Christmas Day in the Workhouse.
   *The Dagonet and Other Poems* (1903)

**SITWELL, Dame Edith**
British poetess
(1887–1964)

4
The fire was furry as a bear.
   'Dark Song', *Façade* (1922)

5
Another little drink wouldn't do us any harm.
   'Scotch Rhapsody' in *ib.*
*See also SONG TITLES 408:2.*

1

Still falls the Rain –
Dark as the world of man, black as our loss –
Blind as the nineteen hundred and forty nails
Upon the cross.
*Still Falls the Rain* (1940)

2

*On novelist Ethel Mannin:*
I do not want Miss Mannin's feelings to be hurt by the fact that I have never heard of her . . . At the moment I am debarred from the pleasure of putting her in her place by the fact that she has not got one.
Quoted in J. Pearson, *Façades*
*Used subsequently about various other targets.*

3

*On Virginia Woolf:*
I enjoyed talking to her, but thought *nothing* of her writing. I considered her 'a beautiful little knitter'.
Letter to G. Singleton, 11 July 1955

### SITWELL, Sir Osbert
British writer
(1892–1969)

4

Educated: in the holidays from Eton.
Entry in *Who's Who*

### SKELTON, Noel
British Conservative politician
(1880–1935)

5

. . . To state as clearly as may be what means lie ready to develop a property-owning democracy, to bring the industrial and economic status of the wage-earner abreast of his political and educational, to make democracy stable and four-square.
Article in the *Spectator*, 19 May 1923
*The phrase 'property-owning democracy' was later popularized by Anthony Eden and Winston Churchill (1946).*

# SLOGANS
## (in alphabetical order)

1

All human life is there.
*Advertising slogan for the* News of the World, *1958–9. A quotation from Henry James.*

2

All power to the soviets.
*Workers in Petrograd, 1917.*

3

Any time, any place, anywhere.
*Martini ads., UK, 1970s.*

4

At sixty miles an hour the loudest noise in this new Rolls-Royce comes from the electric clock.
*Rolls-Royce ads., US, from 1958. From a car test by the Technical Editor of the* Motor.

5

Avoid 'five o'clock shadow'.
*Slogan for Gem Razors and Blades, US, from the 1930s on.*

6

B.O. ('Body odour')
*Lifebuoy soap ads., US, from 1933.*

7

Balfour must go.
*Probably the first such slogan (c.1905) – followed later by 'Eden Must Go' (1956) and 'Marples Must Go' (1962/3).*

8

Ban the bomb.
*Slogan of nuclear disarmament campaigners, initially in the US, from c.1953.*

1

Beanz meanz Heinz.
*Heinz Baked Beans ads., UK, from 1960s.*

2

Berlin by Christmas.
*Anti-German slogan, in Britain, 1914.*

3

Better red than dead.
*Slogan of the British nuclear disarmament movement, from c.1958.*

4

The big one.
*Circus slogan, dating from 1907 amalgamation of Ringling Brothers Circus with Barnum and Bailey.*

5

Black is beautiful.
*US civil rights slogan, from c.1962 (when used by Stokely Carmichael).*

6

Black power.
*US civil rights slogan (used by Stokely Carmichael in 1966).*

7

(Is it true . . .) blondes have more fun?
*Clairol (hair colouring) ads., in US, from 1957.*

8

Blow some my way.
*Chesterfield cigarette ads., US, from 1926.*

9

Bombs away with Curt Lemay.
*Peace chant, US (1967).*

1
Britain can take it.
*British wartime slogan, 1940.*

2
Burn, baby, burn!
*Black extremist slogan, US, 1965.*

3
Burn your bra!
*Feminist slogan from US, c.1970.*

4
Can *you* tell Stork from butter?
*Slogan for Stork margarine, UK, c.1956.*

5
Careless talk costs lives.
*British wartime security slogan, from mid-1940.*

6
Clunk, click, *every* trip.
*Car seat-belt ads., UK, from 1971.*

7
Come on, Aussie, come on.
*Australian slogan, from song by Alan Johnston and Alan Stuart Morris, 1978.*

8
Coughs and sneezes spread diseases.
*UK wartime health slogan, from c.1942.*

9
Daddy, what did *you* do in the Great War?
*Daughter to father in First World War recruiting poster. This became the catchphrase, 'What did you do in the Great War, Daddy?'*

1

Desperation, Pacification, Expectation, Acclamation, Realization.
*UK ads for Fry's chocolate, from 1920s on.*

2

Does she . . . or doesn't she? Only her hairdresser knows for sure.
*Clairol (hair colour) ads., US, from 1955.*

3

Don't ask a man to drink and drive.
*UK road safety slogan, from 1964.*

4

Don't forget the fruit gums, mum.
*UK ads. for Rowntree's Fruit Gums, 1958–61.*

5

Drinka pinta milka day.
*Slogan for the National Milk Publicity Council of England and Wales, 1958.*

6

Dull it isn't.
*UK recruiting ads. for Metropolitan police, 1972.*

7

The East is red.
*Chinese communist slogan, in song, from 1960s.*

8

Ein Reich, ein Volk, ein Führer ('One realm, one people, one leader').
*German Nazi slogan, from 1934.*

9

Enosis ('Union').
*Call for unification of Cyprus with mainland Greece, from 1952.*

1
Even your best friends won't tell you.
*US ads. for Listerine mouthwash.*

2
Export or die.
*UK slogan, 1940s.*

3
The eyes and ears of the world.
*Paramount News (cinema newsreel), UK, 1927–57.*

4
The family that prays together stays together.
*Devised by Al Scalpone for the Roman Catholic Rosary Crusade in the US (1947).*

5
Food shot from guns.
*Slogan for Quaker Puffed Wheat and Puffed Rice, originally in the US, from the early 1990s.*

6
Go for gold.
*Olympic slogan, from 1980, especially in the US.*

7
Go to work on an egg.
*Slogan for British Egg Marketing Board, 1958.*

8
Gone for a Burton.
*Slogan possibly used to promote a Bass beer in the UK, in the 1930s, giving rise to the Second World War expression meaning to have gone missing, presumed dead. No evidence survives.*

9
Guinness is good for you.
*Guinness beer, UK, from 1929.*

1
Gung ho.
*Chinese for 'Work together', adopted by US Marines under General Carlson during the Second World War. Gung Ho! was the title of a US film about the Marines in 1943.*

2
Hang the Kaiser!
*Slogan promoted by Northcliffe newspapers and others at the time of the Versailles Peace Conference, 1919.*

3
Hearts and minds.
*US Government slogan of sorts – meaning what had to be won – in the Vietnam War.*

4
Heineken refreshes the parts other beers cannot reach.
*Heineken lager ads., UK, from 1975.*

5
Hell no, we won't go!
*US anti-war chant, 1965.*

6
Hey, hey, LBJ, how many kids did you kill today?
*Anti-President Johnson chant during Vietnam War, c.1966.*

7
I like Ike.
*Republican slogan, supporting Dwight D. Eisenhower's bid for the US Presidency, from 1947.*

8
I love New York.
*Slogan, originally for the New York State Department of Commerce, from 1977.*

1

Illegitimi(s) non carborundum ('Don't let the bastards grind you down').
*Cod Latin phrase used by US General 'Vinegar Joe' Silwell as his motto during the Second World War, although he did not devise it. 'Carborundum' is the trade name for silicon carbide, used in grinding.*

2

I'm backing Britain.
*Campaign slogan, UK, 1968.*

3

I'm only here for the beer.
*Slogan for Double Diamond beer, in the UK, from 1971.*

4

Is your journey really necessary?
*British wartime travel slogan, from 1939.*

5

It beats . . . as it sweeps . . . as it cleans.
*Slogan for Hoover carpet sweepers, originally in the US, from 1919.*

6

I thought . . . until I discovered Smirnoff.
*Slogan for Smirnoff vodka in the UK, from 1970–5.*

7

It's fingerlickin' good.
*Ads for Kentucky Fried Chicken, originally US, 1960s on.*

8

It's so bracing.
*Ads, for Skegness, UK holiday resort, with jolly fisherman symbol, from 1909.*

9

I was a seven stone weakling.
*Line from Charles Atlas body-building advertising – originally in the US – from 1920s on.*

1
Keep on truckin'.
*Slogan of cartoon character devised by Robert Crumb and generally popular from late 1960s.*

2
Labour isn't working.
*British Conservative Party slogan 1978/9, on poster showing dole queue.*

3
Let's get America moving again.
*Slogan used by John F. Kennedy in US Presidential election, 1960.*

4
Life's better with the Conservatives . . . don't let Labour ruin it.
*British Conservative Party slogan, 1959.*

5
LS/MFT ('Lucky Strike means finer tobacco').
*Lucky Strike cigarette ads., US, from 1940s?*

6
Make do and mend.
*US wartime slogan, 1940s, based on Royal Navy expression for free time devoted to mending clothes.*

7
Make love, not war.
*'Peacenik'/'Flower Power' slogan from mid-1960s.*

8
The man you love to hate.
*Referring to the actor, Erich von Stroheim, for his role in the film* The Heart of Humanity *(1918).*

9
Mean! Moody! Magnificent!
*Ads., US, for Jane Russell film* The Outlaw *(1943).*

1

Nation shall speak unto nation.
*First motto of the BBC (1927), suggested by Dr Montague Rendall, and echoing Micah 4:3: 'Nation shall not lift up a sword against nation.'*

2

Never again.
*Slogan of the Jewish Defence League, from 1960s. Referring to the 'holocaust' of the Second World War – though it had been used generally about wars before this.*

3

Never knowingly undersold.
*Sales policy of John Lewis Partnership, UK, from 1920s on.*

4

Nice one, Cyril.
*Line from TV ad. for Wonderloaf bread, in the UK, 1972. Later taken up by supporters of footballer, Cyril Knowles.*

5

No more war.
*Recurrent slogan during the century.*

6

Nothing over sixpence.
*Slogan for Woolworth stores in UK, from after 1909.*

7

Often a bridesmaid, but never a bride.
*US ads. for Listerine mouthwash, from 1923 on.*

8

Out of the closets and into the streets.
*Slogan for US Gay Liberation Front, from c.1969.*

**1**
Power to the people.
*Slogan of the US Black Panther movement, 1969 – later taken up by others.*

**2**
Put a tiger in your tank.
*Slogan for Esso petroleum, worldwide, from c.1964. Possibly inspired by the song '(I want to put a) tiger in your tank' (by W. Dixon).*

**3**
Safety first.
*British Conservative Party slogan, General Election, 1929 – but earlier road safety use.*

**4**
Save water – bath with a friend.
*Semi-official slogan, UK, from mid-1970s.*

**5**
Say it with flowers.
*Slogan originally devised for the Society of American Florists, 1917.*

**6**
Second front now.
*Demand for invasion of the European mainland (with Soviet help), current 1942–3.*

**7**
Snap . . . crackle . . . pop!
*Line from Kellogg's Rice Krispies advertising, originally in the US, from c.1928.*

**8**
Someone, somewhere, wants a letter from you.
*UK Post Office slogan, 1960s.*

1
Stop me and buy one.
*Slogan for vendors of T. Walls & Sons ice cream, UK, from 1923.*

2
That'll do nicely, sir.
*UK ads. for American Express credit card, 1970s.*

3
That's a h\*\*l of a way to run a railroad!
*Advertising for Boston & Maine railroad (in the 1930s). Derived from cartoon in a US magazine (c.1932) showing two trains about to collide. A signalman comments: 'Tch-tch – what a way to run a railroad!'*

4
Thirteen wasted years (of Tory misrule).
*Unofficial Labour Party slogan, UK, prior to 1964 General Election.*

5
Today . . ., tomorrow the world!
*Probable origin is in 'Heute Presse der Nationalsozialitsen, Morgen Presse der Nation' ('Today the press of the Nazis, tomorrow the press of the nation'), slogan for the National Socialist Press in Germany, in the early 1930s.*

6
Top people take *The Times*.
*Slogan for the London paper, from 1957.*

7
Try it, you'll like it.
*Waiter encouraging customer to indulge himself, in Alka-Seltzer ads., US, from 1971.*

8
Votes for women.
*Slogan of the Women's Social and Political Union (suffragettes), in UK, from October 1905.*

1
Walls have ears.
*British wartime security slogan, early 1940s.*

2
The weekend starts here.
*UK TV pop show,* Ready, Steady, Go!, *from 1963.*

3
We never closed.
*Windmill Theatre, London, ref. to the Blitz in the Second World War.*

4
We shall overcome.
*From a song with a long history, revived 1946, becoming the civil rights anthem of the 1960s.*

5
We want eight and we won't wait.
*Popular cry in UK, 1908, for building of more Dreadnought battleships.*

6
When you got it, flaunt it.
*Line from advertising for US Braniff airline, c.1969.*

7
Where's the beef?
*Wendy Hamburgers, US, 1984.*

8
Which twin has the Toni?
*Headline from advertising for Toni home perms, originally US, from early 1950s.*

9
Who dares, wins.
*Motto of UK Special Air Service regiment, from 1940s on.*

1
Yesterday's men.
*Labour Party election slogan (referring to Conservative leaders),
1970.*

2
You don't have to be Jewish . . .
*Used to promote Levy's rye bread, US, from 1967 – but a show with
this title had run on Broadway in 1965.*

3
You'll wonder where the yellow went
When you brush your teeth with Pepsodent.
*Pepsodent toothpaste ads., US, from 1950s.*

4
You too can have a body like mine.
*Slogan for Charles Atlas body-building courses – originally in the US
– from 1920s on.*

5
Your country needs you!
*Advertisement on cover of* London Opinion, *5 September 1914, and
subsequently used on recruiting posters.*

6
Your king and country need you.
*Advertisement in newspapers, 5 August 1914.*

7
You're never alone with a Strand.
*Notably unsuccessful slogan for Strand cigarettes, UK, 1960.*

8
You've come a long way, baby.
*Virginia Slims cigarette ads., US, from 1968.*

9
You want the best seats, we have them.
*Keith Prowse ticket agency, UK, from 1925.*

## SMITH, Alfred E.
US politician
(1873–1944)

1

*Referring to Hearst press support for a rival:*
The kiss of death.
    Speech, 1926

2

*On the folly of attacking Government benefit programmes:*
Nobody shoots at Santa Claus
    Campaign speeches, 1936

3

No matter how thin you slice it, it's still baloney.
    *Ib.*

## SMITH, Bessie
US blues singer
(1894–1937)

4

When my bed is empty,
Makes me feel awful mean and blue.
My springs are getting rusty,
Living single like I do.
    Song, 'Empty Bed Blues' (*c.*1928)

## SMITH, Cyril
British Liberal politician
(1928–   )

5

If the fence is strong enough I'll sit on it.
    Quoted in the *Observer*, 15 September 1974

## SMITH, F.E.
(later 1st Earl of Birkenhead)
British lawyer and Liberal politician
(1872–1930)

1

*To judge who asked who George Robey was:*
Mr George Robey is the Darling of the music-halls, m'lud.
   Quoted in W. Churchill, *Great Contemporaries*

2

*When Labour MP J.H. Thomas complained he "ad a 'eadache':*
Try taking a couple of aspirates.
   Attrib.

3

*To judge who complained that he was no wiser at the end than when
he had started hearing one of Smith's cases:*
Possibly not, My Lord, but far better informed.
   Quoted in Birkenhead, *Life of F.E. Smith*

4

*On Winston Churchill:*
Winston has devoted the best years of his life to preparing his
impromptu speeches.
   Attrib.

5

The world continues to offer glittering prizes to those who have stout
hearts and sharp swords.
   Rectorial Address, Glasgow University, 7 November 1923

## SMITH, Ian
Rhodesian Prime Minister
(1919–   )

6

We have the happiest Africans in the world.
   Quoted in the *Observer*, 28 November 1971

1

Let me say again, I don't believe in black majority rule ever in Rhodesia. Not in a thousand years.

   Radio broadcast, 20 March 1976
*It came about in 1979.*


## SMITH, Logan Pearsall
US writer
(1865–1946)

2

Thank heavens, the sun has gone in, and I don't have to go out and enjoy it.

   *Afterthoughts* (1931)

3

People say that life is the thing, but I prefer reading.
   *Ib.*

4

A best-seller is the gilded tomb of a mediocre talent.
   Attrib.


## SMITH, Stevie
British poetess
(1902–71)

5

Not Waving, But Drowning.
   Title of poem (1957)


## SNAGGE, John
British broadcaster
(1904–   )

6

I don't know who's ahead – it's either Oxford or Cambridge.
   Radio commentary on Oxford and Cambridge University Boat Race, 1949

## SNOW, C.P.
(later Lord Snow)
British novelist and scientist
(1905–80)

1

The official world, the corridors of power, the dilemmas of conscience and egotism – she disliked them all.

*Homecomings* (1956)
*Snow later used 'Corridors of Power' as the title of a novel (1964).*

2

The Two Cultures and the Scientific Revolution.

Title of Rede Lecture, Cambridge (1959)
*'The two cultures' had been used earlier as the title of an article in the New Statesman (6 October 1956) and became a way of describing the lack of understanding between the camps of science and literature/religion.*

## SNOWDEN, Philip
(later Viscount Snowden)
British socialist politician
(1864–1937)

3

I hope you have read the Election programme of the Labour Party. It is the most fantastic and impracticable programme ever put before the electors . . . This is not Socialism. It is Bolshevism run mad.

Radio election broadcast, 17 October 1931
*Snowden, who had been Chancellor of the Exchequer in the 1929 Labour Government, was now supporting the National Government.*

## SOME LIKE IT HOT
*US film 1959. Script by Billy Wilder and I.A.L. Diamond. With Joe E. Brown.*

4

*Last line:*
*JEB (to Jack Lemmon who has confessed that he is not a woman):*

Nobody's perfect.
  Soundtrack


## SOMOZA, Anastasio
Nicaraguan dictator
(1925–80)


1
You won the elections. But I won the count.
  Quoted in the *Guardian*, 17 June 1977


# SONG TITLES

2
Another little drink wouldn't do us any harm
*By Clifford Grey, included in the show* The Bing Boys Are Here
(1916)

3
(If you want to know the time) Ask a p'liceman
*By E.W. Rogers (1864–1913).*

4
C'mon, baby, light my fire (1967)
*By Jim Morrison (1943–71).*

5
Down in the Forest (Something Stirred)
*Words by H. Simpson, music by Sir Landon Ronald.*

6
I Took My Harp to a Party (But Nobody Asked Me to Play)
*A Carter-Noel Gay composition.*

7
Life is just a bowl of cherries (1931)
*By Lew Brown in the musical* Scandals.

1
Naughty, but nice
*There is more than one song incorporating this idea, starting with 'It's naughty, but it's nice', a US song of the 1890s (Minnie Schultz sang it). It was used as a film title in 1939. There followed a Mercer/Warren composition for* Belle of New York *in 1952.*

2
Non, je ne regrette rien
*Lyrics by Michael Vaucaire. Popularized by Edith Piaf (1915–63).*

3
Open the door, Richard! (1947)
*Words by 'Dusty' Fletcher and John Mason.*

4
Pennies from Heaven
*Written by Johnny Burke. Music by A. Johnston.*

5
Praise the Lord, and pass the ammunition (1942)
*Used as the title of a song, this is supposed to have been said originally by an American naval chaplain during the Japanese attack on Pearl Harbor. Howell M. Forgy (1908–83) and W.H. Maguire are possible perpetrators.*

6
See you later, alligator (1956)
*Written by Robert Guidry.*

7
She's a Bird in a Gilded Cage
*Written by J. Lamb (1870–1928)*

8
There'll always be an England (1939)
*By Ross Parker and Hughie Charles.*

**1**
(Mais apart ça, Madame la Marquise) Tous va très bien (1936)
*By 'Misraki'.*

**2**
Where have all the flowers gone? (1961)
*By Pete Seeger (1919–  ).*

**3**
A Whiter Shade of Pale
*Written by Garry Brooker/Keith Reid and recorded by Procol Harum
(1967).*

## SOUTHERN, Terry
### US novelist
### (1924–  )

**4**
While the hopeless ecstasy of his huge pent-up spasm began . . . sweet
Candy's melodious voice rang out through the temple in truly mixed
feelings: 'GOOD GRIEF – IT'S DADDY!'
  *Candy* (1958).
*Last lines. Written with Mason Hoffenberg and originally published
as by 'Maxwell Kenton'.*

**5**
*She* says, 'Listen, who do I have to fuck to get *off* this picture?'
  *Blue Movie* (1970)
*Also attributed to Shirley Wood of NBC TV in the 1960s as 'Who do
you have to fuck to get out of show business?'*

## SPARK, Muriel
### British novelist
### (1918–  )

**6**
I am putting old heads on young shoulders . . . and all my pupils are
the crème de la crème.
  *The Prime of Miss Jean Brodie* (1961)

1

Give me a girl at an impressionable age, and she is mine for life.
   *Ib.*
*Compare the old Jesuit saying: 'Give us a child until it is seven and it is ours for life.'*


## SPENDER, Stephen
(later Sir Stephen)
British poet
(1909–   )

2

I think continually of those who were truly great –
The names of those who in their lives fought for life,
Who wore at their hearts the fire's centre.
   'I Think Continually of Those Who Were Truly Great' (1930–3)


## SPOONER, Rev. William
British academic
(1844–1930)

3

*To Oxford undergraduate after the First World War:*
Was it you or your brother who was killed in the war?
   Attrib.

4

Through a dark glassly . . .
   Attrib. by James Laver, in conversation with the author (1969)
*The word 'spoonerism' had already been coined by 1900 and most of the famous examples must have occurred by that date.*

5

*To Sir Julian Huxley:*
It is no further from the north coast of Spitsbergen to the North Pole than it is from Land's End to John of Gaunt.
   Quoted in W. Hayter, *Spooner*

1

Poor soul – very sad; her late husband, you know, a very sad death –
eaten by missionaries – poor soul.
  *Ib.*

## SPRING-RICE, Sir Cecil
### British diplomat and poet
### (1858–1918)

2

I vow to thee, my country – all earthly things above –
Entire and whole and perfect, the service of my love.
  'I Vow to Thee, My Country' (1918)

3

And there's another country, I've heard of long ago –
Most dear to them that love her, most great to them that know.
  *Ib.*

4

And her ways are ways of gentleness and all her paths are Peace.
  *Ib.*

## SQUIRE, Sir John
### British poet, essayist and critic
### (1884–1958)

5

I'm not so think as you drunk I am.
  'Ballad of Soporific Absorption'

## *STAGE DOOR*

*US film 1937. Script by Morrie Ryskind and Anthony Veiller, based
on a play by Edna Ferber and George S. Kaufman. With Katherine
Hepburn.*

6

*KH (in a play within the film):* The Calla lilies are in bloom again.
Such a strange flower, suitable to any occasion. I carried them on my
wedding day, and now I place them here in memory of something that
has died.
  Soundtrack

## STALIN, Joseph
Soviet communist leader
(1879–1953)

1

*Pierre Laval, French Foreign Minister, asked Stalin in 1935, 'Can't you do something to encourage religion and the Catholics in Russia? It would help me so much with the Pope.' Stalin replied:*
Oho! The Pope! How many divisions has he got?
    Quoted in W.S. Churchill, *The Second World War*

2

He who is not with us is against us.
    Attrib.

3

Gaiety is the most outstanding feature of the Soviet Union.
    Attrib.

## STALLINGS, Laurence
US writer
(1894–1968)

4

Hollywood – a place where the inmates are in charge of the asylum.
    Attrib.
*See also ROWLAND 371:1 and GEORGE, David Lloyd 187:3.*

## STANTON, Colonel Charles E.
US soldier
(1859–1933)

5

*On the arrival of the American Expeditionary Force in France:*
Here and now, in the presence of the illustrious dead, we pledge our hearts and our honour in carrying this war to a successful issue. Lafayette, we are here!
    Speech at tomb of Lafayette, Paris, 4 July 1917
*General Pershing may have originated the phrase, though – according to Bartlett – he disclaimed having said 'anything so splendid'.*

## STARTREK

*US TV science fiction series, from 1966–9. With William Shatner as Captain Kirk.*

1

Space – the final frontier. These are the voyages of the starship *Enterprise*. It's five-year mission: to explore strange new worlds, to seek out new life and new civilizations, to boldly go where no man has gone before.

　Introductory statement

2

*Kirk (to Lt. Commander 'Scotty' Scott, chief engineer):*
Beam me up, Scotty.

　Stock phrase

## STAR WARS

*US film 1977. Script by George Lucas.*

3

May the Force be with you.

　Repeated phrase

### STEFFENS, Lincoln
US journalist
(1866–1936)

4

*After a visit to the Soviet Union in 1919:*
I have seen the future and it works.

　*Autobiography* (1931)
*It is said that Steffens had been rehearsing this formula even before he went to the Soviet Union. Initially he said, 'I have been over into the future, and it works.'*

## STEIN, Gertrude
US poetess
(1874–1946)

**1**
Rose is a rose is a rose is a rose.
 'Sacred Emily' (1913)
*Frequently this is misquoted as 'A rose is etc'. It may refer to Sir
Francis Rose, an English painter.*

**2**
*Last words:*
What *is* the answer? . . . In that case, what is the question?
 Quoted in D. Sutherland, *G.S., a Biography of Her Work*
*There is more than one version of what she said.*

## STEINBECK, John
US writer
(1902–68)

**3**
*On critics:*
Unless the bastards have the courage to give you unqualified praise, I
say ignore them.
 Quoted in J.K. Galbraith, *A Life in Our Times*

## STEPTOE AND SON
*UK TV comedy series (BBC), from 1964–73. Script by Alan Simpson
and Ray Galton. With Harry S. Corbett as the Younger Steptoe.*

**4**
*Younger Steptoe (to father):* You dirty old man.
 Stock phrase

# STEVENSON, Adlai
US Democratic politician
(1900–1965)

1

Eggheads of the world unite; you have nothing to lose but your yolks.
Attrib. in 1952

*'Egghead' as a synonym for 'intellectual' was popularized by the columnist Joseph Alsop during the 1952 US Presidential campaign.*

2

I suppose flattery hurts no one – that is, if he doesn't inhale.
*Meet the Press*, TV broadcast, 29 March 1952

3

Someone asked me as I came down the street, how I felt, and I was reminded of a story that a fellow townsman used to tell – Abraham Lincoln. They asked him how he felt once after an unsuccessful election. He felt like a little boy who had stubbed his toe in the dark. He said that he was too old to cry, but it hurt too much to laugh.
Speech, conceding defeat, 5 November 1952

4

A politician is a statesman who approaches every question with an open mouth.
Attrib.

*Also ascribed to Arthur Goldberg, on diplomats.*

5

*Of the Republican Party:*
[Needs to be] dragged kicking and screaming into the twentieth century.
Quoted in K. Tynan, *Curtains*

# STOCKWOOD, Mervyn
British Anglican bishop
(1913–   )

6

A psychiatrist is a man who goes to the Folies-Bergère and looks at the audience.
Quoted in the *Observer*, 15 October 1961

### STORY, Jack Trevor
British novelist
(1917–  )

**1**
Live Now, Pay Later.
  Title of screenplay (1962)

### STRACHEY, Lytton
British biographer
(1880–1932)

**2**
*When appearing before military tribunal as a conscientious objector in the First World War, he was asked what he would do if he saw a German soldier trying to rape his sister. He replied:*
I would try to get between them.
  Quoted in R. Graves, *Goodbye To All That*

### SULLIVAN, 'Big Tim'
US trade union leader

**3**
I don't care what the papers say about me as long as they spell my name right.
  Quoted in W. Safire, *Political Dictionary*

### *THE SUN*
*London newspaper*

**4**
GOTCHA!
  Headline, 4 May 1982 (first edition only)
*On the sinking of the Argentine cruiser* General Belgrano *during the Falklands war.*

### *SUNSET BOULEVARD*

*US film 1950. Script by Charles Brackett, Billy Wilder and D.M.*
*Marshman. With Gloria Swanson as Norma Desmond and William*
*Holden as Joe Gillis.*

1
*Joe:* You used to be big in pictures.
*Norma:* I *am* big. It's the pictures that got small.
  Soundtrack

## SVEVO, Italo
### Italian novelist
### (1861–1928)

2
There are three things I always forget. Names, faces, and – the third I
can't remember.
  Attrib.

## SWAFFER, Hannen
### British journalist
### (1879–1962)

3
Freedom of the press in Britain is freedom to print such of the
proprietor's prejudices as the advertisers don't object to.
  In conversation with Tom Driberg, *c.*1928

## SYLVESTER, Victor
### British ballroom orchestra conductor
### (1902–78)

4
Slow, slow, quick, quick, slow [foxtrot tempo].
  Stock phrase

# T

## TAKE IT FROM HERE
*UK radio comedy series (BBC), from 1948 on. Script by Frank Muir and Denis Norden. With Jimmy Edwards, Dick Bentley as Ron and June Whitfield as Eth.*

1
*Edwards:* Black mark, Bentley!
   Catchphrase

2
*Edwards:* Gently, Bentley!
   Catchphrase

3
*Eth:* Oh, Ron . . .
*Ron:* Yes, Eth?
   Catchphrase in 'The Glums' sketches

## TARZAN THE APE MAN
*US film 1932. Script by Ivor Novello. With Johnny Weissmuller as Tarzan.*

4
## Me Tarzan, you Jane.
*In fact he says simply 'Tarzan . . . Jane'. Nor does the line occur in the original novel by Edgar Rice Burroughs.*

### TEBBIT, Norman
British Conservative politician
(1931– )

5
*Of his father who had grown up in the 1930s:*
He didn't riot. He got on his bike and looked for work and he kept looking till he found it.
   Speech, Conservative Party Conference, 15 October 1981
*A recipe for dealing with unemployment, popularly rendered as 'Get on yer bike'.*

## TELEGRAMS AND CABLES

1

HAVE STRONG SUSPICIONS THAT CRIPPEN LONDON CELLAR MURDERER AND ACCOMPLICE ARE AMONGST SALOON PASSENGERS MOUSTACHE TAKEN OFF GROWING BEARD ACCOMPLICE DRESSED AS BOY VOICE MANNER AND BUILD UNDOUBTEDLY A GIRL BOTH TRAVELLING AS MR AND MASTER ROBINSON.

From Captain Kendall to Scotland Yard, 22 July 1910
*This was the first time a wireless telegraphy message from a ship at sea led to the apprehension of criminals.*

2

*Magazine editor to Cary Grant's agent: HOW OLD CARY GRANT?*
*Grant: OLD CARY GRANT FINE. HOW YOU?*
*Probably apocryphal*

3

WINSTON'S BACK.
*Signal to all ships of the Royal Navy from the Admiralty when Winston Churchill was reappointed First Lord, 3 September 1939.*

4

VERY SORRY CAN'T COME. LIE FOLLOWS BY POST.
*Lord Charles Beresford (1846–1919) to the Prince of Wales after receiving a dinner invitation at short notice. The same joke occurs in Proust, Le Temps Retrouvé (1927), as 'Impossible venir, mensonge suit.'*

5

TO HELL WITH YOU. OFFENSIVE LETTER FOLLOWS.
*To Sir Alec Douglas-Home.*

6

SPREAD ALARM AND DESPONDENCY.
*Wireless message to Vladimir Peniakoff c.18 May 1942 (using phrase from Army Acts).*

See also BENCHLEY 50:6, CHESTERTON 97:1, COWARD 120:6, and PARKER 334:1.

# TELEVISION PROGRAMME TITLES

**1**
The Last of the Summer Wine
*This was writer Roy Clarke's provisional title for the series, it stuck, and it is not a quotation.*

**2**
Murder, She Wrote
*US series (mid-1980s) featuring Angela Lansbury as a crime writer. Originally, the title was given to a 1961 film of Agatha Christie's story 4.50 from Paddington. In turn this title must echo that of Frank Loesser song, 'Murder, He Says' (see 279:4), also the title of a film in 1945.*

**3**
The Name of the Game
*This US series (1968–71) grew out of the TV movie* Fame Is the Name of the Game *(1966) and helped launch a cliché phrase of the late 1960s.*

**4**
Not So Much a Programme, More a Way of Life
*A fairly original coinage which spawned many a 'Not so much a . . .' derivative.*

**5**
Only Fools and Horses
*From an old Cockney expression, 'Only fools and horses work.'*

**6**
Only in America
*This short series (1980) concerned immigration to the US and indeed this is the 'immigrants' testament', especially used by those of Jewish stock. It is an exclamation short for 'Only in America could this happen . . .'*

1
Softly, Softly
*'Softly, softly, catchee monkee' has been described as a Negro proverb. More particularly, in this case, the title derives from the saying's use as motto of the Lancashire Constabulary Training School which inspired the TV series.*

2
Some Mothers Do 'Ave 'Em
*An old Northern English expression, popularized in the 1950s and 60s by the comedian Jimmy Clitheroe (1916–73) in radio shows as 'Don't some mothers 'ave 'em?'*

## THATCHER, Margaret
British Conservative Prime Minister
(1925–    )

3
I owe nothing to Women's Lib.
    Attrib. in the *Observer*, 1 December 1974

4
Ladies and gentlemen, I stand before you tonight in my green chiffon evening gown, my face softly made up, my fair hair gently waved . . . the Iron Lady of the Western World. Me? A cold war warrior? Well, yes – if that is how they wish to interpret my defence of values, and freedoms fundamental to our way of life.
    Speech, Dorking, 31 January 1976
*Reacting to Soviet criticism contained in the paper* Red Star *which invented the name 'Iron Lady', although she had been referred to as 'the Iron Maiden' in the UK before this.*

5
Let us make this a country safe to work in. Let us make this a country safe to walk in. Let us make it a country safe to grow up in. Let us make it a country safe to grow old in. And [the message of the 'other'

Britain] says, above all, may this land of ours, which we love so much, find dignity and greatness and peace again.

Political broadcast, 30 April 1979

*The final sentence contains an unattributed quotation from Noel Coward. See 121:6.*

1

(There is no easy popularity in that but I believe people accept) there is no alternative.

Speech, Conservative Women's Conference, 21 May 1980

*'That' refers to her economic policies which included harsh measures such as cuts in public spending, increased unemployment, etc. Sometimes rendered by the acronym: 'TINA'.*

2

To those waiting with bated breath for that favourite media catchphrase, the U-turn, I have only one thing to say. You turn if you want to. The lady's not for turning.

Speech, Conservative Party Conference, 1980

3

Failure? Do you remember what Queen Victoria once said? 'Failure? – the possibilities do not exist.'

TV news interview, at start of Falklands War, 5 April 1982

*Queen Victoria had been speaking during the 'Black Week' of the Boer War in December 1899 when British forces were being repulsed.*

4

*On the recapture of South Georgia, to newsmen outside 10 Downing Street:*

Just rejoice at that news and congratulate our forces and the Marines. Goodnight. Rejoice!

TV news coverage, 25 April 1982

5

*On her feelings in church the Sunday after she had escaped death in the IRA bomb explosion at Brighton:*

This was the day I was meant not to see.

TV interview, October 1984

1
*On reviewing candidates for appointments:*
Is he one of us?
   Attrib.


### THAT WAS THE WEEK THAT WAS
*UK TV satire series (BBC), 1962–3. Scripts by various.*

2
That Was The Week That Was.
   Title
*Said to have been suggested by the actor John Bird in imitation of the
'That's Shell – That Was' advertisements dating from the early 1930s.*

3
Well, it was satire, wasn't it? . . . You can say bum, you can say po,
you can say anything . . . Well, he said it! The thin one! He said bum
one night. I heard him! Satire!
   Sketch, 'Close Down' (by Keith Waterhouse and Willis Hall)

*See also FROST 178:3.*


### THEROUX, Paul
US writer
(1941–   )

4
Ever since childhood, when I lived within earshot of the Boston and
Maine, I have seldom heard a train go by and not wished I was on it.
   *The Great Railway Bazaar* (1975)

### THE THIRD MAN

*UK film 1949. Script by Graham Greene and Carol Reed. With Orson Welles as Harry Lime.*

1

*Harry Lime:* You know what the fellow said – in Italy, for thirty years under the Borgias, they had warfare, terror, murder and bloodshed, but they produced Michelangelo, Leonardo da Vinci and the Renaissance. In Switzerland, they had brotherly love; they had five hundred years of democracy and peace – and what did that produce? The cuckoo clock.
    Soundtrack.
*Welles contributed this part of the script, as Graham Greene confirmed to the author (1978).*

## THOMAS, Dylan
Welsh poet
(1914–53)

2

And Death Shall Have No Dominion.
    Title of poem (1943)

3

Time held me green and dying
Though I sang in my chains like the sea.
    'Fern Hill' (1946)

4

Do not go gentle into that good night.
Rage, rage against the dying of the light.
    'Do Not Go Gentle Into That Good Night' (1952)

5

It is spring, moonless night in the small town, starless and bible-black.
    *Under Milk Wood* (1954)

**1**
The land of my fathers – my fathers can have it.
Quoted in J. Ackerman, *Dylan Thomas*

**2**
Someone's boring me. I think it's me.
Quoted in R. Heppenstall, *Four Absentees* (1960)

**3**
An alcoholic is someone you don't like who drinks as much as you do.
Attrib.

**4**
*Boast to girlfriend towards the end of his life:*
I've had eighteen straight whiskies. I think that's the record . . . After thirty-nine years, this is all I've done.
Attrib.
*He had probably only had four or five.*

### THOMAS, George
(later Viscount Tonypandy)
British Labour politician)
(1909–    )

**5**
*As Speaker of the House of Commons:*
Order, order!
*The traditional cry became very much his own when radio broadcasts of proceedings in Parliament began on 3 April 1978.*

### THOMPSON, William Hale 'Big Bill'
US politician and Mayor of Chicago
(1867–1944)

**6**
*If ever King George V were to set foot in Chicago:*
## I'd punch him in the snoot.
*No direct quotation exists of what he did say when running for a third term in 1927 – 'poke in the snoot', 'bust in the snoot' are other reported versions – but his Anglophobia was very real.*

### THOMSON, Roy
(later Lord Thomson)
Canadian-born industrialist
(1894–1976)

1

*To a neighbour in Edinburgh just after the opening of Scottish Television (a commercial TV company he had founded) in August 1957:*
You know, it's just like having a licence to print your own money.
   Quoted in R. Braddon, *Roy Thomson*

### THORPE, Jeremy
British Liberal politician
(1929–   )

2

*On Harold Macmillan's 'Night of the Long Knives', when he sacked half his Cabinet, 1962:*
Greater love hath no man than this, that he lay down his friends for his life.
   Speech, House of Commons, 1962

3

*After a General Election which resulted in no party having a clear majority:*
Looking around the House, one realizes that we are all minorities now.
   Speech, House of Commons, 6 March 1974

4

*To Norman Scott:*
Bunnies *can* (and *will*) go to France.
   Private letter dated 13 February 1961, published 1976
*Scott later alleged they had had a homosexual relationship. Thorpe was acquitted in 1979 of plotting to murder Scott.*

## THURBER, James
US cartoonist and writer
(1894–1961)

1

All right, have it your way – you heard a seal bark.
Caption to cartoon 'The Seal in the Bedroom' (1932)

2

Early to rise and early to bed makes a male healthy and wealthy and dead.
'The Shrike and the Chipmunks', *Fables for Our Time* (1940)

3

It's a Naive Domestic Burgundy without Any Breeding, But I Think You'll be Amused by its Presumption.
Caption to cartoon in *Men, Women and Dogs* (1943)

4

Well, if I Called the Wrong Number, Why Did You Answer the Phone?
*Ib.*


## TILL DEATH US DO PART
*UK TV comedy series (BBC), from 1964–74. Script by Johnny Speight. With Warren Mitchell as Alf Garnett.*

5

*Alf (to his wife):* You silly (old) moo!
Catchphrase


## TIME
*US news magazine*

6

World War II began last week at 5.20 a.m. (Polish time) Friday, September 1, when a German bombing plane dropped a projectile on Puck, fishing village and air base in the armpit of the Hel Peninsula.
Report, 11 September 1939
*Others, more cautiously, were only talking of 'the war in Europe' at this time.*

## THE TIMES
London newspaper

1

On the accession of King Edward VII:
We shall not pretend that there is nothing in his long career which those who respect and admire him would wish otherwise.
  Leading article, January 1901

2

\#\#   Small earthquake in Chile. Not many dead.
  Quoted in C. Cockburn, *I Claud*
*Cockburn claimed to have won a competition for dullness among sub-editors with this headline in the 1930s. However, an exhaustive search has failed to find it in the paper.*

3

IT *IS* A MORAL ISSUE
  Title of leading article about the Profumo affair, 11 June 1963

4

At social gatherings he was liable to engage in heated and noisy arguments which could ruin a dinner party, and made him the dread of hostesses on both sides of the Atlantic. The tendency was exacerbated by an always generous, and occasionally excessive alcoholic intake.
  Obituary of Randolph Churchill, 7 June 1968
*Said to have been written by Malcolm Muggeridge.*

5

Lord George-Brown drunk is a better man than the Prime Minister [Harold Wilson] sober.
  Leading article, 6 March 1976


## THE TIMES LITERARY SUPPLEMENT
London journal

6

*Reviewing Kenneth Grahame's* The Wind in the Willows *(1908):*
As a contribution to natural history, the work is negligible.
  Quoted in Green, *The Life of Kenneth Grahame*

### TO BE OR NOT TO BE

*US film 1942. Script by Edwin Justis Mayer. With Jack Benny as Joseph Tura, Sig Rumann as Colonel Ehrhardt.*

1

*Ehrhardt (to Tura, in disguise):* What he [Tura] did to Shakespeare, we are doing now to Poland.

   Soundtrack

2

*Tura (disguised as Ehrhardt):* So, they call me Concentration Camp Ehrhardt?!

   Soundtrack

### TO HAVE AND HAVE NOT

*US film 1945. Script by Jules Furthman and William Faulkner from the novel by Ernest Hemingway. With Lauren Bacall as Slim and Humphrey Bogart as Steve.*

3

*Slim:* You know you don't have to act with me, Steve. You don't have to say anything, and you don't have to do anything. Not a thing. Oh, maybe just whistle. You know how to whistle, don't you, Steve? You just put your lips together and blow.

   Soundtrack

### TOLKIEN, J.R.R.
British novelist and academic
(1892–1973)

4

In a hole in the ground there lived a hobbit.

   *The Hobbit* (1937)

1

Nearly all marriages, even happy ones, are mistakes: in the sense that almost certainly (in a more perfect world, or even with a little more care in this very imperfect one) both partners might have found more suitable mates. But the real soul-mate is the one you are actually married to.

Letter to Michael Tolkien, 6–8 March 1941

## TOMALIN, Nicholas
British journalist
(1931–73)

2

The only qualities essential for real success in journalism are rat-like cunning, a plausible manner, and a little literary ability.

Article in the *Sunday Times Magazine*, 26 October 1969

## *TO TELL THE TRUTH*
*US TV panel game, from 1956–66.*

3

*Host:* Will the real [*person's name*], please stand up!
   Stock phrase
*The panel tried to guess which two of three challengers were impostors.*

## TOYNBEE, Arnold
British historian
(1889–1975)

4

*Pressing for a greater British voice in UNO, 1947:*
No annihilation without representation.
   Attrib.

1

America is a large, friendly dog in a very small room. Every time it wags its tail it knocks over a chair.

Attrib.

## TOYTOWN

*UK radio children's drama series (BBC), 1940s/50s. Scripts from books by S. Hulme-Beaman. With Ralph de Rohan as Mr Grouser and Derek McCulloch as Larry the Lamb.*

2

*Mr Growser:* It is disgraceful – it ought not to be allowed.

Stock phrase

3

*Larry (bleating):* Larry the Lammmmb!

Stock phrase

### TREE, Sir Herbert Beerbohm
British actor-manager
(1853–1917)

4

Sir, I have tested your machine [a gramophone]. It adds new terror to life and makes death a long-felt want.

Quoted in H. Pearson, *Beerbohm Tree*

5

*Pointing at stamp in middle of sheet, at Post Office:*
I'll have that one, please.

Ib.

6

*To man carrying a grandfather clock:*
My poor fellow, why not carry a watch?

Ib.

1
My nose bleeds for you.
   *Ib.*

2
*Of Israel Zangwill:*
He is an old bore; even the grave yawns for him.
   *Ib.*

3
A committee should consist of three men, two of whom are absent.
   *Ib.*

4
*To unsuitable actresses:*
Ladies, just a little more virginity, if you don't mind.
   Attrib.


### TRINDER, Tommy
### British comedian
### (1909–   )

5
You lucky people!
   Catchphrase


### TROUP, Bobby
### US songwriter
### (1919–   )

6
If you ever plan to motor west,
Travel my way, take the highway, that's the best,
Get your kicks on Route 66.
   Song, 'Route 66' (1946)

## TRUMAN, Harry S.
US Democratic President
(1884–1972)

1

*To journalists, on succeeding F.D. Roosevelt:*
I don't know whether you fellows ever had a load of hay fall on you,
but when they told me yesterday what had happened, I felt like the
moon, the stars, and all the planets had fallen on me.
Attrib.

2

If you can't stand the heat, get out of the kitchen.
Quoted *Time*, 28 April 1952
*Possibly a cleaned-up version of an earlier expression, referring to
another room in the house.*

3

The buck stops here.
Motto
*On a sign displayed on his desk in the Oval Office.*

4

*To Omar Bradley, of General MacArthur:*
The son of a bitch isn't going to resign on me, I want him fired.
Attrib.
*When Truman sacked MacArthur from his command of UN forces in
Korea, 1951.*

5

It's a recession when your neighbour loses his job: it's a depression
when you lose yours.
Quoted in the *Observer*, 13 April 1958

## 'TWAIN, Mark'
US writer
(1835–1910)

6

Golf is a good walk spoiled.
Attrib.

1
Always do right. This will gratify some people, and astonish the rest.
  Talk to young people, Brooklyn, 16 February 1901

2
*Quoting Disraeli:*
There are lies, damn lies – and statistics.
  *Autobiography* (1924)


## THE TWO RONNIES
*UK TV comedy series, from 1970s on. Script by various. With
Ronnie Barker and Ronnie Corbett.*

3
*Corbett:* It's goodnight from me . . .
*Barker:* And it's goodnight from him.
  Stock closing routine


## 2001: A SPACE ODYSSEY
*UK film 1968. Script by Stanley Kubrick and Arthur C. Clarke. With
Keir Dullea as David Bowman.*

4
*Stranded astronaut Dave, to computer:* Open the pod-bay doors, Hal!
  Soundtrack


## TYNAN, Kenneth
British critic
(1927–80)

5
*On Noel Coward (1953):*
Forty years ago he was Slightly in Peter Pan, and you might say that he
has been wholly in Peter Pan ever since.
  *Curtains* (1961)

1

Even the youngest of us will know, in fifty years' time, exactly what we mean by 'a very Noel Coward sort of person'.

*Ib.*

2

*On Greta Garbo (1953):*

What, when drunk, one sees in other women, one sees in Garbo sober.

*Ib.*

# U

## UPTON, Ralph R.

**1**
*Notice at US railway crossings, 1912:*
Stop; look; listen.
   Quoted in R. Hyman, *Dictionary of Famous Quotations*


## USTINOV, Peter
### British actor and writer
### (1921–   )

**2**
A diplomat these days is nothing but a head-waiter who's allowed to sit down occasionally.
   *Romanoff and Juliet* (1956)

# V

## VALENTI, Jack
US film executive and Presidential aide
(1921–   )

1

I sleep each night a little better, a little more confidently, because Lyndon Johnson is my President. For I know he lives and thinks and works to make sure that for all America and, indeed, the growing body of the free world, the morning shall always come.

   Speech, Boston, June 1965

## *VARIETY*
*US show business newspaper*

2

*On the Wall Street crash:*
WALL ST. LAYS AN EGG
   Headline, 30 October 1929

3

STICKS NIX HICKS PIX.
   Headline, 1920s?
*Meaning that cinema-goers in rural areas were not attracted to films with bucolic themes.*

4

EGGHEAD WEDS HOURGLASS.
   Headline, 1956
*On marriage of playwright Arthur Miller to Marilyn Monroe.*

## VAUGHAN, Norman
British comedian
(1927–   )

**1**
Dodgy!
  Catchphrase, from 1960s

**2**
Swingin'!
  Catchphrase, from 1960s

**3**
A touch of the . . .
  Stock format phrase

## VICTORIA, HM Queen
British sovereign
(1819–1901)

**4**
*Last word:*
Bertie!
  Attrib.
*Referring to her son and heir, Albert Edward, rather than to Prince Albert, her late husband.*

## VIDAL, Gore
US novelist
(1925–   )

**5**
*When asked whether the first person he had slept with was male or female:*
I was far too polite to ask.
  Attrib.

**1**

Never miss a chance to have sex or appear on television.
  Attrib.

**2**

*On William F. Buckley Jnr:*
Looks and sounds not unlike Hitler, but without the charm.
  Attrib.

**3**

*Of Edward F. Kennedy:*
Every country should have at least one King Farouk.
  Attrib.

**4**

Whenever a friend succeeds, a little something in me dies.
  Quoted in *Sunday Times Magazine*, 16 September 1973

## VON STERNBERG, Joseph
Austrian-born film director
(1894–1969)

**5**

*On Hollywood:*
You can seduce a man's wife there, attack his daughter and wipe your
hands on his canary, but if you don't like his movie, you're dead.
  Attrib.

## VON ZELL, Harry
US broadcaster and actor
(1906–81)

**6**

*Introducing radio broadcast by President Herbert Hoover:*
Ladies and gentlemen – the President of the United States, Hoobert
Herver.
  Quoted in *Current Biography* (1944)

## VREELAND, Diana
US fashion journalist
(1906– )

1
*Speaking in 1965:*
I love London. It is the most swinging city in the world at the moment.

Quoted in B. Hillier, *The Style of the Century 1900–1980*
*As a result of this remark, the* Weekend Telegraph *ran an article on 30 April 1965 which probably put together the words 'Swinging London' for the first time.*

2
[The] beautiful people.

Coinage attrib. in *Current Biography* (1978)

# W

## WALKER, James J.
### US politician and Mayor of New York
### (1881–1946)

1

A reformer is a guy who rides through a sewer in a glass-bottomed boat.
  Speech, New York, 1928

## WALLACE, George
### US Democratic politician
### (1919–  )

2

Segregation now, segregation tomorrow and segregation forever.
  Inaugural speech as Governor of Alabama, January 1963

3

Pointy-headed intellectuals who can't park their bicycles straight.
  Customary jibe
*Sometimes it was 'pointed-headed professors'.*

4

Send them a message.
  Slogan when campaigning for the Presidency (1972)
*An invitation to vote symbolically when a candidate has little chance of winning.*

## WALLACE, Henry
### US Democratic Vice-President
### (1888–1965)

5

The century on which we are entering – the century which will come out of this war – can be and must be the century of the common man.
  Speech, 8 May 1942

## WARHOL, Andy
US artist
(1927–    )

1

In the future everyone will be world-famous for fifteen minutes.
  Exhibition catalogue, Stockholm (1968)

## WARING, Eddie
British broadcaster
(1909–86)

2

Up and under!
  Stock phrase
*A Rugby League football term, used by him in TV commentaries.*

## WARNER, Jack
British actor and entertainer
(1895–1981)

3

Mind my bike!
  Catchphrase, *Garrison Theatre*, BBC Radio, 1940s

4

Evenin' all.
  Stock phrase
*As 'PC George Dixon' in BBC series* Dixon of Dock Green *(1955–76).*

## WATERGATE TRANSCRIPTS

5

Expletive deleted.
  Stock phrase
*Used when deleting an obscenity from transcripts of conversations between President Nixon and his aides, published as* The White House Transcripts *(1974).*

## WATERHOUSE, Keith
British journalist and novelist
(1929– )

1

I cannot bring myself to vote for a woman who has been voice-trained to speak to me as though my dog has just died.
  Attrib. 1979

*See also* THAT WAS THE WEEK THAT WAS *424:3.*

## WAUGH, Evelyn
British novelist
(1903–66)

2

Mr Salter's side of the conversation was limited to expressions of assent. When Lord Copper was right he said, 'Definitely, Lord Copper'; when he was wrong, 'Up to a point.'
  *Scoop* (1938)

3

Feather-footed through the plashy fen passes the questing vole.
  *Ib.*

4

'I have been here before,' I said; I had been there before; first with Sebastian more than twenty years ago on a cloudless day in June, when the ditches were creamy with meadowsweet and the air heavy with all the scents of summer.
  *Brideshead Revisited* (1945)

5

*On Winston Churchill:*
Simply a radio personality who outlived his prime.
  Quoted in C. Sykes, *Evelyn Waugh*

1
*When Randolph Churchill went into hospital to have a lung removed
and the trouble was not malignant:*
A typical triumph of modern science to find the only part of Randolph
that was not malignant and remove it.
   *Diaries* (entry for March 1964)

### WEBB, Jim
US songwriter
(1946–   )

2
Someone left the cake out in the rain.
I don't think that I can take it
'Cos it took so long to bake it
And I'll never have that recipe again. Oh no.
   Song, 'MacArthur Park' (1968)

3
Up, Up and Away.
   Title of song (1967)

### WEBB, Sidney
(later Lord Passfield)
British socialist writer
(1859–1947)

4
The inevitability of gradualness.
   Speech to Labour Party Conference, 1920

## WEIGHELL, Sidney
British trade union leader
(1922– )

1

If you want it to go out . . . that you now believe in the philosophy of the pig trough – those with the biggest snouts get the largest share – I reject it.

Speech at Labour Party Conference, Blackpool, 6 October 1978

2

I don't see how we can talk with Mrs Thatcher . . . I will say to the lads, come on, get your snouts in the trough.

Remark, London, 10 April 1979

## WEINER, Herb
US songwriter

3

Nobody knows where my Johnny has gone.

Song, 'It's My Party' (1963)
*Written with John Gluck Jr and Wally Gold.*

4

It's my party and I'll cry if I want to.

*Ib.*

## WELLES, Orson
US film director and actor
(1915–85)

5

*On seeing a Hollywood studio:*
It's the biggest train set a boy ever had.

Attrib.

*See also* CITIZEN KANE *pp. 109–10 and* THE THIRD MAN *p. 425.*

## WELLS, H.G.
British novelist and writer
(1866–1946)

**1**

\#\#   The war to end wars.
*The actual title of Wells's book was* The War That Will End War *(1914).*

**2**

\#\#   In the country of the blind the one-eyed man is king.
*Wells wrote a story with the title* The Country of the Blind *(1904) but the saying dates back to the sixteenth century at least.*

**3**

The Shape of Things to Come.
   Title of book (1933)

## WESKER, Arnold
British playwright
(1932–   )

**4**

Chips With Everything.
   Title of play (1962)
*Popularized the expression.*

## WEST, Mae
US film actress
(1892–1980)

**5**

*Replying to exclamation, 'Goodness, what beautiful diamonds!':*
Goodness had nothing to do with it, dearie.
   *Night After Night* (1932)
*Film script by Vincent Laurence, from novel by Louis Bromfield.*

1
## Come up and see me some time.
*In the film* She Done Him Wrong *(1933), based on her play* Diamond Lil, *what she said was: 'Why don't you come up some time and see me?' In later films, she used the catchphrase in the easier-to-say form.*

2
Tall, dark and handsome.
*Also used in* She Done Him Wrong, *but not original to Mae West.*

3
Beulah, peel me a grape.
  *I'm No Angel* (1933)

4
It's not the men in my life, but the life in my men that counts.
  Attrib.

5
I always say, keep a diary and some day it'll keep you.
  Attrib.

6
Marriage is a great institution, but I'm not ready for an institution yet.
  Attrib.

7
Is that a gun in your pocket or are you just pleased to see me?
  Attrib.


## WEST, Rebecca
(later Dame Rebecca)
British writer
(1892–1983)

8
*On H.G. Wells:*
The Old Maid among novelists; even the sex obsession that lay clotted

on Ann Veronica and The New Machiavelli like cold white sauce was merely Old Maid's mania.

In *Freewoman*, 19 September 1912


1
She said she was attracted [to H.G. Wells] because he smelt of walnuts.

Reference in the *Guardian*, 16 March 1983


2
*Of Michael Arlen:*
Every other inch a gentleman.

Attrib.

*Also attributed to Alexander Woollcott.*


## WESTMINSTER GAZETTE
### London newspaper

3
*Correct challenge to win a newspaper cash prize:*
You are Mr Lobby Lud – I claim the *Westminster Gazette* prize.

First used 1 August 1927

*Later adopted and adapted by other papers.*


## WHAT'S MY LINE?
### US TV panel game, from 1950 onwards.

4
*Host:* Would the next challenger sign in, please?

Stock phrase


5
*Steve Allen (panellist):* Is it bigger than a breadbox?

Stock question

# WHEELER, Jimmy
British comedian
(1910–73)

**1**
Aye, aye, that's yer lot!
 Catchphrase

# WHEELER, Sir Mortimer
British archaeologist
(1890–1976)

**2**
The archaeologist is digging up not *things*, but people.
 *Archaeology from the Earth* (1954)

# WHELDON, Sir Huw
British boadcaster and TV executive
(1916–86)

**3**
*Advice to TV producers:*
The crime is not to avoid failure. The crime is not to give triumph a
chance.
 Attrib.
*Often encapsulated as 'The right to fail'.*

**4**
The job of the producer is to pursue excellence – to take his subject
and tell it as a tale.
 Attrib.

## WHITE, E.B.
US humorist
(1899–1985)

1

*A mother at table says, 'It's broccoli, dear,' and her daughter replies:*
I say it's spinach, and I say the hell with it.
   The *New Yorker*, 8 December 1928
*Caption for cartoon by Carl Rose.*

2

Across the Street and Into the Bar.
   Title of satire on Ernest Hemingway.
*See HEMINGWAY 221:6.*

## WHITE HEAT
*US film 1949. Script by various. With James Cagney as Cody Jarrett.*

3

*Cody:* Made it, Ma, [to the top] of the world.
*Last words of character, shooting it out from the top of an oil tank.*

## WHITEHORN, Katharine
British journalist
(1928–   )

4

*On making rude noises:*
If there is nothing you can do by constriction of throat or rectum to
head them off, try to move away from the group you are with ('I must
find an ashtray' or 'I *say*, look at that squirrel!') and create
diversionary noises – snap a handbag, scrape a foot. Tummy rumbles
are for some reason more OK – laugh if you can.
   *Whitehorn's Social Survival* (1968)

1

Outside every thin girl there is a fat man trying to get in.
    Revived by her on *Quote . . . Unquote*, BBC Radio, 27 July 1985

### WHITELAW, William
(later Viscount Whitelaw)
British Conservative politician
(1918–   )

2

*Of Harold Wilson:*
He is going round the country stirring up apathy.
    Variously cited 1974/5

3

## A short, sharp shock.
    Speech, Conservative Party Conference, 10 October 1979
*Referring to method of hard treatment for young offenders. This expression had been used by Home Secretaries before him and is a quotation from W.S. Gilbert,* The Mikado *(1885).*

### WHITING, G.
US songwriter

4

When You're All Dressed Up and No Place to Go.
    Title of song (1912).
*Popularized by US comedian Raymond Hitchcock (c.1915).*

## WHITLAM, Gough
### Australian Labour Prime Minister
### (1916–   )

1

*After the Governor-General's secretary had read a proclamation dissolving Parliament, effectively dismissing Whitlam as Prime Minister:*
Well may we say 'God Save the Queen', because nothing will save the Governor-General . . . Maintain your rage and your enthusiasm through the campaign for the election now to be held and until polling day.

   Speech, Canberra, 11 November 1975

## WILDER, Billy
### US film director
### (1906–   )

2

*On actor, Cliff Osmond:*
He has Van Gogh's ear for music.
   Attrib.

3

*On working with Marilyn Monroe:*
It was like going to the dentist making a picture with her. It was hell at the time, but after it was all over, it was wonderful.
   Quoted in E. Wilson, *The Show Business Nobody Knows*

## WILHELM II, Kaiser
### German Emperor
### (1859–1941)

4

We have fought for our place in the sun and won it. Our future is on the water.
   Speech at Elbe, June 1901
*The phrase 'place in the sun', referring to German colonial ambitions, had been coined by Count von Bülow in 1897.*

1

*When an English visitor told him that Edward VII was at Windsor Castle:*

Ah, I thought he was boating with his grocer [Sir Thomas Lipton].

  Quoted in W. Churchill, *Great Contemporaries*

*An example of his contempt for the English monarch.*


2

## It is my Royal and Imperial command that you concentrate your energies for the immediate present upon one single purpose, and that is that you address all your skill and all the valour of my soldiers to exterminate first, the treacherous English [and] walk over General French's contemptible little army.

  Quoted in BEF Routine Orders, 24 September 1914

*Giving rise to the BEF nickname 'The Old Contemptibles', this order appears never to have been given by the Kaiser – indeed, he later denied doing so – and it is now accepted that it was a propaganda ploy devised at the War Office by Sir Frederick Maurice.*


## WILLANS, Geoffrey
### British writer
### (1911–58)

3

This is me e.g. nigel molesworth the curse of st custard's which is the skool i am at. It is uterly wet and weedy . . .

  The only good things about skool are the BOYS wizz who are noble brave fearless etc. although you hav various swots, bulies, cissies, milksops, greedy guts and oiks with whom i am forced to mingle hem-hem.

  In fact any skool is a bit of a shambles
        AS YOU WILL SEE.

  *Down With Skool!* (with Ronald Searle) (1953)


4

There is no better xsample of a goody-goody than fotherington-tomas in the world in space. You kno he is the one who sa Hullo Clouds Hullo Sky and skip about like a girly.

  *How To Be Topp* (1954)

## WILLIAM, Capt. Lloyd S.
US soldier

1

*When advised by the French to retreat, shortly after his arrival at the Western Front in the First World War:*
Retreat? Hell, no! We just got here!
  Attrib.

## WILLIAMS, Kenneth
British actor and entertainer
(1926–    )

2

Stop messin' abaht!
  Catchphrase, from 1950s

## WILSON, Charles E.
US Republican politician
(1890–1961)

3

\#\#   What's good for General Motors is good for the country.
  Senate Committee on Armed Services, January 1953
*In fact what the former President of General Motors said when asked whether there might be a conflict of interest if he became Secretary of Defense was, 'I cannot conceive of one because for years I thought what was good for our country was good for General Motors, and vice versa. The difference did not exist.'*

4

*Of the new type of H-bomb tested at Bikini (1954):*
[It gives] a bigger bang for a buck.
  Quoted in W. Safire, *Political Dictionary*

# WILSON, Harold
(later Lord Wilson of Rievaulx)
British Labour Prime Minister
(1916–   )

**1**

The school I went to in the north was a school where more than half the children in my class never had any boots or shoes to their feet. They wore clogs, because they lasted longer than shoes of comparable price.

Speech, Birmingham, 28 July 1948

*Abbreviated reports led to the suggestion that Wilson's schoolmates had gone barefoot.*

*See also BULMER-THOMAS 76:4.*

**2**

All the little gnomes in Zurich and other finance centres.

Speech, House of Commons, 12 November 1956

*The term 'Gnomes of Zurich', used to describe tight-fisted speculators in the Swiss financial capital who questioned Britain's creditworthiness, became popular again after 1964.*

**3**

Every time Mr Macmillan comes back from abroad, Mr Butler goes to the airport and grips him warmly by the throat.

Attrib.

**4**

I have always deprecated . . . in crisis after crisis, appeals to the Dunkirk spirit as an answer to our problems.

Speech, House of Commons, 26 July 1961

*Compare 457:5 below.*

**5**

This party is a moral crusade, or it is nothing.

Speech, Labour Party Conference, 1962

1

We are redefining and we are restating our socialism in terms of the scientific revolution . . . the Britain that is going to be forged in the white heat of this revolution will be no place for restrictive practices or outdated methods on either side of industry.

Speech, Labour Party Conference, 1 October 1963
*Phrase usually remembered as 'the white heat of the technological revolution'.*

2

What we are going to need is something like what President Kennedy had after years of stagnation – a programme of a hundred days of dynamic action.

Speech, Election campaign, 1964
*In fact, Kennedy had specifically ruled out a 'hundred days', saying in his Inaugural Address that his programmes could not be carried out in a thousand days.*

3

*On an MP who had run an allegedly racist campaign:*
Smethwick Conservatives can have the satisfaction of having topped the poll, of having sent a member who, until another election returns him to oblivion, will serve his time here as a Parliamentary leper.

Speech, House of Commons, 4 November 1964

4

A week is a long time in politics.

To parliamentary lobby correspondents, autumn 1964
*Because meetings of the lobby are 'off the record', no one appears quite certain when or why this celebrated aphorism was first uttered.*

5

I believe that the spirit of Dunkirk will once again carry us through to success.

Speech, Labour Party Conference, 12 December 1964
*Compare 456:5 above.*

1

The cumulative effect of the economic and financial sanctions [against Rhodesia] might well bring the rebellion to an end within a matter of weeks rather than months.

> Final communiqué of the Commonwealth Prime Ministers' Conference at Lagos, 12 January 1966

*Employing a phrase used by Wilson earlier that day.*

2

Now one encouraging gesture from the French Government – which I welcome – and the Conservative leader rolls on his back like a spaniel.

> Speech, Bristol, 18 March 1966

3

*On communist influence in a national seamen's strike:*
It is difficult for us to appreciate the pressures which are put on men I know to be realistic and responsible, not only in their executive capacity but in their highly organized strike committees in the ports, by this tightly knit group of politically motivated men.

> Speech, House of Commons, 22 June 1966

4

Every dog is allowed one bite, but a different view is taken of a dog that goes on biting all the time. He may not get his licence returned when it falls due.

> Speech to Parliamentary Labour Party, 2 March 1967

5

*After a devaluation of the pound:*
## The pound in your pocket.

> Broadcast address, 19 November 1967

*In fact what he said was: 'From now on the pound abroad is worth 14 per cent or so less in terms of other currencies. That doesn't mean, of course, that the pound here in Britain, in your pocket or purse or in your bank, has been devalued.'*

6

I'm an optimist, but I'm an optimist who takes his raincoat.

> Attrib.

**1**

Cohorts of distinguished journalists have been combing obscure parts of the country with a mandate to find anything, true or fabricated, to use against the Labour Party.
  Attrib. September 1974

**2**

*To journalists at press conference marking his retirement:*
I forgive you all.
  Remark, March 1976

<br>

**WILSON, Mary**
(later Lady Wilson)
Wife of above
(1916–   )

**3**

If Harold has a fault it is that he will drown everything with HP sauce.
  Interviewed by the *Sunday Times*, 1962

<br>

**WILSON, Woodrow**
US Democratic President
(1856–1924)

**4**

*On film* The Birth of a Nation *(1915):*
It is like writing history with lightning. And it's all true.
  Quoted in D. Boorstin, *The Image*

**5**

*Asking for a declaration of war:*
The world must be safe for democracy. Its peace must be planted upon trusted foundations of political liberty.
  Speech to Congress, 2 April 1917
*Usually remembered as 'The world must be made safe for democracy.'*

## WILTON, Robb
British comedian
(1881–1957)

**1**

The day war broke out . . .
   Catchphrase, from 1940s onwards

## WINCHELL, Walter
US journalist and broadcaster
(1897–1972)

**2**

Good evening, Mr and Mrs North America, and all the ships at sea.
Let's go to press!
   Standard start to radio newscasts, from 1932 onwards

## WINDSOR, Duchess of
(formerly Mrs Wallis Simpson)
American-born wife of the Duke of Windsor
(1896–1986)

**3**

I married the Duke for better or worse but not for lunch.
   Quoted in J. Bryan III and J.V. Murphy, *The Windsor Story*

**4**

You can never be too rich or too thin.
   Attrib.

## WISE, Ernie see MORECAMBE, Eric and WISE, Ernie

# WODEHOUSE, P.G.
## (later Sir Pelham)
### British novelist and lyricist
### (1881–1975)

1

Proceed, old gargoyle . . . you have our ear.
*The Inimitable Jeeves* (1923)

2

Jeeves coughed one soft, low, gentle cough like a sheep with a blade of grass in its throat.
*Ib.*

3

I turned to Aunt Agatha, whose demeanour was now rather like that of one who, picking daisies on the railway, has just caught the down express in the small of the back.
*Ib.*

4

'What ho!' I said, 'What ho!' said Motty. 'What ho! What ho!' 'What ho! What ho! What ho!' After that it seemed rather difficult to go on with the conversation.
'Jeeves and the Unbidden Guest', *Carry On Jeeves* (1925)

5

'Do you know, Jeeves, you're – well, you absolutely stand alone!'
'I endeavour to give satisfaction, sir,' said Jeeves.
*Ib.*

6

He spoke with a certain what-is-it in his voice, and I could see that, if not actually disgruntled, he was far from being gruntled.
*The Code of the Woosters* (1938)

### WOLFE, Humbert
British poet and critic
(1885–1940)

1
You cannot hope
  to bribe or twist,
thank God! the
  British journalist.

But, seeing what
  the man will do
unbribed, there's
  no occasion to.
  'Over the Fire', *The Uncelestial City* (1930)


### WOLFE, Tom
US writer
(1931–  )

2
Radical Chic.
  Title of book (1970)

3
The Right Stuff.
  Title of book (1979)
*Referring to the qualities needed by early members of the US space
programme.*


### WOODHOUSE, Barbara
British animal trainer
(1910–  )

4
*When training dogs:*
Walkies! . . . Sit!
  Stock phrases, TV shows, 1980s

## WOODROOFFE, Tommy
British broadcaster
(1899–1978)

**1**

*Describing the illumination of the Fleet on the night of the Coronation Naval Review at Spithead:*
At the present moment, the whole Fleet's lit up. When I say 'lit up', I mean lit up by fairy lamps.
  BBC radio broadcast, 20 May 1937
*Woodrooffe always denied that he had been 'lit up', too.*

## WOOLF, Virginia
British novelist
(1882–1941)

**2**

A Room of One's Own.
  Title of book (1929)

## WOOLLCOTT, Alexander
US writer and critic
(1887–1943)

**3**

All the things I really like to do are either illegal, immoral, or fattening.
  *The Knock at the Stage Door* (1933)

**4**

[Michael] Arlen, for all his reputation, is not a bounder. He is every other inch a gentleman.
  Quoted in R.E. Drennan, *Wit's End*
*See also WEST 449:2.*

1
There is absolutely nothing wrong with Oscar Levant that a miracle cannot fix.

    Quoted in M.C. Harriman, *The Vicious Circle*

2
Germany was the cause of Hitler just as much as Chicago is responsible for the *Chicago Tribune*.

    Radio broadcast, 1943
*Last words before the microphone. He died after the broadcast.*

*See also BENCHLEY 50:3.*

# Y

**YEATMAN, R.J.** see **SELLAR, W.C.** and **YEATMAN, R.J.**

## YEATS, W.B.
### Irish poet
### (1865–1939)

1

*On Rupert Brooke:*
He is the handsomest man in England, and he wears the most
beautiful shirts.
   Attrib. January 1913

2

Things fall apart; the centre cannot hold;
Mere anarchy is loosed upon the world . . .
The best lack all conviction, while the worst
Are full of passionate intensity.
   'The Second Coming' (1921)

3

A terrible beauty is born.
   'Easter 1916' (1921)

4

Cast a cold eye
On life, on death.
Horseman, pass by!
   'Under Ben Bulben' (1936–9)
*Later carved on his gravestone.*

## YOUNG, Jimmy
British singer and broadcaster
(1923–   )

**1**
Orft we jolly well go.
　Stock phrase at start of show, BBC Radio, 1960s

**2**
Sur le continong . . . sur le telephoneo.
　Stock phrases, 1960s

**3**
B.F.N. – 'Bye for now.
　Catchphrase

## 'YORK, Peter'
British journalist
(1947–   )

**4**
The Sloane Rangers, usually known by other regiments as the Headscarf Brigade or the Knightsbridge Knotteds, after what they wear on their heads . . . are the nicest British girl.
　Article in *Harpers & Queen*, October 1975
*The appellation 'Sloane Ranger' was actually coined by Martina Margetts, a sub-editor on the magazine.*

# Z

### ZAPPA, Frank
US rock musician
(1940–   )

1
Rock journalism is people who can't write interviewing people who can't talk for people who can't read.
   Attrib.

### ZIEGLER, Ron
US White House press spokesman
(1939–   )

2
*Euphemism for lie, at time of Watergate:*
This is the operative statement. The others are inoperative.
   Press conference, Washington, 17 April 1973

# Index of Key Words

In the index, most of the quotations have been edited or condensed. See the dictionary for the full and correct text. Key words appear in the index as they should be written, i.e. "ole" under **Hole**, 'viskey' as **Whiskey**, etc.

**A**

**Ablaze**
set Europe a., 103:3

**Abyss**
world now stands on the brink of the final a., 316:3

**Across**
A. the River and Into the Trees, 221:6

**Act**
can't a., can't sing, slightly bald . . . can dance a little, 21:7
everybody wants to get into da a., 145:2

**Actor**
a.'s a guy who . . . ain't talking about him, ain't listening, 70:3
scratch an a., 332:4

**Actors**
a. should be treated like cattle, 226:1
send me some good a. – cheap, 44:2

**Actual**
that's yer a. French, 370:4

**Admiral**
still call me A., 23:5

**Adopt**
a., adapt, improve, 149:3

**Adventure**
to die will be an awfully big a., 41:3

**Advertise**
it pays to a., 20:2

**Advertising**
a. is the most fun you can have with your clothes on, 136:7
half the money I spend on a. is wasted, 278:3

**Aerials**
(TV) a. removed . . . moral equivalent of a prostate operation, 317:6

**Aesop**
A. was writing for the tortoise market, 74:1

**Affluent**
A. Society, 181:4

**Afraid**
Who's A. of Virginia Woolf, 342:2

**Africans**
we have the happiest A. in the world, 405:6

**After**
a. you, Claude . . . a. you, Cecil, 237:1

**Against**
fifth of the people a. everything all the time, 255:4
he who is not with us is a. us, 413:2

**Age**
a. shall not weary them, nor the years condemn, 60:4
I prefer old a. to the alternative, 98:6

**Aggressors**
US a. and all their running dogs, 295:5

**Agnew**
Spiro A. is not a household name, 11:1

**Agony**
ee, it was a., Ivy, 355:5

**Agreeable**
what could be more a., 111:1

**Ahead**
a. – it's either Oxford or Cambridge, 406:6

**Aim**
what is our a. . . . victory, 102:3

**Alarm**
spread a. and despondency, 420:6

**Albert**
A. had married beneath his station, 124:5

**Alcoholic**
a. someone you don't like who drinks as much as you do, 426:3
excessive a. intake, 429:4

**Algeria**
Long live French A., 135:6

**Allergy**
dreaded lergy, 197:4

**Alligator**
see you later, a., 409:6

**Alone**
I want to be a., 183:3
never a. with a Strand, 403:7
she sleeps a. at last, 50:5
very well, a., 284:1
when he's a. in a room, there's nobody there, 256:3

**Alphabet**
eat a. soup and shit better lyrics, 304:4

**Alternative**
there is no a., 423:1

**Am**
I a. what I a., 342:4

**Amazing**
pretty a., 138:3

**Amen**
so goodbye, dear, and a., 344:4

**America**
A. like large, friendly dog, 432:1
Only in A., 421:6

**American**
chief business of A. people is business, 118:2
truth, justice and the A. way, 90:4

**Americans**
all A. as blind as you, 385:5
A. have plenty of everything and the best of nothing, 250:8

**Ammunition**
praise the Lord, and pass the a., 409:5

**Amuse**
talent to a., 122:5

**Anger**
telegrams and a., 175:2

**Angry**
A. Young Man, 335:3

**Animal**
into a. husbandry until they caught him, 273:2

**Animals**
all a. are equal, 328:3
never work with a. or children, 21:1

**Annihilation**
no a. without representation, 431:4

**Another**
never be a., 306:1

**Answer**
a. is in the plural and they bounce, 285:2
a., my friend, is blowin' in the wind, 146:1
I think the a. lies in the soil, 60:1
what is the a., what is the question, 415:2

**Anything**
A. Goes, 343:5

**Anywhere**
any time, any place, a., 391:3

**Apathy**
going round country stirring up a., 452:2

**Apologize**
never complain and never a., 169:4

**Aphrodisiac**
fame is a powerful a., 201:1
power is the ultimate a., 261:7

**Appalling**
I put . . . my own view with a. frankness, 38:5

**Appeasement**
limitation of armaments by political a., 282:6

**Apple**
she could eat an a. through a tennis racquet, 124:3

**April**
A. is the cruellest month, 153:7

**Archaeologist**
a. digging up not things but people, 450:2
a. is the best husband any woman can have, 99:4

**Archangel**
if I were A. Gabriel, you would not be in my constituency, 303:5

**Argentina**
Don't Cry for Me, A., 363:3

**Arm**
a. round your waist and his eye on the clock, 29:5

**Armed**
we are not at war . . . we are in a. conflict, 148:3

**Armful**
pint, that's very nearly an a., 211:3

**Army**
contemptible little a., 454:2

**Aroma**
faint a. of performing seals, 215:2

**Arrest**
sergeant, a. most of these people, 258:3

**Arrived**
I've a. and, to prove it, I'm here, 79:4

**Ars**
A. Gratia Artis, 138:4

**Arse**
I would kick him up the a., Alfred, 107:7
politician is an a., 127:1

**Arsenal**
great a. of democracy, 367:7

**Art**
as the a. mistress said to the gardener, 359:4
only interested in a., 386:2
portrait is remarkable example of modern a., 109:2

**Arthur**
speak for England, A., 16:1

**Ascribe**
never a. to an opponent motives meaner than your own, 42:4

**Ask**
a. not what your country can do for you, 253:3

**Asked**
I only a., 71:2

**Asleep**
fall a. halfway through her name, 52:5

**Aspirates**
try taking a couple of a., 405:2

**Assassinates**
not satisfied until somebody a. him, 250:1

**Assassination**
a. is the extreme form of censorship, 384:7

**Astonish**
a. me, 138:2

**Asylum**
inmates are in charge of the a., 413:4
lunatic a. run by lunatics, 187:3
lunatics have taken over the a., 371:1

**Atheist**
a. is a man who has no invisible means of support, 76:2
I am still an a., thank God, 77:1

**August**
A. for the people, 32:2

**Aunt**
A. Edna, 355:4

**Aussie**
come on, A., come on, 393:7

**Barney**
give 'im the money, B., 339:3

**Bastard**
all my eggs in one b., 334:2
we knocked the b. off, 224:4

**Bastards**
don't let the b. grind you down, 397:1
that'll hold the little b., 83:6

**Battle**
France has lost a b. but not the war, 135:1
never-ending b. for truth, justice and the
American way, 90:4

**BBC**
BBC('s) excessive sensitivity . . . posture
of a hedgehog at bay, 18:4

**Be**
Let It B., 276:7

**Beaches**
we shall fight on the b., 102:5

**Beam**
b. me up, Scotty, 414:2

**Beans**
B. meanz Heinz, 392:1

**Bear**
B. of Very Little Brain, and long words
Bother me, 307:5

**Beast**
beauty killed the b., 258:4

**Beastliness**
(Masturbation) is called in our schools b.,
35:4

**Beastly**
Don't Let's Be B. to the Germans, 123:2

**Beat**
really a b. generation, 256:1
so we b. on, borne against the current,
169:6

**Beatles**
(B.) greatest composers since Beethoven,
76:3
B.'s first LP, 266:6

**Beats**
b. as it sweeps as it cleans, 397:5

**Beautiful**
b. downtown Burbank, 269:6
b. girls, walk a little slower when you
walk by me, 24:5
b. people, 441:2
inordinately, devastatingly, immortally
. . . b., 73:6
saying, 'Oh, how b.' and sitting in the
shade, 261:6
Small Is B., 378:5

**Beauty**
born with my b. and your brains, 385:6
me old b., me old pal, 26:3
it was b. killed the beast, 258:4
terrible b. is born, 465:3

**Because**
b. it's there, 294:1

**Bed**
get up early, if you want to get out of b.,
112:4
never go to b. with a woman whose
troubles are greater, 12:3
not having more than one man in b.,
131:2
rather cup of tea than go to b., 186:4
should have stood in b., 239:2

**Bedpost**
Does the Spearmint Lose Its Flavour on
the B. Overnight, 369:1

**Beds**
getting into other people's b., 316:1

**Bee**
queen b. crossed with Fresian bull, 193:1

**Beef**
where's the b., 402:7

**Beer**
I'm only here for the b., 397:3

**Beethoven**
B.'s Fifth Symphony . . . most sublime
noise ever, 175:3

**Before**
here and now, b. your very eyes, 28:6
I have been here b., 444:4

**Begin**
now vee may perhaps to b., 370:2

**Beginning**
in my b. is my end, 155:2
this is the b. of a beautiful friendship, 87:4

**Beguine**
when they begin the b., 344:2

**Belgium**
If It's Tuesday, This Must Be B., 166:7

**Believe**
B. It or Not, 364:2
if you b. (in fairies), clap your hands, 41:4

**Believed**
justice seen to be b., 45:4

**Belt**
can't see a b. without hitting below it, 29:3

**Berlin**
B. by Christmas, 392:2

**Berliner**
ich bin ein B., 254:3

**Bert**
B., I'm proud of you, 85:3

**Bertie**
B., 439:4
I'm Burlington B., 214:4

**Best**
b. lack all conviction, 465:2

**Best-seller**
b.-s. the gilded tomb of a mediocre talent, 406:4

**Better**
b. drowned than duffers if not duffers won't drown, 355:1
b. the cold blast of winter than hot breath, 351:1
every day . . . I am getting b. and b., 119:3

**Betting**
keeps horses from b. on people, 165:7

**Best**
why not the b., 84:4

**Betray**
guts to b. my country, 175:4

**Between**
try to get b. (German soldier raping sister), 417:2

**Bewitched**
B., Bothered and Bewildered, 215:4

**B.F.N.**
B.F.N. – 'Bye for now, 466:3

**Bias**
b. against understanding, 61:2

**Bible**
searching through the B. for loopholes, 165:8

**Bible-Black**
starless and b.-b., 425:5

**Bien**
tout va très b., 410:1

**Big**
B. Brother is watching you, 328:6
b. one, 392:4
b. ones, small ones, some as b. as your head, 219:4

**Bigger**
b. than both of us, 259:1
b. they come, the harder they fall, 170:3

**Big-hearted**
b.-h. Arthur, that's me, 28:3

**Bike**
got on his b. and looked for work, 419:5
mind my b., 443:3

**Bill**
write 'Emily I love you' on the back of the b., 133:2

**Billboard**
never see a b. lovely as a tree, 321:1

**Bills**
have the b. to prove it, 277:5

**Bippy**
you bet your sweet b., 269:7

**Bird**
cannot catch a b. of paradise, 257:3
it's a b., it's a plane, it's Superman, 90:3
She's a B. in a Gilded Cage, 409:7

**Birds**
b. do it, bees do it, 343:1

**Bunk**
history is more or less b., 173:5

**Bunnies**
b. can (and will) go to France, 427:4

**Burbank**
beautiful downtown B., 269:6

**Burden**
bear any b., 252:3

**Buried**
they b. him among the Kings, 159:1

**Burn**
b., baby, b., 393:2
b. your bra, 393:3

**Burning**
Keep the Home Fires B., 325:2

**Burton**
gone for a B., 395:8

**Bury**
B. My Heart at Wounded Knee, 64:4
we will b. you, 257:1

**Bus**
(Hitler) missed the b., 94:2

**Business**
b. as usual, 380:4
chief b. of American people is b., 118:2
How to Succeed in B. Without Really
Trying, 280:3
no b. like show b., 55:5

**Butcher**
Prime Minister has to be a b., 78:2

**Butler**
b. did it, 89:3

**Butter**
big b.-and-egg man, 204:1
b. for the Royal slice of bread, 307:1
b. will only make us fat, 192:4
b. wouldn't melt in mouth, or anywhere
else, 264:3
guns before b., 192:3
tell Stork from b., 393:4

**Butterfly**
float like a b., 13:1

**Buy**
would you b. a used car from this man,
23:6

# C

**Cabbages**
sits among the c. and peas, 376:3

**Cabots**
Lowells talk only to C., and the C. talk
only to God, 68:3

**Cake**
face looks like wedding c., 33:3
someone left the c. out in the rain, 445:2

**Calamity**
oh, c., 214:3

**Calcutta**
Oh, C., 341:7

**Calibre**
man of my c., 211:1

**Call**
let's c. the whole thing off, 189:3

**Callous**
word C. engraved on her heart, 381:2

**Calls**
if anybody c., say I'm designing St Paul's,
54:1

**Cambridge**
C. people . . . urban, squat, and packed
with guile, 72:5

**Camel**
'take my c., dear', said my aunt Dot,
287:2

**Camera**
I am a c., 236:3

**Can**
he who c. does, he who cannot, teaches,
384:5

**Canada**
don't know what street C. is on, 83:3

**Canary**
you can wipe your hands on his c., 440:5

**Complain**
never c. and never apologise, 169:4
never c. and never explain, 38:7

**Composers**
(Beatles) greatest composers since Beethoven, 76:3

**Compris**
je vous ai c., 135:6

**Concentrate**
I am unable to c., 186:1

**Concentration**
they call me C. Camp Ehrhardt, 430:2

**Concorde**
like C. is a spin-off of the Tiger Moth, 201:4

**Conditions**
dese are de c. dat prevail, 145:1

**Conduct**
C. Unbecoming, 341:3

**Confederacy**
C. of Dunces, 64:5

**Confessed**
poured himself a drink and after a few minutes c., 216:4

**Conflict**
never in the field of human c., 103:3

**Confused**
anyone who isn't c. . . . doesn't understand what's going on, 24:7

**Conked**
c. out, 274:1

**Connect**
only c., 175:1

**Conscience**
c. warns that somebody may be looking, 303:2
not cut my c. to fit fashions, 220:1

**Consent**
full-hearted c. of Parliament and people, 218:5

**Consequently**
c. this country is at war with Germany, 94:1

**Conservatives**
life's better with the C., 398:4

**Constant**
C. Weader fwowed up, 331:4

**Consultation**
customary processes of c., 292:6

**Contemptible**
General French's c. litle army, 454:2

**Continent**
sur le c. . . . sur le telephoneo, 466:2

**Continued**
c. page 94, 348:4

**Contraception**
not leave c. on the long finger too long, 285:4
best c. is a glass of cold water, 23:7

**Conventional**
c. wisdom, 182:1

**Convictions**
man of no c., at least, I think I am, 210:2

**Cookie-wise**
way it crumbles, c.-w., 26:1

**Cooks**
as good c. go, she went, 375:1

**Coolidge**
C. only snored, 302:5

**Cop**
I'm a c. . . . my name's Friday, 142:1

**Corn**
c. is as high as an elephant's eye, 208:4

**Corner**
some c. of a foreign field that is for ever England, 73:3

**Corpse**
the sort of greeting a c. would give an undertaker, 38:2

**Corridors**
c. of power, 407:1

**Cough**
c. like a sheep with a blade of grass in its throat, 461:2

**Coughing**
c. well, tonight, 174:3

**Cry**
c. all the way to the bank, 278:4
too old to c., but it hurt too much to
laugh, 416:3

**Cuckoo**
One Flew Over the C.'s Nest, 167:4

**Cuckoo clock**
In Switzerland . . . what did 500 years of
democracy produce – the c.c., 425:1

**Cult**
c. of personality, 256:5

**Culture**
hear the word 'c.', and I reach for my
revolver, 246:1

**Cultures**
Two C. and the Scientific Revolution,
407:2

**Cure**
is no c. for this disease, 49:4

**Curtain**
so I face the final c., 18:1

**Customer**
c. is always right, 380:3

**Cut**
two things should be c., 124:4
will not c. my conscience to fit this year's
fashions, 220:1

**Cycle**
life is a glorious c. of song, 334:5

**D**

**Daddy**
good grief, it's D., 410:4
what did you do in the Great War, d.,
393:9

**Daffodils**
what d. were to Wordsworth, 267:2

**Daft**
d. as a brush, 340:4

**Dame**
There Is Nothin' Like a D., 209:2

**Damn**
d. you, England, 329:4
frankly, I don't give a d., 196:2
if we believe a thing to be bad . . . and d.
the consequences, 308:2

**Dance**
can d. a little, 21:7
D. to the Music of Time, 64:6

**Dangerous**
when they ask us how d. it was, 342:5

**Dares**
who d. wins, 402:9

**Dark**
clean your teeth in the d., 241:3
d. night of the soul, 170:1
don't want to go home in the d., 222:4
It Was a D. and Stormy Night, 378:3
through a d. glassly, 411:4

**Darkness**
Heart of D., 115:5

**Darling**
George Robey is the D. of the music-
halls, 405:1

**Darlings**
goodnight, my d., 125:3
hello, my d., 142:3

**Daughter**
don't put your d. on the stage, Mrs
Worthington, 122:5

**Day**
d. I was meant not to see, 423:5
our d. will come, 235:5
things done better in my d., 255:6
today is the first d. of the rest of your life,
134:2

**Destiny**
I felt as if I were walking with d., 107:5

**Destroy**
whom the gods wish to d., 115:1

**Detected**
d. only once in the use of an argument, 53:2

**Diamonds**
D. Are a Girl's Best Friend, 284:5
D. are Forever, 65:1

**Diary**
keep a d., and some day it'll keep you, 448:5

**Dictionary**
like Webster's D., we're Morocco bound, 364:4

**Die**
(troops must) d. on the spot rather than give way, 243:1
not afraid to d. . . . don't want to be there when it happens, 15:1
not here to d. for your country, 304:6
proud to d. in service of this nation, 182:4
to d. will be an awfully big adventure, 41:3

**Died**
he d. as he lived – at sea, 21:8
what can you say about 25-year-old girl who d., 283:2

**Different**
something completely d., 313:3

**Difficulties**
little local d., 291:4

**Dime**
brother, can you spare a d., 212:4

**Dined**
I am a man more d. against than dining, 69:3

**Dinner**
best number for a d. party is two, 204:3

**Diplomat**
d. a head-waiter who's allowed to sit down, 437:2

**Direction**
did not care which d. . . . so long as he was driver, 47:3

**Dirt**
after four years the d. doesn't get any worse, 125:5
get all the d. off the front of your shirt, 94:3

**Dirty**
d. British coaster, 299:5
you d. old man, 415:4
you d. rat, 81:1
you d. rotten swine, you, 198:4

**Discomfiture**
d. as a result of . . . elements of refurbishment, 20:1

**Disease**
I've got Bright's d. and he's got mine, 336:5

**Diseases**
coughs and sneezes spread d., 393:8

**Disgrace**
d. of the single life . . . more airy, 24:6

**Disgraceful**
it is d. – it ought not to be allowed, 432:2

**Disgruntled**
if not d., he was far from being gruntled, 461:6

**Disorder**
policeman is there to preserve d., 130:4

**Diver**
don't forget the d., 237:5

**Divisions**
how many d. has the Pope got, 413:1

**Do**
anything you can d., I can d. better, 55:7
can I d. you now, sir, 237:4
d. not d. unto others as you would they should d., 384:3
let's d. it, let's fall in love, 343:1
man's gotta d. what a man's gotta d., 382:3

**Doc**
what's up, D., 92:3

**Empire**
Great Britain has lost an e. and not yet found a role, 9:2
how is the E., 186:2

**Enchanted**
Some E. Evening, 209:3

**End**
e. of civilization as we know it, 110:4
in my e. is my beginning, 155:3
is this the e. of Rico, 278:5
it is, perhaps, the e. of the beginning, 104:7
not the e. of anything, this is the beginning of everything, 357:6
Keep Right On to the E. of the Road, 268:2

**England**
close my eyes and think of E., 225:2
damn you, E., 329:4
for ever E., 73:3
good evening, E. . . . G. Potter speaking to you in English, 345:7
Our E. is a garden, 261:6
pulseless lot that make up E. today, 270:2
speak for E., Arthur, 16:1
there'll always be an E., 409:8
things I've done for E., 349:6
wake up, E., 184:4

**English**
G. Potter speaking to you in E., 345:7
mobilized the E. language, 254:2, 318:4
pretty exciting to be E., 121:7
sort of E. up with which I will not put, 107:3
under an E. heaven, 73:4

**Englishman**
E. drawn first prize in the lottery of life, 362:1

**Englishmen**
mad dogs and E., 122:3

**Enigma**
mystery inside an e., 102:1

**Enjoy**
people enjoy their own handwriting as their own farts, 33:2

**Enosis**
e., 394:9

**Enough**
e. is e., 129:6

**Entertainment**
stage is a world of e., 139:4
That's E., 139:3

**Equal**
all animals are e., but some more e. than others, 328:3

**Establishment**
The E., 161:2

**Eton**
educated in the holidays from E., 390:4

**Etonne**
é.-moi, 138:2

**Europe**
lamps going out all over E., 202:2
set E. ablaze, 103:2

**Evening**
e. all, 443:4

**Everest**
(climbed E.) because it's there, 294:1

**Everyday**
e. story of country folk, 26:2

**Evil**
banality of e., 26:4
we are origin of all coming e., 248:4

**Exchanged**
e. many frank words, 116:2

**Exciting**
it is still pretty e. to be English, 121:7

**Excuse**
reporter made an e. and left, 336:4

**Exercise**
whenever I feel like e., I lie down until feeling passes, 232:2

**Explain**
mission to e., 241:1
never complain and never e., 38:7
never e., your friends don't need it, enemies won't believe it, 200:6

**Expletive**
e. deleted, 443:5

**Exploit**
not going to e. my opponent's youth,
357:4

**Exploitation**
e. of man by man, 25:8

**Export**
e. or die, 395:2

**Exporting**
e. is fun, 292:2

**Express**
just caught the down e. in the small of the
back, 461:3

**Exterminate**
e., e., 143.1

**Extremism**
e. in the defence of liberty no vice, 194:2

**Eye**
less in this than meets the e., 40:2

**Eyeball**
e. to e., and the other fellow just blinked,
372:3

**Eyebrows**
(e. like) skins of small mammal not large
enough to be mats, 49:1

**Eyes**
e. and ears of the world, 395:3
my e. are dim, 20:5


# F

**Fabians**
good man fallen among F., 274:6

**Face**
f. looks like a wedding cake left out in the
rain, 33:3
f. that she keeps in a jar by the door, 276:3
I wish I loved its silly f., 354:1
never forget f., but make an exception in
your case, 298:4

**Facts**
all we want is the f., ma'am, 142:2
f. are sacred, 379:1

**Fade**
they just f. away, 286:5

**Fag-end**
I belong to the f.-e. of Victorian liberalism, 175:5

**Fail**
right to f., 450:3

**Failure**
all political lives . . . end in f., 347:1
f., the possibilities do not exist, 423:3
utterly unspoiled by f., 122:6
what we've got here is a f. to communicate, 117:2

**Fair**
F. Shares for All, is Labour's Call, 240:2

**Fairies**
every time a child says 'I don't believe in
f.', 41:2
f. at the bottom of our garden, 180:3
if you believe (in f.), clap your hands,
41:4

**Faith**
If you break f. with us who die, 289:1

**Fallen**
good man f. among politicians, 130:1
he's f. in the water, 197:6

**Falls**
still f. in the rain, 390:1

**Fame**
f. is a powerful aphrodisiac, 201:1

**Family**
f. that prays together stays together,
395:4
we're not a f., we're a firm, 186:3

**Famine**
f. in the land, know who caused it, 386:1

**Famous**
everyone will be world-f. for fifteen
minutes, 443:1

**Fantasy**
artist has won through f. . . . honour,
power, love of women, 177:2

**Faraway**
quarrel in f. country between people of
whom we know nothing, 93:2

**Farce**
(dying) not as hard as f., 205:1

**Farewell**
and so we say f., 170:2

**Fart**
can't f. and chew gum, 245:2

**Farts**
enjoy smell of their own f., 33:2
every man likes smell of his own f., 351:3

**Fasten**
f. your seatbelts . . . going to be a bumpy night, 13:4

**Fat**
f. man trying to get in, 452:1
f. white woman whom nobody loves, 118:7
imprisoned in every f. man, 114:4

**Fate**
Flying Fickle Finger of F., 269:1

**Father**
Lloyd George knew my f., 365:1

**Fathers**
land of my f., my f. can have it, 426:1

**Favourite**
these are a few of my f. things, 209:8

**Fear**
let us never negotiate out of f., 252:4
only thing we have to f. is f. itself, 367:3

**Feast**
Paris is a moveable f., 221:1

**Feather**
like f. pillow, bears marks of last person to sit, 206:2

**Feather-footed**
f.-f. through the plashy fen passes the questing vole, 444:3

**Feeds**
it f. the hand that bites it, 338:2

**Fees**
answered as they took their f. . . . 'is no cure for disease', 49:4

**Feet**
better to die on f. than live on your knees, 233:2

**Fell**
no wonder George Eliot's husband f. into the Grand Canal, 314:5

**Fellow**
and so, my f. Americans, 253:3

**Female**
f. of the species more deadly than the male, 261:4
interviewing a faded f. in a damp basement, 213:4

**Fence**
if f. is strong enough I'll sit on it, 404:5
sat so long on f. that iron has entered his soul, 187:5

**Fences**
good f. make good neighbours, 179:3

**Fetters**
men arise to the noise of f. breaking, 261:6

**Few**
so much owed by so many to so f., 103:3

**Fickle**
Flying F. Finger of Fate, 269:1

**Fiction**
newspaper . . . one form of continuous f., 59:3

**Fidelity**
your idea of f. is not having more than one man in bed, 131:1

**Field**
never in the f. of human conflict, 103:3

**Fifth**
f. column, 310:4

**Fifty**
f. million Frenchmen can't be wrong, 20:4

**Fight**
f. and f. and f. again, 181:2
f. between two bald men over a comb, 68:2
here stand and f., there will be no further withdrawal, 312:2
in no circumstances f., 330:2
we shall f. on the beaches, 102:5

**Film**
every f. should have beginning, middle and end, 192:2

**Final**
f. solution, 227:4
so I face the f. curtain, 18:1

**Finest**
this was their f. hour, 103:1

**Finger**
Flying Fickle F. of Fate, 269:1
not leave contraception on long f., 285:4
time we pulled our f. out, 338:3
whose f., 129:5

**Fingerlicking**
it's f. good, 397:7

**Finger-nails**
if you don't stop biting your f.-n., 366:3

**Fings**
F. Ain't Wot They Used T'Be, 341:4

**Finish**
I've started so I'll f., 300:2

**Fire**
c'mon, baby, light my f., 408:4
no more water, the f. next time, 37:1

**Firm**
not a family, we're a f., 186:3

**First**
always travels f. class, 168:5
F. Hundred Thousand, 217:2
f. ninety minutes are the most important, 365:4

**Fish**
dead f. before it has had time to stiffen, 329:1
f. fuck in it, 165:3
Martin, Barton and F., 367:6

**Five**
f. – four – three – two – one, 80:1
I'll give it f., 322:1

**Flannelled**
f. fools at the wicket, 260:2

**Flat**
very f., Norfolk, 121:1

**Flattery**
f. hurts no one, if he doesn't inhale, 416:2

**Flaunt**
when you got it, f. it, 402:6

**Flea**
English literature's performing f., 326:3

**Fleet**
whole F.'s lit up, 463:1

**Flew**
One F. Over the Cuckoo's Nest, 167:4

**Float**
f. like a butterfly, sting like a bee, 13:1

**Floreat**
F. Etona, 41:6

**Flowers**
let a hundred f. bloom, 295:3
say it with f., 400:5
where have all the f. gone, 410:2

**Flutter**
spirits of woodcock . . . f. and bear him up the Norfolk sky, 57:1

**Fly**
do not remove f. with hatchet, 351:2
if God had intended us to f., 171:4

**Foe**
his f. was folly and his weapon wit, 229:3

**Fog**
yellow f. that rubs its back upon the window panes, 153:2

**Fold**
do not f., spindle or mutilate, 22:2

**Follow**
I must f. them, I am their leader, 270:1

**Foolish**
these f. things remind me of you, 299:3

**Fool**
F. There Was, 166:4

**Fools**
flannelled f. at the wicket, 260:2
f. give you reasons, wise men never try, 209:4
Only F. and Horses, 421:5

**Foot**
putting your f. in it, 338:4

**Football**
f. more serious than life and death, 382:4

**Force**
may the F. be with you, 414:3

**Ford (G.)**
(G.F.) can't fart and chew gum at the same time, 245:2
I am a F., not a Lincoln, 172:4
(F.) like guy in science fiction movie, 179:5

**Foreign**
send F. Secretary . . . naked into the conference chamber, 58:5

**Forest**
Down in the F. (Something Stirred), 408:5

**Forget**
don't f. the fruit gums, mum, 394:4
three things I always f., 418:2

**Forgive**
f. but never forget, 254:5
f. you all, 459:2

**Forty**
clinging on to (f.) for dear life, 114:2
Life Begins at F., 340:3

**Forward**
One Step F., Two Steps Back, 274:3

**Fourteen**
I'll have f. kidnapped grandchildren, 189:6

**Fourteenth**
f. Mr Wilson, 141:2

**Fragments**
these f. have I shored against my ruins, 154:1

**France**
certaine idée de la F., 135:3
F. has lost a battle, but F. has not lost the war, 135:1

**Frankly**
f., my dear, I don't give a damn, 196:2

**Free**
f. at last, f. at last, 258:1
I'm f., 27:1
I'm not a number, I'm a f. man, 348:1

**Freedom**
f. of press, to print proprietor's prejudices, 418:3

**French**
F. Without Tears, 355:2
yer actual F., 370:4

**Frenchmen**
fifty million F. can be wrong, 204:2
fifty million F. can't be wrong, 20:4

**Freud**
F. never played Glasgow Empire on a Friday night, 140:2

**Friday**
my name's F., 142:1

**Friend**
for yourself and a f., if you have one, 101:2
I expect you know my f., Evelyn Waugh, 100:2

**Friends**
even your best f. won't tell you, 395:1
f. are God's apology for relations, 259:4
little help from my f., 276:5

**Friendship**
beginning of a beautiful f., 87:4

**Frightened**
going to make sure my children f. of me, 185:3

**Frontier**
stand on the edge of a New F., 251:4

**Frumpish**
f. and banal, 317:4

**Fuck**
fish f. in it, 165:3
they f. you up, your mum and dad, 266:7
who do I have to f. to get off this picture, 410:5
you couldn't write f. on a dusty venetian blind, 75:5
zipless f. is rarer than the unicorn, 247:1

**Gentleman**

every other inch a g., 463:4; 449:2

g. in Whitehall really does know better, 240:3

hereabouts died a very gallant g., 158:4

**Gentlemen**

g. lift the seat – a loyal toast, 305:3

G. Prefer Blondes, 282:3

**Gently**

g., Bentley, 419:2

**George**

G., don't do that, 202:1

**Germans**

Don't Let's Be Beastly to the G., 123:3

**Germany**

G. calling, 217:1

**Get**

let's g. on with it, 91:1

**Gets**

g. off with women because can't get on with them, 272:4

**Gin**

bottle of Gordon's g., 63:3

of all the g. joints . . . she walks into mine, 86:4

**Gipper**

win this one for the G., 262:4

**Girl**

G. like I, 283:4

**Girls**

good g. go to heaven, bad g. go everywhere, 74:4

**Glad**

g., g., g., 277:6

never g. confident morning again, 61:1

**Gladdies**

wave your g., possums, 231:3

**Glasses**

girls who wear g., 332:3

**Glint**

everywhere the g. of gold, 84:3

**Glittering**

g. prizes, 405:5

**Global**

a g. village, 290:3

**Glory**

goodbye, my friends, I go to g., 144:2

**Gnomes**

little g. in Zurich, 456:2

**Gnu**

gnot a gnother g., 171:3

**Go**

do not pass 'g.', 311:2

g. for gold, 395:6

g., g., g., said the bird, 155:1

g. to it, 315:2

g. to work on an egg, 395:7

I g. – I come back, 238:1

let my people g., 374:3

Let's All G. Down the Strand, 88:1

let us g. then, you and I, 152:5

**Goal**

g. of landing a man on the moon, 253:4

**God**

Fear G. and Dread Nought, 168:6

G. be thanked who has matched us with His hour, 73:2

G. can stand being told . . . he doesn't exist, 347:4

G. finally caught his eye, 250:5

G. Protect Me From My Friends, 65:5

G.'s apology for relations, 259:4

he didn't love G., he just fancied him, 25:7

if G. had intended us to fly . . . never given us railways, 171:4

isn't G. a shit, 100:1

nearer G.'s heart in a garden, 204:4

not only is there no G., but try getting a plumber, 14:3

there, but for the grace of G., goes G., 106:4

when I pray to (G.) I find I'm talking to myself, 41:1

where it will end, knows G., 190:4

why G. withheld sense of humour from women, 82:4

**Goebbels**

G. has no balls at all, 22:5

**Goering**
G. has two (balls), but very small, 22:5

**Going**
I'm g. down now, sir, 238:2
when the g. gets tough, the tough get g., 254:6

**Gold**
everywhere the glint of g., 84:3
go for g., 395:6
there's g. in them thar hills, 91:7

**Golden**
g. rule is that there are no g. rules, 384:4
g. rules for an orchestra: start together and finish together, 48:3

**Goldfish**
g. in the privacy of bowls do it, 343:2

**Golf**
g. is a good walk spoiled, 434:6

**Gone**
G. With the Wind, 65:6

**Gongs**
certain women should be struck regularly like g., 121:2

**Good**
g. evening, each, 360:2
g. evening, Mr and Mrs North America, let's go to press, 460:2
g. morning . . . nice day, 237:6
G. Thing, 380:6
he's very g., you know, 197:7
never had it so g., 292:1
what's g. for General Motors is g. for the country, 455:3

**Goodbye**
g., children . . . everywhere, 289:2
G. To All That, 200:1
so g., dear, and amen, 344:4

**Goodness**
g., gracious me, 381:5
g. had nothing to do with it, 447:5

**Goodnight**
g. and good luck, 318:3
g. from me, g. from him, 435:3
g., Mrs Calabash – wherever you are, 145:3
say g., Gracie . . . g. Gracie, 77:2

**Gossamer**
trip to the moon on g. wings, 344:4

**Gotcha**
g., 417:4

**Govern**
go out and g. New South Wales, 50:1

**Government**
do not criticize your g. when out of the country, 106:6
G. brought down by action of two tarts, 292:5
G. looks with favour upon . . . national home for Jewish people, 39:2
smack of firm g., 130:2

**Gradualness**
inevitability of g., 445:4

**Gramophone**
(g.) adds new terror to life, 432:4

**Grandmama**
what G. would have thought of Labour Government, 185:1

**Grandmother**
I would walk over my g. if necessary, 114:1

**Grape**
keep the change . . . I trod on a g., 159:4

**Grass**
g. will grow in the streets, 229:1

**Gravy**
(mother's) g. used to move about a bit, 211:2

**Gray**
these little g. cells, 99:2

**Great**
think continually of those were truly g., 411:2

**Great Britain**
G.B. . . . has lost an empire and not yet found a role, 9:2

**Greatest**
G. Motion Picture Ever Made, 196:4
g. week in the history of the world since the Creation, 323:5
I am the g., 12:4

**Greatness**
country will find dignity and g., 121:6
I want to get out with my g. intact, 13:2

**Greeks**
G. had a word for it, 11:5

**Greeting**
Curzon (gave) . . . g. a corpse would give to an undertaker, 38:2

**Grief**
good g., Charlie Brown, 378:2

**Grocer**
boating with his g., 454:1

**Gromyko**
plan to be the G. of the Labour Party, 218:3

**Grow**
they shall g. not old as we that are left g. old, 60:4

**Grub**
lovely g., lovely g., 238:5

**Grumbler**
I have always been a g., 347:5

**Guard**
they're changing g. at Buckingham Palace, 306:6

**Guests**
play a round of Get the G., 12:1

**Guido**
G. Nadzo is nadzo g., 250:3

**Guinness**
G. is good for you, 395:9
trying for G. Book of Records, 207:3

**Gum**
any g., chum, 88:2

**Gumdrops**
goody, goody, g., 89:4

**Gums**
don't forget the fruit g., mum, 394:4

**Gun**
drop the g., Louis, 87:3
g. in your pocket, or just pleased to see me, 448:7
political power grows out of the barrel of a g., 295:1

**Gung Ho**
g. h., 396:1

**Guns**
g. before butter, 192:3
g. will make us powerful, butter only fat, 192:4

**Guts**
(g.=) grace under pressure, 221:2
hope I should have g. to betray my country, 175:4
people had to leave (g.) on ground at Goose Green, 260:1

**Guttersnipe**
draggle-tailed g., 384:9

# H

**Had**
Dear Mary, we all knew you h. it in you, 334:1

**Hair**
h. upon his chest . . . but, sister, so has Lassie, 345:1
never get on in politics with that h., 31:1

**Hairdresser**
only her h. knows for sure, 394:2

**Hairy**
small, h. individual, 19:2

**Half**
h. mad baronet, h. beautiful woman, 77:4

**Half-naked**
(h.-n.) fakir, 101:4

**Half-quote**
don't h.-q. me to reinforce your prejudices, 110:6

**Helicopters**
son, they are all my h., 245:5

**Hell**
go to h., Babe Ruth – American, you die, 22:4
h. is other people, 377:1
h. no, we won't go, 396:5
'H.' said the Duchess, 99:3
made an excursion to h. and came back glorious, 347:3
to h. with you, offensive letter follows, 420:5
yours till h. freezes over, 169:3

**Hello**
h., folks, and what about the workers, 197:5
h., good evening and welcome, 178:4
h., I must be going, 298:3
h., Mrs, 140:4
touch of h. folks and what about the workers, 313:5

**Help**
get by with a little h. from my friends, 276:5

**Herod**
oh, for an hour of H., 229:2

**Heroes**
make Britain a land fit for h., 187:2

**Hidden**
H. Persuaders, 331:1

**Hierarchy**
in h., employee tends to rise to level of incompetence, 338:1

**High**
be ye never so h., the law is above you, 137:4
corn is as h. as an elephant's eye, 208:4

**Hills**
h. are alive with the sound of music, 209:7

**Himmler**
H. has something similar, 22:5

**Historians**
h. repeat each other, 39:3, 203:3

**History**
end of a thousand years of h., 181:3
h. does not repeat itself . . . , 39:3
h. is more or less bunk, 173:5
H. Man, 69:5
h. repeats itself; historians repeat each other, 203:3
like writing h. with lightning, 459:4

**Hit**
write a h. same way you write a flop, 277:4

**Hitler**
H. has only got one ball, 22:5
not unlike H. but without the charm, 440:2
wouldn't believe H. was dead, even if he told me, 377:5

**Hi-yo**
h.-y., Silver, 89:6, 281:1

**Hobbit**
in hole in the ground there lived a H., 430:4

**Hobson (H.)**
H.H. barking up the wrong tree, 190:5

**Hockey-sticks**
jolly h.-s., 360:1

**Hole**
if you knows of a better h., go to it, 36:2
in h. in the ground there lived a Hobbit, 430:4

**Hollow**
we are the h. men, 154:2

**Hollywood**
H. is a world with personality of a paper cup, 95:2
H. where inmates are in charge of the asylum, 413:4
H. . . . where people from Iowa mistake themselves for movie stars, 14:1

**Home**
house is not a h., 10:4
I think I go h., 183:2
sodomy and drug addiction I can get at h., 116:3

**Homeward**
Look H., Angel, 66:1

**Husband**
archaeologist is best h., 99:4
if you were my h., I'd poison your coffee, 101:1
my h. and I, 157:3, 157:4

**Husbands**
h. I have had apart from my own, 181:1

**Hush**
h., h., nobody cares! Christopher Robin has fallen downstairs, 45:1
ought to have said 'h.' just once, 83:2

# I

**Idea**
good i., son, 79:3
seemed like a good i. at the time, 267:3

**Idol**
one-eyed yellow i. to the North of Khatmandu, 217:4

**Ike**
I like I., 396:7

**Illegal**
i., immoral or fattening, 463:3
when the President does it, not i., 324:7

**Illegitimi**
I. non carborundum, 397:1

**Illumination**
for support rather than i., 265:2

**Illusion**
La Grande I., 166:5

**Imagine**
i. there's no heaven, 275:3

**Imitation**
i. rough diamond, 29:6

**Impossible**
in two words – i., 195:3

**Impostors**
treat those two i. just the same, 261:1

**Impressionable**
give me a girl at an i. age and she is mine for life, 411:1

**Impressive**
few more i. sights than a Scotsman on the make, 42:1

**Imprisoned**
i. in every fat man, 114:4

**Impropriety**
no i. in my acquaintanceship with Miss Keeler, 350:1

**Impromptu**
(Churchill) preparing his i. speeches, 405:4

**Improved**
enormously i. by death, 375:2

**Incest**
everything except i. and folk-dancing, 44:1

**Inch**
every other i. a gentleman, 449:2, 463:4

**Include**
i. me out, 195:1

**Income**
with private i. better things to do than love mankind, 259:3

**Incompetence**
rise to his level of i., 338:1

**Individual**
small, hairy i. and, out of curiosity, one climbed on, 19:2

**Indoors**
'er i., 308:3

**Indubitably**
i., 214:2

**Ineligible**
honourably i. for the struggle of life, 114:3

**Inexactitude**
risk of terminological i., 100:4

**Infamy**
date which will live in i., 368:1

**Inferiors**
where does she find (i.), 332:5

**Inflation**
little i. is like being a little pregnant, 222:2

**Jim**
Force made him Sunny J., 211:4
ha-harr, J., lad, 210:4
I'm worried about J., 316:5

**Job**
gi' us a j., I could do that, 62:2

**John**
J. Willie, come on, 174:4

**John Bull**
if it's in J.B., it is so, 69:2

**Johnny**
heeeeere's J., 89:5
J. head-in-air, 352:3
nobody knows where my J. has gone,
446:3

**John Thomas**
J. Thomas says good-night to Lady Jane,
270:5

**Join**
you can't see the j., 313:7

**Jokes**
like Parsifal without the j., 123:7

**Jolly**
everyone should be j. at my funeral, 316:4
j. hockey-sticks, 360:1

**Josephine**
not tonight, J., 233:3

**Journalism**
Christianity, yes, but why j., 39:1
j. consists in saying 'Lord Jones Dead',
98:5
qualities essential for j., 431:2
rock j. is for people who can't read, 467:1

**Journalist**
cannot bribe or twist British j., 462:1

**Journalists**
cohorts of distinguished j., 459:1
j. say a thing they know isn't true, 53:1
(j.) more attentive to minute hand of
history, 287:1

**Journey**
is your j. really necessary, 397:4
J.'s End, 341:5

**Joy**
Politics of J., 231:2

**Joyful**
one can't exactly be j. at the prospect
before us, 111:2

**Juantorena**
J. opens wide his legs and shows his class,
25:4

**Judge**
here come de j., 269:2

**June**
J. Is Bustin' Out All Over, 208:5

**Justice**
j. . . . not only seen to be done but . . .
seen to be believed, 45:4
j. open to all, like the Ritz hotel, 300:4
j. should be seen to be done, 224:1

# K

**Kaiser**
'arf a mo', K., 88:5
hang the K., 396:2

**K.B.O.**
(keep buggering on), 104:1

**Keep**
regardless of what they say, we are going
to k. it, 323:1

**Kennedy (Jackie)**
(K.) on yacht of Greek petrol millionaire,
136:2

**Kennedys**
K. don't cry, 255:3

**Kettle**
here's a pretty k. of fish, 299:1

**Keynsham**
K. – spelt K.E.Y.N.S.H.A.M., 43:3

**Kick**
I get a k. out of you, 343:6
I get no k. from champagne, 343:6

**Kicking**
dragged k. and screaming into the twentieth century, 416:5

# L

**Labour**
Fair Shares for All, is L.'s Call, 240:2
I wonder what (Grandmama) would have thought of a L. Government, 185:1
L. isn't working, 398:2
rootless intellectuals who call themselves the L. Party, 52:3

**Lady**
nicest old l. I ever met, 162:4
that's why the l. is a tramp, 215:3
when she says yes, she is no l., 137:5

**Lafayette**
L., we are here, 413:5

**Laid**
all young girls at Yale Prom l. end to end, 334:4

**Lamp-post**
what l.-p. feels about dogs, 210:3

**Lamps**
l. are going out all over Europe, 202:2

**Land**
come by l., sea and air, 235:3
l. fit for heroes, 187:2
l. flow with milk and honey, 193:1
L. of Hope and Glory, Mother of the free, 53:4
l. of my fathers, 426:1
this l. of ours which we love so much, 422:5

**Land's End**
from L. E. to John of Gaunt, 411:5

**Landslide**
damned if I'm going to pay for a l., 251:3

**Language**
l. of Shakespeare, Milton and the Bible, 385:1
two countries separated by the same l., 383:3

**Larry**
L. the lamb, 432:3

**Lassie**
I Love a L., 268:1

**Late**
too little and too l., 321:4

**Later**
it is l. than you think, 382:1

**Laughed**
I l. all the time, 119:4

**Laughter**
born with the gift of l. and sense that the world was mad, 374:1

**Law**
l. is above you, 137:4

**Lawrence (T.E.)**
Dear 338171, 122:1

**Lawyer**
l. with his briefcase can steal more, 353:3

**Lay**
(space) to l. a hat and a few friends, 333:7

**LBJ**
hey, hey, LBJ, how many kids did you kill today, 396:6

**Liberty**
l., so precious it must be rationed, 274:4

**Licence**
l. to print money, 427:1
may not get his (dog) l. renewed, 458:4

**Lie**
l. can be halfway round the world before truth has got its boots on, 82:1
l. follows by post, 420:4
masses more easily fall to a big l. than to a small one, 226:3

**Leader**
follow them, I am their l., 270:1
take me to your l., 91:6

**Machinery**
m. takes place of every profession, 139:5

**Mack**
M. the Knife, 70:4

**Mad**
Anthony (Eden) – half m. baronet, half beautiful woman, 77:4
don't get m., get even, 255:1
don't get me m., see, 81:2
m. as hell and I'm not going to take this, 321:3
m. dogs and Englishmen, 122:2
sense that the world was m., 374:1

**Madam**
call me m., 337:2

**Madeira**
have some m., m'dear, 171:2

**Madeleine**
taste of the little crumb of m., 350:3

**Magic**
That Old Black M., 304:2

**Magistra**
placetne, m., 377:4

**Maid**
being an old m. is like death by drowning, 163:3
Old M. among novelists, 448:8

**Maintain**
m. your rage, 453:1

**Make**
go ahead, m. my day, 358:2
it's m. your mind up time, 201:3
m. love, not war, 398:7
man who could not m. up his mind, 138:1

**Maker**
I am ready to meet my M., 108:1

**Malignant**
remove only part of Randolph that was not m., 445:1

**Man**
brotherhood of m. under the fatherhood of God, 365:5
it's that m. again, 237:1
m. hands on misery to m., 267:1
m. is as old as the woman he feels, 298:6
M. who (committed some solecism or other), 43:4
remembered as m. about whom all is forgotten, 54:2
you'll be a M., my son, 261:3

**Manchester**
if you haven't been to M., you haven't lived, 356:2
shortest way out of M., a bottle of Gordon's gin, 63:3

**Mankind**
came in peace for all m., 235:2
giant leap for m., 27:3

**Many**
m., m., times, 370:5

**Margaret**
come on, M., 151:1

**Market Harborough**
am in M.H. . . . . where ought I to be, 97:1

**Marriage**
m. is a great institution but I'm not ready, 448:6
m. is popular . . . combines maximum of temptation with opportunity, 384:6

**Marriages**
nearly all m. are a mistake, 431:1

**Married**
I don't sleep with happily m. men, 152:4
I was born in 1896, and my parents m. in 1919, 9:3
m. beaneath me . . . all women do, 30:7
m. Duke for better or worse but not for lunch, 460:3
m. women and single men, 302:4
spent m. lives getting into other people's beds, 316:1

**Marry**
lesson not to m. ladies in high positions, 16:3
why did He not m., 312:1

**Marrying**
m. a princess – or someone royal . . . they know what happens, 95:4

**Martin**
M., Barton and Fish, 367:6

**Martini**
m., shaken, not stirred, 193:2
out of wet clothes and into a dry m., 50:3

**Marvellous**
just too m. for words, 303:6

**Masochism**
spirt of national m. prevails, 11:3

**Masters**
we are the m. now, 386:5

**Masturbation**
(M.) is called in our schools 'beastliness', 35:4
m. is the thinking man's television, 210:1
m. . . . sex with someone you love, 14:6

**Matched**
m. us with His hour, 73:2

**Matches**
to read economic documents I have to have box of m., 141:1

**Matilda**
who'll come a-waltzing M. with me, 335:2

**Mating**
come here often? . . . only in the m. season, 197:3

**Matters**
nothing m. very much and very few things matter at all, 39:4

**Matzo**
isn't there another part of the m. you can eat, 311:4

**Mayor**
good m. of Birmingham in an off-year, 187:4

**Mayors**
one hundred and fifty Lord Mayors . . . all look the same, 185:2

**Mean**
all depends what you m. by, 242:3
down these m. streets a man must go, 94:5
m., moody, magnificent, 398:9

**Measured**
m. out my life with coffee spoons, 153:3

**Mecca**
New York is not M., just smells like it, 388:3

**Medals**
no more bloody m., 298:7

**Mediocre**
gilded tomb of a m. talent, 406:4
only m. are always at their best, 191:3
titles distinguish the m., 384:1

**Medium**
m. because neither rare nor well done, 263:3
m. is the message, 290:4
TV . . . a m. because nothing's well done, 9:1

**Medley**
play us a m. of your hit, 278:1

**Meek**
m. shall inherit earth, but not mineral rights, 189:7

**Member**
are you now or have you been a m. of the Communist Party, 26:5

**Men**
m. are m., but Man is a woman, 97:7
not the m. in my life, but the life in my m., 448:4
where do we get such m., 71:3

**Mend**
make do and m., 398:6

**Meredith**
M., we're in, 262:2

**Merrygoround**
no go the m., 293:1

**Mess**
another fine m. you've gotten me into, 214:1

**Music**
don't know anything about m., 48:6
how potent cheap m. is, 121:5
m. is the brandy of the damned, 383:7
play the m. and open the cage, 158:3
stoppa da m., 145:4
Van Gogh's ear for m., 453:2

**Musical**
(going to bed with Ivor Novello) – musical, 101:6
m. equivalent of the towers of St Pancras station, 48:2
(kind of) m. Malcolm Sargent, 48:5

**Music-Halls**
Darling of the M.-H., 405:1

**Music-lovers**
thank you, m.-l., 246:3

**My**
I did it m. way, 18:1

**N**

**Nacht**
N. und Nebel, 227:3

**Naff**
why don't you n. off, 19:5

**Naive**
N. Domestic Burgundy, Amused by its Presumption, 428:3

**Naked**
eight million stories in the n. city, 320:2
N. Ape, 314:3
n. into the conference chamber, 58:5

**Name**
as long as you spell my n. right, 113:1
don't care, if spell n. right, 417:3
in the n. of God, go, 16:2
like to change your Christian n., 47:6
my n. is Jimmy Carter and I'm running for President, 85:1
N. of the Game, 421:3
needs no n. on the door, 380:5
Spiro Agnew is not a household n., 11:1
their n. liveth for evermore, 158:5
(played) under an assumed n., 250:6

**Names**
only the n. have been changed to protect the innocent, 142:1

**Naming**
n. of parts, 359:1

**Nannies**
n. are so hard to come by these days, 25:1

**Nasty**
something n. in the woodshed, 190:2

**Nation**
n. shall speak peace unto n., 399:1
n. talking to itself, 305:2

**Nattering**
n. nabobs of negativism, 11:4

**Natural**
negligible as contribution to n. history, 429:6

**Naturally**
doin' what comes n., 55:6

**Naughty**
n., but nice, 409:1

**Navy**
N.'s here, 334:6
we joined the N. to see the world, 55:2

**Necessarily**
It Ain't N. So, 189:1

**Need**
will you still n. me when I'm sixty-four, 276:4

**Needed**
by Jove, I n. that, 140:3

**Needle**
n., nardle, noo, 198:1

**Negativism**
nattering nabobs of n., 11:4

**Negotiate**
let us never fear to n., 252:4

**Neigh**
people expect me to n., grind my teeth
. . . swish my tail, 19:3

**Nerves**
it's me n., 239:4

**Never**
n. again, 399:2
n. eat at a place called Mom's, 12:3

**News**
no n. is good n. . . . no journalists is even
better, 54:4

**Newspaper**
good n. is a nation talking to itself, 305:2
it would be fun to run a n., 110:2
n. . . . my one form of continuous fiction,
59:3

**New York**
I love N.Y., 396:8

**New Zealand**
I went to N.Z. but it was closed, 21:3

**Nice**
be n. to people on the way up, 309:4
haven't anything n. to say, come and sit
by me, 281:5
he's not as n. as he looks, 107:1
n. guys finish last, 145:5
n. legs, shame about the face, 91:2
n. one, Cyril, 399:4
n. to get up in the mornin', 268:6
n. to see you, to see you, n., 176:2
seems like a n. boy, doesn't he, 200:5
together we can, being so n. and so
talented, work it out, 241:2

**Nicely**
that'll do n., sir, 401:2

**Nicest**
two of the n. people if ever there was one,
52:1

**Nicht**
It's a Braw Brecht Moonlecht N., 268:4
it's a braw bricht moonlicht n., 89:7

**Night**
It Was a Dark and Stormy N., 378:3
n. and day you are the one, 343:3
N. and Fog, 227:3
N. Has a Thousand Eyes, 66:5
n. is your friend . . . the 'V' is your sign,
72:3
N. Mail . . . bringing the cheque and the
postal order, 32:3
N. of Broken Glass, 180:2
N. of the Long Knives, 226:4
'tain't a fit n. out for man or beast, 162:2

**Nightingale**
N. Sang in Berkeley Square, 299:3

**Nightmare**
our long national n. is over, 173:1

**Nikky**
n., nokky, noo, 140:6

**Nixon**
only person standing between N. and the
White House, 252:1
you won't have N. to kick around any
more, 323:3

**No**
woman can't say n. in any (language),
333:2

**Nobody**
n. we know, dear, 75:4

**Noise**
loud n. at one end, no sense of responsibility at other, 262:3
n. . . . and the people, 22:7

**Noises**
create diversionary n., 451:4

**Nomination**
shall not seek, nor accept, the n. of my
party, 245:7

**Non**
n., 136:1

**None**
N. But the Lonely Heart, 66:6

**Onion**
takes out o., 349:5

**Open**
o. the door, Richard, 409:3

**Opera**
(Parsifal) is kind of o., 354:3
o. in English as sensible as baseball in Italian, 302:6
o. isn't over till the fat lady sings, 352:1

**Opportunity**
never miss o. to relieve yourself, 150:1
never missed occasion to let slip an o., 383:2

**Optimist**
o. who takes his raincoat, 458:6

**Oral**
o. contract not worth paper it's written on, 195:2

**Orchestra**
golden rules for an o., 48:3

**Order**
o., o., 426:5

**Orders**
I was only obeying o., 90:5

**Organ**
when the o. grinder is present, 58:4

**Origin**
we are o. of all coming evil, 248:4

**Orphan**
defeat is an o., 109:5

**Orwell (G.)**
(O.) would not blow nose without moralizing, 115:4

**Others**
now (dead girl) is like the others, 135:2

**Otis**
Miss O. regrets she's unable to lunch today, 343:4

**Outside**
going o., and I may be some time, 326:1

**Outspoken**
o. by whom, 332:1

**Overboard**
throw man o. not much good if heading for rocks, 191:1

**Overcome**
we shall o., 402:4

**Overpaid**
O., overfed, oversexed and over here, 22:3

**Owes**
world o. me a living, 139:6

**Ownership**
common o. of means of production, distribution and exchange, 264:1

**Oxford**
clever men at O. know all there is to be knowed, 199:6

# P

**Paddy**
keep P. behind the big mixer, 286:1

**Pageant**
all part of life's rich p., 296:1

**Pain**
(Queen's speaking) a p. in the neck, 15:3

**Pakistan**
(P. place where) everyone should send his mother-in-law, 68:4

**Pale**
p. hands I loved beside the Shalamar, 229:4

**Panic**
don't p., 10:1

**Paper**
here is the p. which bears his name . . . as well as mine, 93:3
it's only a p. moon, 212:3
p. tigers, 295:2

**Paper cup**
Hollywood is world with personality of a p. c., 95:2

**Penny**
not a p. off the pay, not a minute on the day, 116:1

**People**
for God's sake look after our p., 379:5
forward with the p., 129:2
interested in p., but I've never liked them, 301:3
noise and the p., 22:7
not many p. know that, 81:4
presenting the p. to the p., 338:5

**Peoria**
it'll play in P., 150:5

**Perfect**
nobody's p., 407:4

**Performance**
nothing to be fixed except your p., 120:6

**Period**
p. of silence on your part would be welcome, 31:3

**Permission**
p. to speak, sir, 128:2

**Permissive**
p. society . . . is the civilized society, 241:4

**Perpendicular**
p. expression of horizontal desire, 386:3

**Perspiration**
ninety-nine per cent p., 149:2

**Persuaders**
Hidden P., 331:1

**Petrol**
price of p. has been increased by one penny, 129:3

**Phew**
P., what a scorcher, 348:5

**Philadelphia**
I went to P. and found that it was closed, 165:1
on the whole I'd rather be in P., 164:4

**Phone**
E.T., p. home, 148:2
most historic p. call ever made, 323:4
p. for the fish knives, Norman, 57:4
why did you answer the p., 428:4

**Phoney**
everything about you is p. . . . . even your hair, 22:6

**Photographed**
I was p. and interviewed and p. again, 120:2

**Pianist**
Shoot the P., 168:1

**Piano-player**
Shoot the P.-P., 168:1

**Pickle**
weaned on a p., 281:6

**Picture**
one p. is worth ten thousand words, 351:8

**Pictures**
I am big, p. got small, 418:1

**Pie**
put in a p. by Mrs McGregor, 345:6
you don't want no p. in the sky, 13:3
you'll get p. in the sky when you die, 224:3

**Pile**
p. it high, sell it cheap, 113:2

**Pint**
p. – that's very nearly an armful, 211:3

**Pips**
squeeze until you can hear the p. squeak, 184:1

**Piss**
isn't worth a pitcher of warm p., 184:4

**Pisser**
si je pouvais p. comme il parle, 112:2

**Pissing**
economics like p. down your leg, 245:4
inside my tent p. out, 245:3

**Pistol**
I don't have a p. (in a drawer), 324:4

**Pits**
you are the p. of the world, 289:3

**Place**
great God, this is an awful p., 379:3
in p. of fear, 58:1
In P. of Strife, 87:6
our p. in the sun, 453:4

**Placidly**
go p. amid the noise and haste, 151:2

**Play**
He no p. da game. He no make-a da rules,
79:1
if she can stand it, I can . . . p. it, 86:5
(game of chance) – not the way I p. it,
165:5
p. it again, Sam, 86:2, 86:3, 86:5
this p. what I have wrote, 314:1

**Played**
how you p. the game, 362:5

**Playmates**
hello, p., 28:5

**Plough**
I must p. my own furrow alone, 369:2

**Plumber**
try getting a p. on weekends, 14:3

**Plumbers**
country needs good p., 324:5

**Po**
pee p. belly bum drawers, 171:7

**Pocket**
pecker in my p., 244:3, 245:6

**Pod-bay**
open the p.-b. doors, Hal, 435:4

**Poem**
p. lovely as a tree, 257:4

**Poems**
you provide the prose p. . . . I'll provide
the war, 110:4

**Poetry**
line of p. makes skin bristle, 230:2
only man who has never written p., 98:1
p. is the pity, 330:1

**Point**
up to a p., Lord Copper, 444:2

**Pointy-headed**
p.-h. intellectuals who can't park bicycles
straight, 442:3

**Poles**
I desire the P. carnally, 85:5

**Policeman**
if you want to know the time, ask a p.,
408:3
p. is there to preserve disorder, 130:4

**Polite**
far too p. to ask (sex), 439:5

**Political**
not going to exploit for p. purposes my
opponent's youth, 357:4
p. (problems) are insoluble . . . economic
ones incomprehensible, 141:3

**Politician**
p. approaches every question with an
open mouth, 416:4
p. is an arse upon which everyone has sat,
127:1

**Politicians**
good man fallen among p., 130:1

**Politics**
I'm in p. . . . play the piano in a whorehouse, 21:5
never get on in p. with that hair, 31:1
p. is the art of the possible, 78:3
p. is too important to be left to the
politicians, 134:3
P. of Joy, 231:2
week is a long time in p., 457:4

**Ponces**
wriggling p. of the spoken word, 71:4

**Poodle**
Mr Balfour's p., 186:5

**Poop-poop**
O bliss, o p.-p., 199:5

**Poor**
P. Little Rich Girl, 120:3

**Pop**
into p. to get rich, get famous and get laid,
184:3

**Pope**
anybody can be P., 243:3
how many divisions has (P.) got, 413:1
wake up and remember I am the P., 243:2

**Poppa**
P. wins, 118:4

**Poppies**
in Flanders fields the p. blow, 288:4

**Porcupine**
like fucking a p. – a hundred pricks
against one, 310:1

**Pornography**
kind of show that gives p. a bad name,
40:6

**Portrait**
p. is a remarkable example of modern art,
109:2

**Positive**
Power of P. Thinking, 336:1

**Possible**
politics is the art of the p., 78:3

**Possums**
wave your gladdies, p., 231:3

**Poster**
Kitchener a great p., 29:2

**Postillion**
P. Struck by Lightning, 67:2

**Post-industrial**
The Coming of P.-I. Society, 49:2

**Potent**
strange how p. cheap music is, 121:5

**Pound**
p. in your pocket, 458:5

**Power**
p. is the ultimate aphrodisiac, 261:7
p. . . . like a dead sea fruit, 292:4
p. to the people, 400:1
p. without responsibility – the prerogative of the harlot, 37:3

**Practise**
I p. a lot when I'm on my own, 14:4

**Praise**
p. the Lord, and pass the ammunition,
409:5
unless (critics give) unqualified p., ignore
them, 415:3

**Pray**
p. for us now and at the hour of our birth,
154:5

**Prayer**
comin' in on a wing and a p., 10:3

**Prayers**
Christopher Robin is saying his p., 307:2

**Prays**
family that p. together stays together,
395:4

**Prejudices**
don't half-quote me to reinforce your p.,
110:6

**Prepared**
Be P., 35:1

**Preside**
p. over the liquidation of the British
Empire, 104:6

**Presidency**
cancer within close to the P., 134:1

**President**
All the P.'s Men, 63:4
anybody could become P. . . . . I'm beginning to believe it, 131:4
I do not choose to run for P., 118:3
I'm running for P., 85:1
when P. does it, not illegal, 324:7

**Press**
let's go to p., 460:2

**Presumption**
Amused by its P., 428:3

**Price**
pay any p., bear any burden, 252:3
p. of petrol has been increased, 129:3

**Pricks**
hundred p. against one, 310:1

**Priggish**
utterances . . . of a p. schoolgirl, 15:4

# Q

**Quarrel**
q. in faraway country, 93:2

**Que**
Q., 163:2

**Quebec**
vive le Q. libre, 136:3

**Queen**
(Q.) whom we love because she is herself, 108:3

**Queerer**
universe is q. than we suppose, 207:2

**Question**
Irish secretly changed the q., 381:3

**Quiet**
All Q. on the Western Front, 360:5
revolution so q., 219:2

**Quitter**
I am not a q., 323:2

**Quotation**
no more able to resist q. than refuse a drink, 329:2

**Quotations**
going to find that this is full of q., 142:4
it is gentlemanly to get one's q. very slightly wrong, 362:4
old fags and cabbage-stumps of q. from the Bible, 270:3

**Quote**
if I had a good q., I'd be wearing it, 146:6

# R

**Race**
human r., to which so many of my readers belong, 97:6
I wish I loved the Human R., 354:1

**Radical**
R. Chic, 462:2
r. is man with both feet planted in the air, 367:4

**Radio**
I had the r. on, 311:3
(Churchill) r. personality who outlived his prime, 444:5
steam r., 113:4

**Rage**
maintain your r., 453:1

**Railroad**
hell of a way to run a r., 401:3

**Rainbow**
somewhere over the r., 212:5

**Random**
R. Harvest, 67:3

**Raped**
anyone here been r. and speaks English, 24:1

**Rapists**
all men are r., 177:1

**Raspberries**
I'm the one who gets the r., 110:5

**Rat**
all right to r., but you can't re-r., 105:4
first time a r. has come to the aid of sinking ship, 25:5
r. swimming out to join a sinking ship, 105:7
you dirty r., 81:1

**Rat-like**
r.-l. cunning, 431:2

**Ravish**
can't r. a tin of sardines, 270:4

**Reactionaries**
all r. are paper tigers, 295:2

**Read**
all I know is just what I r. in the papers, 366:2
I'm sorry I'll r. that again, 90:1
r. any good books lately, 230:1

**Reader**
Dear R., you may be right, 302:2

**Reading**
but I prefer r., 406:3
what exactly is she r., 159:3

# S

**Sack**
s. the lot, 169:2

**Sackville-West (V.)**
(S.-W.) like Lady Chatterley above waist and gamekeeper below, 115:3

**Safety**
s. first, 400:3

**Salmon**
s. are striking back, 156:2

**Salvation**
wot prawce S., nah, 383:6

**Sang**
s. in my chains like the sea, 425:3

**Sanitary**
Golden S. Towel Award Presentation, 329:6

**Sardines**
life like opening a tin of s., 51:4

**Sat**
bears marks of last person who has s. on him, 206:2
you have s. here too long, 16:2

**Satire**
he said bum one night – s., 424:3
purpose of s. . . . to strip off veneer, 171:6
s. is what closes Saturday night, 250:4

**Satisfaction**
can't get no s., 239:3
complete s. or money refunded, 380:2
I endeavour to give s., 461:5
in work the greatest s. lies, 15:2

**Sauce**
will drown everything in HP s., 459:3

**Savaged**
like being s. by a dead sheep, 218:2

**Save**
nothing will s. the Governor-General, 453:1
s. water, bath with a friend, 400:4
to s. the town it became necessary to destroy, 24:4

**Say**
I s., you fellows, 363:5
s. hey, 301:5
s. it with flowers, 400:5

**Saying**
as I was s. when I was interrupted, 87:5

**Schedule**
cannot be a crisis . . . my s. is already full, 262:1

**School**
how explain s. to a higher intelligence, 148:1
st custard's which is the s. i am at, 454:3

**Scorer**
for when the One Great S. comes, 362:5

**Scotsman**
S. on the make, 42:1

**Scout**
S. smiles and whistles under all circumstances, 35:3

**Scratch**
s. an actor and you'll find an actress, 332:4

**Sculptor**
patriotism is the last refuge of the s., 342:3

**Scum**
they are s., 300:5

**Sea**
died as he lived, at s., 21:8
snotgreen s. . . . scrotumtightening s., 247:4
What did we see? We saw the s., 55:2

**Seal**
you heard a s. bark, 428:1

**Seas**
I must down to the s. again, 299:4

**Seat**
get up out of your s., 199:3

**Seatbelts**
fasten your s., 13:4

**Seats**
you want the best s., we have them, 403:9

**Slush**
pure as the driven s., 40:5

**Smack**
s. of firm government, 130:2

**Small**
one s. step for (a) man, one giant leap for mankind, 27:3
S. Is Beautiful, 378:5

**Smile**
(Mona Lisa) has s. of woman who has dined off husband, 145:6
man has a nice s., but iron teeth, 203:1

**Smirnoff**
until I discoverd S., 397:6

**Smoke**
only s. on special occasions, 23:4
S. Gets in Your Eyes, 212:2

**Smoke-filled**
s.-f. room, 132:1

**Snap**
s., crackle, pop, 400:7

**Sniggering**
(Britain) about to sink s. beneath the watery main, 116:4

**Snobbery**
school of s. with violence, 52:2

**Snobs**
effete corps of impudent s., 11:3

**Snoot**
punch him in the s., 426:6

**Snored**
Nero fiddled, but Coolidge only s., 302:5

**Snouts**
biggest s. get the largest share, 446:1
come on, get your s. in the trough, 446:2

**Snow**
Russians with s. on their boots, 20:3

**Snows**
more it s. (tiddely pom), 307:6

**Sober**
better man than Prime Minister s., 429:5
I shall be s. in the morning, 105:6

**Socialism**
s. . . . (means) the conquest of commanding heights of the economy, 59:2

**Society**
upward to the Great S., 244:5

**Sock**
s. it to me, 269:5

**Socialism**
nothing in S. that age or money will not cure, 144:3
S. with a human face, 143:2

**Socialists**
why is it always the intelligent people who are s., 52:4

**Sodomy**
s. and drug addiction I can get at home, 116:3

**Softly**
S., S., 422:1
speak s. and carry a big stick, 368:3

**Soil**
answer lies in the s., 60:1

**Soldier**
S. of the Great War Known unto God, 158:6

**Soldiers**
old s. never die . . . they just fade away, 286:5

**Solution**
not part of the s., part of the problem, 351:5

**Something**
now for s. completely different, 313:3
s. must be done, 150:2
time for a little s., 307:4

**Song**
s. is ended but the melody lingers on, 55:1
With a S. in My Heart, 215:1

**Son-in-Law**
s.-i.-l. also rises, 21:6

**Soufflé**
you can't make a s. rise twice, 282:2

**Soul**
dark night of the s., 170:1

**Stately**
one of the s. homos of England, 126:1
S. Homes of England, 122:7

**Statesmanship**
s. . . . I call it an emotional spasm, 59:1

**Statesmen**
Most British s. have either drunk too
much or womanized, 74:2

**Station**
ideas above her s. . . . how would you say
in French, 355:3
made me feel that Albert had married
beneath his s., 124:5

**Statistics**
lies, damn lies and s., 435:2
uses s. as a drunken man uses lamp-posts,
265:2

**Statue**
no s. ever been put up to a critic, 387:2

**Stay**
come again when you can't s. so long,
387:3

**Steam**
s. radio, 113:4

**Step**
don't s. on my blue suede shoes, 337:1
One S. Forward, Two Steps Back, 274:3
small s. for (a) man, 27:3
take a s. forward, lads . . . it will be
easier, 99:1

**Stick**
speak softly and carry a big s., 368:3
s. with an 'orse's 'ead 'andle, 149:1

**Sticks**
S. Nix Hicks Pix, 438:3

**Still**
at the s. point of the turning world, 154:7

**Sting**
s. like a bee, 13:1

**Stonewall**
want you to s. it . . . cover-up, 324:1

**Stood**
should have s. in bed, 239:2

**Stool**
look as if I was having a difficult s., 109:3

**Stop**
once again we s. the mighty roar of
London's traffic, 235:3
s., look, listen, 437:1
s. me and buy one, 401:1
Stop the World, I Want to Get Off, 342:1

**Store**
famous s. needs no name on the door,
380:5

**Stork**
can you tell S. from butter, 393:4

**Story**
this could have been a one-sentence s.,
366:4
this is where the s. really begins, 197:1

**Strand**
Let's All Go Down the S., 88:1
never alone with a S., 403:7

**Stranger**
look, s., at this island now, 32:4

**Straw**
S. Dogs, 167:8

**Street**
Across the S. and Into the Bar, 451:2
don't even know what s. Canada is on,
83:3

**Streets**
down these mean s., 94:5
grass will grow in the s., 229:1
s. full of water . . . please advise, 50:6

**Streisand (B.)**
(S.) playing herself – and awfully soon for
that, 249:1

**Strife**
In Place of S., 87:6

**Strike**
no right to s. against the public safety,
117:4

**String**
chewing little bits of s., 49:3

**Stroke**
at a s., 219:1

**Titanic**
furniture on the deck of the T., 315:4

**Titles**
t. distinguish the mediocre, 384:1

**Toad**
t. work squat on my life, 266:1

**Toast**
(t.) to the people of Israel . . . Egypt, 173:2

**Today**
t. is first day of rest of your life, 134:2
t. . . ., tomorrow the world, 401:5

**Together**
let us go forward t., 102:4

**Told**
I think we should be t., 349:2

**Tomorrow**
t. is another day, 196:3
t. is first day of rest of your life, 134:2
t. the world, 401:5

**Tonight**
Henry Hall speaking and t. is my guest night, 207:5
not t., Joephine, 233:3

**Tools**
give us the t., and we will finish the job, 103:6

**Toothpaste**
can't put the t. back in the tube, 324:6

**Top**
made it, Ma, [to the] t. of the world, 451:3
t. people take *The Times*, 401:6
You're the T., 344:1

**Tora**
t.-t.-t., 180:1

**Torch**
t. passed to a new generation, 252:3

**Torpedo**
dropped t. . . . most entertaining, 319:1

**Tortoise**
Aesop was writing for the t. market, 74:1

**Touch**
t. of the —, 439:3

**Tough**
t. get going, 254:6

**Toujours**
t. gai is my motto, 296:1

**Towels**
never darken my t. again, 143:4

**Town**
to save the t., it became necessary to destroy it, 24:4

**Tragedies**
two t. in life, to lose your heart's desire, 384:2

**Trahison**
t. des clercs, 51:1

**Train**
biggest t. set a boy ever had, 446:5
only way of catching t. . . . miss the t. before, 97:5
seldom seen t. go by and not wished I was on it, 424:4

**Tramp**
why the lady is a t., 215:3

**Tread**
T. Softly for You T. on My Jokes, 67:7

**Tree**
billboard lovely as a t., 321:1
no, a t. fell on me, 306:5
poem lovely as a t., 257:4

**Trees**
books are t. with squiggles on, 234:3

**Trenches**
out of the t. before Christmas, 173:4

**Tribal**
*Times* is a t. noticeboard, 24:2

**Trip**
t. to the moon on gossamer wings, 344:3

**Trucking**
keep on t., 398:1

**True**
Always T. to You in My Fashion, 345:3

**Trumpet**
t. summons us again, 253:2

**Truth**
before t. has got boots on, 82:1
first casualty when war comes is t., 244:1
t. is the glue that holds government together, 173:1

**Try**
t. everything once, except incest and folk-dancing, 44:1
t. it, you'll like it, 401:7

**Tuesday**
If It's T., This Must Be Belgium, 166:7

**Tunnel**
light at the end of the t., 253:5, 284:2

**Tuppenny**
t. Punch and Judy show, 108:2

**Turn**
t. me over, Jack, 362:3
t. on, tune in, drop out, 271:4

**Turned**
it's t. out nice again, 174:2

**Turning**
lady's not for t., 423:2

**Turnip**
candle in great t. gone out, 106:1

**Twaddle**
better to write t. than nothing at all, 294:4

**Twelve**
t. (apostles) – couldn't we make do with six, 199:1

**Twilight**
t. of empire, 318:1

**Twin**
which t. has the Toni, 402:8

**Twinkletoes**
hello, it's me, T., 71:1

**Twist**
let him t. slowly in the wind, 151:1

**Two**
it takes t. to tango, 351:6

**Tyrant**
village t., 225:2

# U

**U**
U and Non-U, 369:3

**Uganda**
talking about U., 348:7

**Ugly**
he never kissed an u. girl, 298:6

**Umbrella**
love me, love my u., 248:2

**Unacceptable**
u. face of capitalism, 219:3

**Unbeatable**
in defeat u., 108:4

**Unborn**
for all ill-treated fellows u. and unbegot, 230:3

**Uncertain**
this u. summer, 353:4

**Unemployment**
when people are unable to find work, u. results, 228:2

**Undersold**
never knowingly u., 399:3

**Understood**
I have u. you, 135:6

**Undertaking**
no such u. has been received, 94:1

**Underwear**
with suitcase full of clothes and u. I set out for Vienna, 226:2

**Unforgiving**
fill the u. minute, 261:3

**Universe**
u. is queerer than we can suppose, 207:2

**Unknown**
U. Prime Minister by the side of the U. Soldier, 29:1

**Unofficial**
u. English rose, 72:4

**Unprepared**
magnificently u. for the long littleness of life, 118:6

**Unspoiled**
utterly u. by failure, 122:6

**Up**
u. and under, 443:2
u. there, Cazaly, 92:2
u., u. and away, 445:3

**Uplands**
move forward into broad, sunlit u., 102:6

**Urban**
u., squat and packed with guile, 72:5

**Used**
buy a u. car from this man, 23:6

**Utterly**
u. wet and weedy, 454:3

**U-turn**
U-t. if you want to, 423:2

# V

**V**
V. is your sign, 72:3

**Vain**
so v. you probably think this song is about you, 388:1

**Valentine**
My Funny V., 215:6

**Van Gogh**
V. G.'s ear for music, 453:2

**Vast**
v. wasteland, 308:5

**Venice**
V. like eating box of chocolate liqueurs at one go, 83:4

**Vermin**
lower than v., 57:7

**Vicarage**
look like a v. tea-party, 130:3

**Vicars**
arrest several of these v., 258:3

**Victory**
in v., magnanimity; in peace, goodwill, 107:4
this is your v., 104:8
v. finds a hundred fathers, but defeat is an orphan, 109:5
what is our aim – v., 102:3

**Vietnam**
V. was lost in the living rooms of America, 290:5

**View**
V. to a Kill, 168:2

**Village**
global v., 290:3
v. tyrant, 225:2

**Violence**
v. is the repartee of the illiterate, 71:5

**Virgin**
before she became a v., 278:2
knew Doris Day before she was a v., 297:6
Lillian, you should have stayed a v., 86:1

**Virginity**
little more v., if you don't mind, 433:4

**Vole**
passes the questing v., 444:3

**Votes**
v. for women, 401:8

**Vow**
I v. to thee my country, 412:2

**Voyage**
bon v., 195:8

**Voyager**
Now V., 167:2

**Vulture**
one thing a v. can't stand, it's a glass eye, 230:6
resemblance to (v.) doesn't end there, 297:3

# W

**Waggle**
write books, but can you w. your ears, 42:5

**Wagner**
W. is the Puccini of music, 45:5

**Wait**
thought I told you to w. in the car, 40:3
very well, I can w., 378:1
w. and see, 28:7

**Work**
got on his bike and looked for w., 419:5
I ain't gonna w. on Maggie's farm no
more, 146:5
in w. the greatest satisfaction lies . . .
centre of life, 15:2
it all makes w. for the working man to do,
171:5
never w. with animals or children, 21:1
Nice W. If You Can Get It, 189:2
toad w. squat on my life, 266:1
w. expands to fill time available for its
completion, 335:1
w. is much more fun than fun, 124:2

**World**
all the w. owes me a living, 139:6
so when the w. is asleep, 261:6
whole w. in a state o' chassis, 326:2
w. is a beautiful place to be born into,
163:4
w. must be made safe for democracy,
459:5
w. shall hear from me again, 161:1

**Worra**
w.w.w., 308:1

**Worse**
more will mean w., 17:2

**Worst**
own w. enemy . . . not while I'm alive he
ain't, 59:4
w. are full of passionate intensity, 465:2

**Would**
well, he w., wouldn't he, 363:4

**Wriggling**
w. ponces of the spoken word, 71:4

**Write**
better w. twaddle than nothing, 294:4
do not attempt to w. on both sides of the
paper, 381:4
you couldn't w. fuck on a venetian blind,
75:5

**Writer**
w. thinks about critics, 210:3

**Writing**
drawing chair up to w. desk, 23:1
I just do the w., 96:2
not w., that's typing, 83:5
what is the future for my kind of w., 353:4
w. a book . . . neither am I, 117:1

**Writs**
I shall not hesitate to issue w., 350:2

**Wrong**
if anything can go w., it will, 23:3
Month in the W. Country, 123:4
something w. with our bloody ships
today, 45:6
w. war, at the w. place, at the w. time, and
with w. enemy, 70:1

# Y

**Yaks**
(Beethoven's 7th) . . . like a lot of y.
jumping about, 48:4

**Yam**
I y. what I y., 342:4

**Yarooh**
y., 363:5

**Yawns**
even the grave y. for him, 433:2

**Yeh**
y.-y.-y., 275:5

**Yellow**
Follow the Y. Brick Road, 213:1
wonder where the y. went, 403:3

**Yes**
she didn't say y., she didn't say no, 212:1

**Yesterday**
y., all my troubles seemed so far away,
276:2
y.'s men, 403:1

**Youth**
delighted to meet (his youth), 127:2

# Z